The Natural History of Wiltshire

by

John Aubrey

The Echo Library 2006

Published by

The Echo Library

Echo Library
131 High St.
Teddington
Middlesex TW11 8HH

www.echo-library.com

Please report serious faults in the text to complaints@echo-library.com

ISBN 1-40680-716-8

TO

GEORGE POULETT SCROPE, ESQ. M.P., &c, &c. &c.

MY DEAR SIR,

BY inscribing this Volume to you I am merely discharging a debt of gratitude and justice. But for you I believe it would not have been printed; for you not only advocated its publication, but have generously contributed to diminish the cost of its production to the "WILTSHIRE TOPOGRAPHICAL SOCIETY", under whose auspices it is now submitted to the public.

Though comparatively obsolete as regards its scientific, archaeological, and philosophical information, AUBREY'S "NATURAL HISTORY OF WILTSHIRE" is replete with curious and entertaining facts and suggestions, at once characterising the writer, and the age in which he lived, and illustrating the history and topography of his native county. Had this work been revised and printed by its author, as he wished and intended it to have been, it would have proved as useful and important as Plot's "Staffordshire" and "Oxfordshire"; Burton's "Leicestershire"; Morton's "Northamptonshire"; Philipott's "Kent"; or any others of its literary predecessors or contemporaries. It could not have failed to produce useful results to the county it describes; as it was calculated to promote inquiry, awaken curiosity, and plant seeds which might have produced a rich and valuable harvest of Topography.

Aubrey justly complained of the apathy which prevailed in his time amongst Wiltshire men towards such topics ; and, notwithstanding the many improvements that have since been made in general science, literature, and art, I fear that the gentry and clergy of the county do not sufficiently appreciate the value and utility of local history; otherwise the Wiltshire Topographical Society would not linger for want of adequate and liberal support. Aubrey, Bishop Tanner, Henry Penruddocke Wyndham, Sir Richard Colt Hoare, and the writer of this address, have successively appealed to the inhabitants of the county to produce a history commensurate to its wealth and extent, and also to the many and varied objects of importance and interest which belong to it: but, alas ! all have failed, and I despair of living to see my native county amply and satisfactorily elucidated by either one or more topographers.

By the formation of the Society already mentioned, by writing and superintending this volume and other preceding publications, and by various literary exertions during the last half century, I have endeavoured to promote the cause of Topography in Wiltshire ; and in doing so have often been encouraged by your sympathy and support. For this I am bound to offer you the expression of my very sincere thanks; and with an earnest wish that you may speedily complete your projected "History of Castle Combe,"

I am,
My dear Sir,
Yours very truly,
JOHN BRITTON. 1st September, 1847.

EDITOR'S PREFACE.

IN the "Memoir of John Aubrey", published by the Wiltshire Topographical Society in 1845, I expressed a wish that the "NATURAL HISTORY of WILTSHIRE", the most important of that author's unpublished manuscripts, might be printed by the Society, as a companion volume to that Memoir, which it is especially calculated to illustrate.

The work referred to had been then suggested to the Council of the Society by George Poulett Scrope, Esq. M.P., as desirable for publication. They concurred with him in that opinion; and shortly afterwards, through the kind intervention of the Marquess of Northampton, an application was made to the Council of the Royal Society for permission to have a transcript made for publication from the copy of the " Natural History of Wiltshire" in their possession. The required permission was readily accorded; and had not the printing been delayed by my own serious illness during the last winter, and urgent occupations since, it would have been completed some months ago.

When the present volume was first announced, it was intended to print the whole of Aubrey's manuscript; but after mature deliberation it has been thought more desirable to select only such passages as directly or indirectly apply to the county of Wilts, or which comprise information really useful or interesting in itself, or curious as illustrating the state of literature and science at the time when they were written.

Before the general reader can duly understand and appreciate the contents of the present volume it is necessary that he should have some knowledge of the manners, customs, and literature of the age when it was written, and with the lucubrations of honest, but "magotie- headed" John Aubrey, as he is termed by Anthony a Wood. Although I have already endeavoured to portray his mental and personal characteristics, and have carefully marked many of his merits, eccentricities, and foibles, I find, from a more careful examination of his "Natural History of Wiltshire" than I had previously devoted to it, many anecdotes, peculiarities, opinions, and traits, which, whilst they serve to mark the character of the man, afford also interesting memorials of his times. If that age be compared and contrasted with the present, the difference cannot fail to make us exult in living, breathing, and acting in a region of intellect and freedom, which is all sunshine and happiness, opposed to the gloom and illiteracy which darkened the days of Aubrey. Even Harvey, Wren, Flamsteed, and Newton, his contemporaries and friends, were slaves and victims to the superstition and fanaticism of their age.

It has long been customary to regard John Aubrey as a credulous and gossiping narrator of anecdotes of doubtful authority, and as an ignorant believer of the most absurd stories. This notion was grounded chiefly upon the prejudiced testimony of Anthony a Wood, and on the contents of the only work which Aubrey published during his lifetime,- an amusing collection of "Miscellanies" relating to dreams, apparitions, witchcraft, and similar subjects.

Though his " History of Surrey" was of a more creditable character, and elicited the approval of Manning and Bray, the subsequent historians of that county, an unfavourable opinion of Aubrey long continued to prevail. The publication of his " Lives of Eminent Men" tended, however, to raise him considerably in the estimation of discriminating critics; and in my own " Memoir" of his personal and literary career, with its accompanying analysis of his unpublished works, I endeavoured (and I believe successfully) to vindicate his claims to a distinguished place amongst the literati of his times.

That he has been unjustly stigmatised amongst his contemporaries as an especial votary of superstition is obvious, even on a perusal of his most objectionable work, the "Miscellanies" already mentioned, which plainly shews that his more scientific contemporaries, including even some of the most eminent names in our country's literary annals, participated in the same delusions. It would be amusing to compare the "Natural History of Wiltshire" with two similar works on "Oxfordshire" and " Staffordshire," by Dr. Robert Plot, which procured for their author a considerable reputation at the time of their publication, and which still bear a favourable character amongst the topographical works of the seventeenth century. It may be sufficient here to state that the chapters in those publications on the Heavens and Air, Waters, Earths, Stones, Formed stones, Plants, Beastes, Men and Women, Echoes, Devils and Witches, and other subjects, are very similar to those of Aubrey. Indeed the plan of the latter's work was modelled upon those of Dr. Plot, and Aubrey states in his Preface that he endeavoured to induce that gentleman to undertake the arrangement and publication of his "Natural History of Wiltshire". On comparing the writings of the two authors, we cannot hesitate to award superior merits to the Wiltshire antiquary.

A few passages may be quoted from the latter to shew that he was greatly in advance of his contemporaries in general knowledge and liberality of sentiment:-

" I have oftentimes wished for a mappe of England coloured according to the colours of the earth; with markes of the fossiles and minerals." (p. 10.)

"As the motion caused by a stone lett fall into the water is by circles, so sounds move by spheres in the same manner; which, though obvious enough, I doe not remember to have seen in any booke." (p. 18.)

"Phantomes. Though I myselfe never saw any such things, yet I will not conclude that there is no truth at all in these reports. I believe that extraordinarily there have been such apparitions; but where one is true a hundred are figments. There is a lecherie in lyeing and imposing on the credulous, and the imagination of fearfull people is to admiration." [In other words, timid people are disposed to believe marvellous stories.] (p. 122.)

"Draughts of the Seates and Prospects. If these views were well donn, they would make a glorious volume by itselfe, and like enough it might take well in the world. It were an inconsiderable expence to these persons of qualitie, and it would remaine to posterity when their families are gonn and their buildings ruined by time or fire, as we have seen that stupendous fabric of Paul's Church, not a stone left on a stone, and lives now only in Mr. Hollar's Etchings in Sir

William Dugdale's History of Paul's. I am not displeased with this thought as a desideratum, but I doe never expect to see it donn; so few men have the hearts to doe public good to give 4 or 5 pounds for a copper-plate." p. 126.)

With regard to the history of the work now first published, it may be stated that it was the author's first literary essay; being commenced in 1656, and evidently taken up from time to time, and pursued "con amore". In 1675 it was submitted to the Royal Society, when, as Aubrey observed in a letter to Anthony á Wood, it "gave them two or three dayes entertainment which they were pleased to like." Dr. Plot declined to prepare it for the press, and in December 1684 strongly urged the author to "finish and publish it" himself; he accordingly proceeded to arrange its contents, and in the month of June following (in the sixtieth year of his age) wrote the Preface, describing its origin and progress. He states elsewhere that on the 21st of April 1686, he "finished the last chapter," and in the same year he had his portrait painted by "Mr. David Loggan, the graver," expressly to be engraved for the intended publication.

On the 18th of August 1686 he wrote the following Will: " Whereas I, John Aubrey, R.S.S., doe intend shortly to take a journey into the west; and reflecting on the fate that manuscripts use to have after the death of the author, I have thought good to signify my last Will (as to this Naturall History of Wilts): that my will and desire is, that in case I shall depart this life before my returne to London again, to finish, if it pleaseth God, this discourse, I say and declare that my will then is, that I bequeath these papers of the Natural History of Wilts to my worthy friend Mr. Robert Hooke, of Gresham Colledge and R.S.S., and I doe also humbly desire him, and my will is, that the noble buildings and prospects should be engraven by my worthy friend Mr. David Loggan, who hath drawn my picture already in order to it"

This document* shews at once the dangers and difficulties which attended travelling in Aubrey's time, and also that he seriously contemplated the publication of his favourite work.

* [It has been already printed in my Memoir of Aubrey. A note attached to it shews that the author intended to incorporate with the present work some portions of his MS. "Monumenta Britannica"; which was also dedicated to the Earl of Pembroke.]

Neither his fears of death nor his hopes of publication were however then realized: probably the political disturbances attending the Revolution of 1688 interfered with the latter. In the November of the year following that event Aubrey's friend and patron Thomas, Earl of Pembroke, was elected President of the Royal Society, which distinguished office he held only for one year. During that period the author dedicated the " Natural History of Wiltshire " to his Lordship; and there is little reason to doubt that the fair copy, now in the Society's Library, was made by the author, and given to it in the year 1690. About the same time he had resolved to present his other manuscripts, together with some printed books, coins, antiquities, &c., to the Ashmolean Museum at Oxford; and most of them were accordingly deposited there. He however appears to have retained his original manuscript of the " Natural History," in which he made several observations in the year 1691; that being the latest date attached by him to any of the additions.†

† [Some of these additions of 1691 Aubrey afterwards transcribed into certain blank spaces in the Royal Society's copy.]

On the 15th of September in the same year Aubrey sent this work to his learned and scientific friend, John Ray, for his perusal. The latter made a number of notes upon various parts of the manuscript, which he retained till the 27th of the ensuing month; when he returned it with the very judicious letter which will be found printed in this present publication (p. 7.) He had acknowledged the receipt of the work in a previous letter, in which he says: "I have read it over with great pleasure and satisfaction. You doe so mingle "utile dulci" {the useful with the sweet} that the book cannot but take with all sorts of readers: and it is pity it should be suppressed; which, though you make a countenance of, I cannot persuade myself you really intend to do:" and then proceeds to criticise a few pedantic or "new-coyned " words, and also the contents of Chapter VIII. (Part I.) It was probably soon afterwards that Evelyn perused and added some notes to the manuscript;‡ and in February 1694 Aubrey also lent the work to Thomas Tanner (afterwards Bishop of St Asaph), at his earnest request. He seems to have become acquainted with his fellow county-man, Tanner, only a short time before this. The latter, although then only in his twenty-first year, and pursuing his studies at Oxford, had acquired a reputation for knowledge of English antiquities, and with the ardour and enthusiasm of youth evinced much anxiety to promote the publication of this and some of the other works of his venerable friend. He added several notes to the manuscript, and whilst in his possession it was no doubt examined also by Gibson. It is referred to in the notes to the latter's edition of Camden's " Britannia."

‡ [Perhaps in May 1692 ; when he is known to have examined another of Aubrey's works, "An Idea of Education of Young Gentlemen". - Evelyn's notes to the "Wiltshire" are thus referred to in a memorandum by Aubrey on a fly-leaf of the manuscript: "Mdm. That ye annotations to which are prefixed this marke [J. E.] were writt by my worthy friend John Evelyn, Esq. R.S.S. 'Twas pitty he wrote them in black lead; so that I was faine to runne them all over againe with inke. I thinke not more than two words are obliterated."]

Had Aubrey's life been spared a few years longer it is very possible that most of his manuscripts would have been printed, under the stimulus and with the assistance of his youthful friend. His "Miscellanies," which appeared in 1696, seem to have owed their publication to these influences; and in the Dedication of that work to his patron the Earl of Abingdon, Aubrey thus expressly mentions Tanner:- "It was my intention to have finished my Description of Wiltshire (half finished* already), and to have dedicated it to your Lordship, but my age is now too far spent for such undertakings.† I have therefore devolved that task on my countryman Mr. Thomas Tanner, who hath youth to go through with it, and a genius proper for such an undertaking."

* [The work alluded to still remains "half finished," being a Description of the " North Division" only of the county. It has been printed by Sir Thomas Phillipps from the MS. in the Ashmolean Museum. 4to. 1821-1838.]

† [He was then in his 71st year.]

A chapter of the "Natural History" (being "Fatalities of Families and Places"), was at this time detached from the original manuscript to furnish materials for the remarks on "Local Fatality," in the "Miscellanies."

John Aubrey died suddenly in the first week in June 1697, and was buried in the church of St. Mary Magdalen at Oxford, and from the time of his decease the original draught of his Wiltshire History has been carefully preserved in the Ashmolean Museum at Oxford, as the fair copy of 1690 has also in the Library of the Royal Society in London.

Until the "Natural History of Wiltshire" was briefly described in my own "Memoir" of its author, very little was known of it beyond the mere fact of the existence of the two manuscripts. Copying from the original at Oxford, Dr. Rawlinson printed the Preface and Dedication, together with Ray's letter of the 27th October, 1691, as addenda to his edition of Aubrey's "History of Surrey," (1719.) The same manuscript was also noticed by Thomas Warton and William Huddesford in a list of the author's works in the Ashmolean Museum.‡ Horace Walpole referred to the Royal Society's copy in his Anecdotes of Painting (1762); but though his reference seems to have excited the curiosity of Gough, the latter contented himself with stating that he could not find the work mentioned in Mr. Robertson's catalogue of the Society's library.

‡ [This list forms a note to the "Lives of Leland, Hearne, and Wood" (8° 1772). Though it includes the "Natural History," it omits the "Description of North Wiltshire." The latter was known previously, being mentioned by Aubrey himself in his Miscellanies, and also by Dr. Rawlinson; and hence, Warton and Huddesford's list being supposed to be complete, much confusion has arisen respecting these two of Aubrey's works, which have been sometimes considered as identical.]

Some years ago Sir Thomas Phillipps, Bart., contemplated publishing this "Natural History," but he appears to have abandoned his design.

A brief description of the present state of the two manuscripts, with reference to the text of the volume now published, may be desirable. The Oxford copy, which may be termed the author's rough draught, is in two parts or volumes, demy folio, in the original vellum binding.§ Being compiled at various times, during a long series of years, it has a confused appearance, from the numerous corrections and additions made in it by Aubrey. A list of the chapters is prefixed to each volume, whence it appears that Aubrey had intended to include some observations on "Prices of Corne", "Weights and Measures", "Antiquities and Coines", and "Forests, Parks, and Chaces". Most of these topics are adverted to under other heads, but the author never carried out his intention by forming them into separate chapters.

§ [The first volume has two title-pages. On one of them, as well as on the cover, the work is called the "Natural History" of Wiltshire; but the remaining title designates its contents as "Memoires of Natural Remarques" in the county.]

Besides wanting the "Fatalities of Families and Places", taken out by the author in 1696, as already stated, the Oxford manuscript is deficient also in the chapters on "Architecture", "Accidents", and "Seates". So far therefore as Aubrey's own labours are concerned, the Royal Society's copy is the most perfect; but the notes of Ray, Evelyn, and Tanner were written upon the Oxford manuscript after the fair copy was made, and have never been transcribed into the latter. The Royal Society's manuscript is entirely in Aubrey's own hand, and is very neatly and carefully written, being in that respect, as well as in its completeness, much superior to the original. Of the latter it appears to have been an exact transcript; but it wants some of the rude sketches and diagrams with which the original is illustrated. The two parts form only one volume, demy folio, which is paged consecutively from 1 to 373, and is bound in modern Russia leather.

As already stated, a copy of the entire work was made for the purposes of this publication from the Royal Society's volume. The ownership of this copy has since been transferred to George Poulett Scrope, Esq. M.P., of Castle Combe, who has had it collated with the Oxford manuscript, thus making it unique.

Every care has been taken to preserve the strictest accuracy in the extracts now published, and with that view, as well as to correspond with such of Aubrey's works as have been already printed, the original orthography has been retained. The order and arrangement of the chapters, and their division into two parts, are also adhered to. At the commencement of each chapter I have indicated the nature of the passages which are omitted in the present volume, and although such omissions are numerous, it may be stated that all the essential and useful portions of the work are either here printed, or so referred to as to render them easily accessible in future to the scientific student, the antiquary, and the topographer.

With respect to the Notes which I have added, as Editor of the present volume, in correction or illustration of Aubrey's observations, I am alone responsible.* It would have been easy to have increased their number; for every page of the original text is full of matter suggestive of reflection and comment. I am aware that a more familiar acquaintance with the present condition of Wiltshire would have facilitated my task, and added greatly to the importance of these notes. On this point indeed I might quote the remarks of Aubrey in his preface, for they apply with equal force to myself; and, like him, I cannot but regret that no "ingeniouse and publique-spirited young Wiltshire man" has undertaken the task which I have thus imperfectly performed.

* [These are enclosed within brackets [thus], and bear the initials J. B. Some of the less important are marked by brackets only.]

In closing this address, and also in taking leave of the county of Wilts, as regards my literary connection with it, I feel it to be at once a duty and a pleasure to record my acknowledgments and thanks to those persons who have kindly aided me on the present occasion. When I commenced this undertaking I did not anticipate the labour it would involve me in, and the consequent time it would demand, or I must have declined the task; for I have been compelled to neglect a superior obligation which I owe to a host of kind and generous friends who have thought proper to pay me and literature a compliment in my old age, by subscribing a large sum of money as a PUBLIC TESTIMONIAL. In return for this, and to reciprocate the compliment, I have undertaken the laborious and delicate task of writing an AUTO-BIOGRAPHY which will narrate the chief incidents of my public life, and describe the literary works which I have produced. It is my intention to present a copy of this volume to each subscriber, so as to perpetuate the event in his own library and family, by a receipt or acknowledgment commemorative of the mutual sympathy and obligation of the donor and the receiver. Being now relieved from all other engagements and occupations, it is my intention to prosecute this memoir with zeal and devotion; and if health and life be awarded to me I hope to accomplish it in the ensuing winter.*

* [The volume will contain at least fifteen illustrations from steel copper, wood, and stone, and more than 300 pages of letterpress. A copy of the work will be presented to each subscriber, proportionate in value to the amount of the contribution. Hence three different sizes of the volume will be printed, namely: imperial 4to, with India proofs, fur subscribers of 10 [pounds}; medium 4to, with proofs, for those of 3 {pounds} and 5 {pounds}; and royal 8vo, with a limited number of prints, for subscribers of 1{pound} and 2 {pounds}.]

To the MARQUESS OF NORTHAMPTON, a native of Wiltshire, the zealous and devoted President of the Royal Society, my especial thanks are tendered for his influence with the Council of that Society, in obtaining their permission to copy Aubrey's manuscript; and also to

GEORGE POULETT SCROPE, Esq. M.P., for contributing materially towards the expense of the copy, and thereby promoting its publication.

To my old and esteemed friend the REV. DR. INGRAM, President of Trinity College, Oxford, I am obliged for many civilities, and for some judicious corrections and suggestions. His intimate acquaintance with Wiltshire, his native county, and his general knowledge of archaeology, as well as of classical and mediaeval history, eminently qualify him to give valuable aid in all publications like the present.

To JOHN GOUGH NICHOLS, Esq. F.S.A., both myself and the reader are under obligations, for carefully revising the proof sheets for the press, and for several valuable corrections.

To C. R. WELD, Esq. Assistant Secretary to the Royal Society, I am indebted for affording facilities for copying the manuscript.

Lastly, my obligations and thanks are due to MR. T. E. JONES, for the accurate transcript which he made from Aubrey's fair manuscript, for collating the same with the original at Oxford, for selecting and arranging the extracts which are now for the first time printed, and for his scrupulous and persevering assistance throughout the preparation of the entire volume. But for such essential aid, it would have been out of my power to produce the work as it is now presented to the members of the "Wiltshire Topographical Society," and to the critical reader.

JOHN BRITTON.

Burton Street, London.

1st September, 1847.

TABLE OF CONTENTS.

MEMOIRES

OF

NATURALL REMARQUES

IN THE

County of Wilts:
TO WHICH ARE ANNEXED,

OBSERVABLES OF THE SAME KIND

IN THE COUNTY OF SURREY, AND

FLYNTSHIRE.

BY

MR. JOHN AUBREY, R.S.S.
1685.

PSALM 92, v. 5, 6. "0 LORD, HOW GLORIOUS ARE THY WORKES: THY THOUGHTS ARE VERY DEEP. AN UNWISE MAN DOTH NOT WELL CONSIDER THIS: AND A FOOL DOTH NOT UNDERSTAND IT."

PSALM 77, v. 11."I WILL REMEMBER THE WORKES OF THE LORD: AND CALL TO MIND THY WONDERS OF OLD TIME."

GRATII PALISCI CYNEGETICON.
"O RERUM PRUDENS QUANTUM EXPERIENTIA VULGO
MATERIEM LARGILIA BONI, SI VINCERE CURENT
DESIDIAM, ET GRATOS AGITANDO PREBENDERE FINES !
—— DEUS AUCTOR, ET IPSA
AREM ALUIT NATURA SUAM."

TO

THE RIGHT HONOURABLE

THOMAS, EARLE OF PEMBROKE AND MONTGOMERIE,
LORD HERBERT OF CAERDIFFE, &c.;
ONE OF THE PRIVY COUNCELL TO THEIR MAJESTIES, AND PRESIDENT OF THE ROYALL SOCIETIE.

[A page is appropriated in the manuscript to the Author's intended DEDICATION ; the name and titles of his patron only being filled in, as above.

The nobleman named is particularly mentioned by Aubrey in his Chapter on "The Worthies of Wiltshire", printed in a subsequent part of this volume. He was Earl of Pembroke from 1683 till his death in 1733; and was distinguished for his love of literature and the fine arts. He formed the Wilton Collection of marbles, medals, and coins; and succeeded John, Earl of Carbery, as President of the Royal Society, in November, 1689.- J. B.]

PREFACE.

TILL about the yeare 1649,* 'twas held a strange presumption for a man to attempt an innovation in learning; and not to be good manners to be more knowing than his neighbours and forefathers. Even to attempt an improvement in husbandry, though it succeeded with profit, was look't upon with an ill eie. "Quo non Livor abit?"† Their neighbours did scorne to follow it, though not to do it was to their own detriment. 'Twas held a sinne to make a scrutinie into the waies of nature; whereas Solomon saieth, "Tradidit mundum disputationibus hominum": and it is certainly a profound part of religion to glorify GOD in his workes.‡

* Experimentall Philosophy was then first cultivated by a club at Oxon.

† Ovid. Fast.

‡ "Deus est maximus in minimis. Prsæsentemque refert quælibet Herba Deum".

In those times to have had an inventive and enquiring witt was accounted resverie [affectation§], which censure the famous Dr. William Harvey could not escape for his admirable discovery of the circulation of the blood. He told me himself that upon his publishing that booke he fell in his practice extremely.

§ [The words inclosed within brackets are inserted in Aubrey's manuscript above the preceding words, of which they were intended as corrections or modifications. If the work had been printed by the author he would doubtless have adopted those words which he deemed most expressive of his meaning.- J. B.]

Foreigners say of us that we are "Lyncei foris, Talpœ domi". There is no nation abounds with greater varietie of soiles, plants, and mineralls than ours; and therefore it very well deserves to be surveyed. Certainly there is no hunting to be compared with "Venatio Panos"; and to take no notice at all of what is dayly offered before our eyes is grosse stupidity.

I was from my childhood affected with the view of things rare; which is the beginning of philosophy : and though I have not had leisure to make any considerable proficiency in it, yet I was carried on with a strong [secret] inpulse to undertake this taske: I knew not why, unles for my owne private [particular] pleasure. Credit there was none; for it getts the disrespect [contempt] of a man's neighbours. But I could not rest [be] quiet till I had obeyed this secret call. Mr. Camden, Dr. Plott, and Mr. Wood confess the same [like].

I am the first that ever made an essay of this kind for Wiltshire, and, for ought I know, in the nation; having begun it in An°. 1656. In the yeare 1675 I became acquainted with Dr. Robert Plott, who had then his "Naturall Historie of Oxfordshire " upon the loome, which I seeing he did performe so excellently well, desired him to undertake Wiltshire, and I would give him all my papers: as I did [he had] also my papers of Surrey as to the naturall things, and offered him my further assistance. But he was then invited into Staffordshire to illustrate that countie; which having finished in December 1684, I importuned him again to undertake this county: but he replied he was so taken up in [arranging ?] of the Museum Ashmoleanum that he should meddle no more in that kind, unles it were for his native countie of Kent; and therefore wished me to finish and publish what I had begun. Considering therefore that if I should not doe this myselfe, my papers might either perish, or be sold in an auction, and somebody else, as is not uncommon, put his name to my paines; and not knowing any one that would undertake this designe while I live, I have tumultuarily stitch't up what I have many yeares since collected; being chiefly but the observations of my frequent road between South and North Wilts; that is, between Broad Chalke and Eston Piers. If I had had then leisure, I would willingly have searched the naturalls of the whole county. It is now fifteen yeares since I left this country, and have at this distance inserted such additions as I can call to mind, so that methinks this description is like a picture that Mr. Edm. Bathurst, B.D. of Trinity Colledge, Oxon, drew of Dr. Kettle three [some] yeares after his death, by strength of memory only; he had so strong an idea of him: and it did well resemble him. I hope hereafter it will be an incitement to some ingeniouse and publique spirited young Wiltshire man to polish and compleat what I have here delivered rough-hewen; for I have not leisure to heighten my style. And it may seem nauseous to some that I have rak't up so many western vulgar proverbs, which I confess I do not disdeigne to quote,* for proverbs are drawn from the experience and observations of many ages; and are the ancient natural philosophy of the vulgar, preserved in old English in bad rhythmes, handed downe to us; and which I set here as "Instantiæ Crucis" for our curious moderne philosophers to examine and give {Gk: dioti} to their {Gk: hostis}.

* Plinie is not afraide to call them Oracles: (Lib. xviii. Nat. Hist. cap. iv.) "Ac primum omnium oraculis majore ex parte agemus, qua non in alio vite genere plura certiorara sunt."

But before I fly at the marke to make a description of this county, I will take the boldness to cancelleer, and give a generall description of what parts of England I have seen, as to the soiles : which I call Chorographia Super and Subterranea (or thinke upon a more fitting name).

London, Gresham Coll., June 6M, 1685.

[The original of the following LETTER from JOHN RAY to AUBREY is inserted immediately after the Preface, in the MS. at Oxford. It is not transcribed into the Royal Society's copy of the work. -J. B.]

FOR MR. JOHN AUBREY.

Sr,

Black Notley, 8br 27, -91.

Your letter of Octob. 22d giving advice of your safe return to London came to hand, wch as I congratulate with you, so have I observed your order in remitting your Wiltshire History, wch with this enclosed I hope you will receive this week. I gave you my opinion concerning this work in my last, wch I am more confirmed in by a second perusal, and doe wish that you would speed it to ye presse. It would be convenient to fill up ye blanks so far as you can; but I am afraid that will be a work of time, and retard the edition. Whatever you conceive may give offence may by ye wording of it be so softned and sweetned as to take off ye edge of it, as pills are gilded to make them lesse ungratefull. As for the soil or air altering the nature, and influencing the wits of men, if it be modestly delivered, no man will be offended at it, because it accrues not to them by their own fault: and yet in such places as dull men's wits there are some exceptions to be made. You know the poet observes that Democritus was an example -

Summos posse viros, et magna exempla daturos Vervecû in patria, crassoque sub aere nasci.

Neither is yr observation universally true that the sons of labourers and rusticks are more dull and indocile than those of gentlemen and tradesmen; for though I doe not pretend to have become of the first magnitude for wit or docility, yet I think I may without arrogance say that in our paltry country school here at Braintry - "Ego meis me minoribus condiscipulis ingenio prælu[si]": but perchance the advantage I had of my contemporaries may rather be owing to my industry than natural parts; so that I should rather say "studio" or "industria excellui".

I think (if you can give me leave to be free with you) that you are a little too inclinable to credit strange relations. I have found men that are not skilfull in ye history of nature, very credulous, and apt to impose upon themselves and others, and therefore dare not give a firm assent to anything they report upon their own autority; but are ever suspicious that they may either be deceived themselves, or delight to teratologize (pardon ye word) and to make a shew of knowing strange things.

You write that the Museum at Oxford was rob'd, but doe not say whether your noble present was any part of the losse. Your picture done in miniature by Mr. Cowper is a thing of great value, I remember so long agoe as I was in Italy, and while he was yet living, any piece of his was highly esteemed there; and for that kind of painting he was esteemed the best artist in Europe.

What my present opinion is concerning formed stones, and concerning the formation of the world, you will see in a discourse that is now gone to the presse concerning the Dissolution of the World: my present opinion, I say, for in such things I am not fix't, but ready to alter upon better information, saving always ye truth of ye letter of ye scripture. I thank you for your prayers and good wishes, and rest,

Sr, your very humble servant,

JOHN RAY.

I have seen many pheasants in a little grove by the city of Florence, but I suppose they might have been brought in thither from some foreign country by the Great Duke.

Surely you mistook what I wrote about elms. I never to my knowledge affirmed that the most common elm grows naturally in the north: but only thought that though it did not grow there, yet it might be native of England: for that all trees doe not grow in all countreys or parts of England. The wych-hazel, notwithstanding its name, is nothing akin to the "corylus" but a true elm.

The story concerning the drawing out the nail driven crosse the wood-pecker's hole is without doubt a fable.

Asseveres and vesicates are unusuall words, and I know not whether the wits will allow them.

[The name of John Ray holds a pre-eminent place amongst the naturalists of Great Britain. He was the first in this country who attempted a classification of the vegetable kingdom, and his system possessed many important and valuable characteristics. Ray was the son of a blacksmith at Black Notley, near Braintree, in Essex, where he was born, in 1627. The letter here printed sufficiently indicates his natural shrewdness and intelligence. One of his works here referred to is entitled "Three Physico-Theological Discourses concerning Chaos, the Deluge, and the Dissolution of the World," 1692. There is a well- written memoir of Ray in the "Penny CyclopEedia," Aubrey's portrait, by the celebrated miniature-painter Samuel Cooper, alluded to above, is not now extant; but another portrait of him by Faithorne is preserved in the Ashmolean Museum, and has been several times engraved. A print from the latter drawing accompanied the "Memoirs of Aubrey," published by the Wiltshire Topographical Society. Cooper died in 1672, and was buried in the old church of St. Pancras, London. Ray visited Italy between the years 1663 and 1666. J. B.]

INTRODUCTORY CHAPTER.

CHOROGRAPHIA.

[IT has been thought sufficient to print only a few brief extracts from this Introductory Chapter, which in the original is of considerable length. Its title (derived from the Greek words {Gk:choros} and {Gk: grapho}) is analogous to Geography. By far the greater portion of it has no application to Wiltshire, but, on the contrary, consists of Aubrey's notes, chiefly geological and botanical, on every part of England which he had visited; embracing many of the counties. His observations shew him to have been a minute observer of natural appearances and phenomena, and in scientific knowledge not inferior to many of his contemporaries; but, in the present state of science, some of his remarks would be justly deemed erroneous and trivial.

It will be seen that he contends strongly for the influence of the soil and air upon the mental and intellectual faculties or "wits", of individuals; on which point some of his remarks are curious. Ray's comments on this part of his subject will be found in the letter already printed (page 7). "The temper of the earth and air", in the opinion of Aubrey, caused the variance in "provincial pronunciation".

The author's theory of the formation and structure of the earth, which is here incidentally noticed, will be adverted to in the description of Chapter VIII. - J. B.]

PETRIFIED SHELLS.-As you ride from Cricklad to Highworth, Wiltsh., you find frequently roundish stones, as big,, or bigger than one's head, which (I thinke) they call braine stones, for on the outside they resemble the ventricles of the braine; they are petrified sea mushromes. [Fossil Madrepores ?-J. B.]

The free-stone of Haselbury [near Box] hath, amongst severall other shells, perfect petrified scalop-shells. The rough stone about Chippenham (especially at Cockleborough) is full of petrified cockles. But all about the countrey between that and Tedbury, and about Malmesbury hundred, the rough stones are full of small shells like little cockles, about the bigness of a halfpenny.

At Dinton, on the hills on both sides, are perfect petrified shells in great abundance, something like cockles, but neither striated, nor invecked, nor any counter-shell to meet, but plaine and with a long neck of a reddish gray colour, the inside part petrified sand; of which sort I gave a quantity to the R. Society about twenty yeares since; the species whereof Mr. Hooke says is now lost.

On Bannes-downe, above Ben-Eston near Bathe, [Banner-downe, near Bath- Easton.- J. B.] where a battle of king Arthur was fought, are great stones scattered in the same manner as they are on Durnham-downe, about Bristow, which was assuredly the work of an earthquake, when these great cracks and vallies were made.

The like dispersion of great stones is upon the hills by Chedar rocks, as all about Charter House, [Somersetshire,] and the like at the forest at Fountain-Bleau, in France; and so in severall parts of England, and yet visible the remarques of earthquakes and volcanoes; but in time the husbandmen will cleare their ground of them, as at Durnham-downe they are exceedingly diminished since my remembrance, by making lime of them.

The great inequality of the surface of the earth was rendred so by earthquakes: which when taking fire, they ran in traines severall miles according to their cavernes; so for instance at Yatton Keynell, Wilts, a crack beginnes which runnes to Longdeanes, in the parish, and so to Slaughtonford, where are high steep cliffs of freestone, and opposite to it at Colern the like cliffs; thence to Bathe, where on the south side appeare Claverdon, on the north, Lansdon cliffs, both downes of the same piece; and it may be at the same tune the crack was thus made at St. Vincent's rocks near Bristow, as likewise Chedar rocks, like a street. From Castle Combe runnes a valley or crack to Ford, where it shootes into that that runnes from Yatton to Bathe. ——

Edmund Waller, Esq., the poet, made a quaere, I remember, at the Royal Society, about 1666, whether Salisbury plaines were always plaines ?

In Jamaica, and in other plantations of America, e. g. in Virginia, the natives did burn down great woods, to cultivate the soil with maiz and potato-rootes, which plaines were there made by firing the woods to sowe corne. They doe call these plaines Savannas. Who knowes but Salisbury plaines, &c. might be made long time ago, after this manner, and for the same reason ?

I have oftentimes wished for a mappe of England coloured according to the colours of the earth; with markes of the fossiles and minerals. [Geological maps, indicating, by different colours, the formations of various localities, are now familiar to the scientific student. The idea of such a map seems to have been first suggested by Dr. Martin Lister, in a paper on "New Maps of Countries, with Tables of Sands, Clays, &c." printed in the Philosophical Transactions, in 1683. The Board of Agriculture published a few maps in 1794, containing delineations of soils, &c.; and in 1815 Mr. William Smith produced the first map of the strata of England and Wales. Since then G. B. Greenough, Esq. has published a similar map, but greatly improved; and numerous others, representing different countries and districts, have subsequently appeared. - J. B.] ——

The great snailes* on the downes at Albery in Surrey (twice as big as ours) were brought from Italy by ..-.., Earle Marshal about 1638. ——

OF THE INDOLES OF THE IRISH. - Mr. J. Stevens went from, Trinity College in Oxford, 1647-8, to instruct the Lord Buckhurst in grammar; afterwards he was schoolmaster of the Free Schoole at Camberwell; thence he went to be master of Merchant Taylors' Schoole; next he was master of the schoole at Charter House; thence he went to the Free Schoole at Lever Poole, from whence he was invited to be a schoole master of the great schoole at Dublin, in Ireland; when he left that he was schoolmaster of Blandford, in Dorset; next of Shaftesbury; from whence he was invited by the city of Bristoll to be master of the Free Schoole there; from thence he went to be master of the Free Schoole of Dorchester in Dorset, and thence he removed to be Rector of Wyley in Wilts, 1666.

* Bavoli, (i.e.) drivelers.-J. EVELYN.

CHOROGRAPHIA: LOCAL INFLUENCES. 11

He is my old acquaintance, and I desired him to tell me freely if the Irish Boyes had as good witte as the English; because some of our severe witts have ridiculed the Irish understanding. He protested to me that he could not find but they had as good witts as the English; but generally speaking he found they had better memories. Dr. James Usher, Lord Primate of Ireland, had a great memorie: Dr Hayle (Dr. of the Chaire at Oxford) had a prodigious memorie: Sir Lleonell Jenkins told me, from him, that he had read over all the Greeke fathers three times, and never noted them but with his naile. Mr. .... Congreve, an excellent dramatique poet. Mr. Jo. Dodwell hath also a great memorie, and Mr. .... Tolet hathe a girle at Dublin, mathematique, who at eleven yeares old would solve questions in Algebra to admiration. Mr. Tolet told me he began to instruct her at seven yeares of age. See the Journall of the R. Society de hoc. ——

As to singing voyces wee have great diversity in severall counties of this nation; and any one may observe that generally in the rich vales they sing clearer than on the hills, where they labour hard and breathe a sharp ayre. This difference is manifest between the vale of North Wilts and the South. So in Somersettshire they generally sing well in the churches, their pipes are smoother. In North Wilts the milkmayds sing as shrill and cleare as any swallow sitting on a berne:-

> "So lowdly she did yerne, Like any swallow sitting on a berne."-
> CHAUCER.

——

According to the severall sorts of earth in England (and so all the world over) the Indigense are respectively witty or dull, good or bad.

To write a true account of the severall humours of our own countrey would be two sarcasticall and offensive: this should be a secret whisper in the eare of a friend only and I should superscribe here,

"Pinge duos angues -locus est sacer: extra Mei ite." - PERSIUS SATYR.

Well then! let these Memoires lye conceal'd as a sacred arcanum. ——

In North Wiltshire, and like the vale of Gloucestershire (a dirty clayey country) the Indigense, or Aborigines, speake drawling; they are phlegmatique, skins pale and livid, slow and dull, heavy of spirit: hereabout is but little, tillage or hard labour, they only milk the cowes and make cheese; they feed chiefly on milke meates, which cooles their braines too much, and hurts their inventions. These circumstances make them melancholy, contemplative, and malicious; by consequence whereof come more law suites out of North Wilts, at least double to the Southern Parts. And by the same reason they are generally more apt to be fanatiques: their persons are generally plump and feggy: gallipot eies, and some black: but they are generally handsome enough. It is a woodsere country, abounding much with sowre and austere plants, as sorrel, &c. which makes their humours sowre, and fixes their spirits. In Malmesbury Hundred, &c. (ye wett clayy parts) there have ever been reputed witches.

On the downes, sc. the south part, where 'tis all upon tillage, and where the shepherds labour hard, their flesh is hard, their bodies strong: being weary after hard labour, they have not leisure to read and contemplate of religion, but goe to bed to their rest, to rise betime the next morning to their labour.

> —— "redit labor actus in orbem
> Agricolae."-VIRGIL, ECLOG.
> ——

The astrologers and historians write that the ascendant as of Oxford is Capricornus, whose lord is Saturn, a religious planet, and patron of religious men. If it be so, surely this influence runnes all along through North Wilts, the vale of Glocestershire, and Somersetshire. In all changes of religions they are more zealous than other; where in the time of the Rome-Catholique religion there were more and better churches and religious houses founded than any other part of England could shew, they are now the greatest fanaticks, even to spirituall madness: e. g. the multitude of enthusiastes. Capt. Stokes, in his "Wiltshire Rant, "printed about 1650, recites ye strangest extravagancies of religion that were ever heard of since the time of the Gnosticks. The rich wett soile makes them hypochondricall.

> "Thus wind i'th Hypochondries pent,
> Proves but a blast, if downwards sent;
> But if it upward chance to flie
> Becomes new light and prophecy."-HUDIBRAS.

[The work above referred to bears the following title: "The Wiltshire Rant, or a Narrative of the Prophane Actings and Evil Speakings of Thomas Webbe, Minister of Langley Burrell, &c. By Edward Stokes. "4to. Lond. 1652.-J. B.] ——

The Norfolk aire is cleare and fine. Indigente, good clear witts, subtile, and the most litigious of England: they carry Littleton's Tenures at the plough taile. Sir Thorn. Browne, M. D., of Norwich, told me that their eies in that countrey doe quickly decay; which he imputes to the clearness and driness (subtilcness) of the aire. Wormwood growes the most plentifully there of any part of England; which the London apothecaries doe send for.

Memorandum.-That North Wiltshire is very worme-woodish and more litigious than South Wilts,

[A Table of Contents, or List of the Chapters, is prefixed to each Part, or Volume, of the Manuscript, as follows:-]

THE CHAPTERS.

PART I.

1. Air.
2. Springs Medicinall.
3. Rivers.
4. Soiles.
5. Mineralls and Fossills.
6. Stones.
7. Formed Stones.
8. An Hypothesis of the Terraqueous Globe: a digression "ad mentem M{emo}ri", R. Hook, R.S.S.
9. Plants.
10. Beastes.
11. Fishes.
12. Birds.
13. Insects and Reptils.
14. Men and Woemen.
15. Diseases and Cures.
16. Observations on some Register Books, as also the Poore Rates and Taxes of the County, "ad mentem D{omi}ni" W. Petty.

PART II.

1. Worthies.
2. The Grandure of the Herberts, Earles of Pembroke. Wilton House and Garden.
3. Learned Men who received Pensions from the Earles of Pembroke.
4. Gardens - Lavington-garden, Chelsey-garden, &c.
5. Arts - Inventions.
6. Architecture.
7. Agriculture and Improvements.
8. The Downes - Sheep - Shepherds - Pastoralls.
9. Wool.
10. Falling of Rents.
11. History of Cloathing
12. Eminent Cloathiers of this County.
13. Faires and Marketts
14. Hawks and Hawking.
15. The Race.
16. Number of Attorneys in this Countie now and heretofore.
17. Locall Fatality.
18. Accidents.
19. Seates
20. Draughts of the Seates and Prospects [an Appendix].

CHAPTER I.

AIR.

[THIS Chapter contains a variety of matter not apposite to Wiltshire. Besides the passages here quoted, there are accounts of several remarkable hurricanes, hail storms, &c., in different parts of England, as well as in Italy. The damage done by "Oliver's wind "(the storm said to have occurred on the death of the Protector Cromwell) is particularly noticed: though it may be desirable to state on the authority of Mr. Carlyle, the eloquent editor of "Cromwell's Letters and Speeches" (8vo. 1846), that the great tempest which Clarendon asserts to have raged "for some hours before and after the Protector's death", really occurred four days previous to that event. Aubrey no doubt readily adopted the general belief upon the subject. He quotes, without expressly dissenting from it, the opinion of Chief Justice Hale, that "whirlewinds and all winds of an extraordinary nature are agitated by the spirits of air". Lunar rainbows, and meteors of various kinds, are described in this chapter; together with prognostics of the seasons from the habits of animals, and some observations made with the barometer; and under the head of Echoes, "for want of good ones in this county", there is a long description by Sir Robert Moray of a remarkable natural echo at Roseneath, about seventeen miles from Glasgow. On sounds and echoes there are some curious notes by Evelyn, but these are irrelevant to the subject of the work.- J. B.]

BEFORE I enter upon the discourse of the AIR of this countie, it would not be amiss that I gave an account of the winds that most commonly blow in the western parts of England.

I shall first allege the testimony of Julius Cæsar, who delivers to us thus: "Corns ventus, qui magnam partem omnis temporis in his locis flare consuevit". - (Commentaries, lib. v.) To which I will subjoine this of Mr. Th. Ax, of Somersetshire, who hath made dayly observations of the weather for these twenty-five years past, since 1661, and finds that, one yeare with another, the westerly winds, which doe come from the Atlantick sea, doe blowe ten moneths of the twelve. Besides, he hath made observations for thirty years, that the mannours in the easterne parts of the netherlands of Somersetshire doe yield six or eight per centum of their value; whereas those in the westerne parts doe yield but three, seldome four per centum, and in some mannours but two per centum. Hence he argues that the winds carrying these unwholesome vapours of the low country from one to the other, doe make the one more, the other less, healthy.

This shire may be divided as it were into three stories or stages. Chippenham vale is the lowest. The first elevation, or next storie, is from the Derry Hill, or Bowdon Lodge, to the hill beyond the Devises, called Red-hone, which is the limbe or beginning of Salisbury plaines. From the top of this hill one may discerne Our Lady Church Steeple at Sarum, like a fine Spanish needle. I would have the height of these hills, as also Hackpen, and those toward Lambourn, which are the highest, to he taken with the quicksilver barometer, according to the method of Mr. Edmund Halley in Philosophical Transactions, No. 181. ——

Now, although Mindip-hills and Whitesheet, &c., are as a barr and skreen to keep off from Wiltshire the westerly winds and raines, as they doe in some measure repel those noxious vapours, yet wee have a flavour of them; and when autumnal agues raigne, they are more common on the hills than in the vales of this country. ——

The downes of Wiltshire are covered with mists, when the vales are clear from them, and the sky serene; and they are much more often here than in the lowest story or stage.

The leather covers of bookes, &c. doe mold more and sooner in the hill countrey than in the vale. The covers of my bookes in my closet at Chalke would be all over covered with a hoare mouldinesse, that I could not know of what colour the leather was; when my bookes in my closet at Easton- Piers (in the vale) were not toucht at all with any mouldiness.

So the roomes at Winterslow, which is seated exceeding high, are very mouldie and dampish. Mr. Lancelot Moorehouse, Rector of Pertwood, who was a very learned man, say'd that mists were very frequent there: it stands very high, neer Hindon, which one would thinke to stand very healthy: there is no river nor marsh neer it, yet they doe not live long there.

The wheat hereabout, sc. towards the edge of the downes, is much subject to be smutty, which they endeavour to prevent by drawing a cart-rope over the corne after the meldews fall.

Besides that the hill countrey is elevated so high in the air, the soile doth consist of chalke and mawme, which abounds with nitre, which craddles the air, and turns it into mists and water. ——

On the east side of the south downe of the farme of Broad Chalke are pitts called the Mearn-Pitts*, which, though on a high hill, whereon is a sea marke towards the Isle of Wight, yet they have alwaies water in them. How they came to be made no man knowes; perhaps the mortar was digged there for the building of the church.

* Marne is an old French word for marle.

——

Having spoken of mists it brings to my remembrance that in December, 1653, being at night in the court at Sr. Charles Snell's at Kington St. Michael in this country, there being a very thick mist, we sawe our shadowes on the fogg as on a wall by the light of the lanternes, sc. about 30 or 40 foot distance or more. There were several gentlemen which sawe this; particularly Mr. Stafford Tyndale. I have been enformed since by some that goe a bird-batting in winter nights that the like hath been seen: but rarely.

[A similar appearance to that here mentioned by Aubrey is often witnessed in mountainous countries, and in Germany has given rise to many supernatural and romantic legends. The "spectre of the Brocken", occasionally seen among the Harz mountains in Hanover, is described by Mr. Brayley in his account of Cumberland, in the Beauties of England and Wales, to illustrate some analogous appearances, which greatly astonished the residents near Souterfell, in that county, about a century ago.- J. B.] ——

The north part of this county is much influenc't by the river Severne, which flowes impetuously from the Atlantick Sea. It is a ventiduct, and brings rawe gales along with it: the tydes bringing a chilnesse with them. ——

On the top of Chalke-downe, 16 or 18 miles from the sea, the oakes are, as it were, shorne by the south and south-west winds; and do recline from the sea, as those that grow by the sea-side. ——

A Wiltshire proverb:-

"When the wind is north-west,
The weather is at the best:
If the raine comes out of east
'Twill raine twice twenty-four howres at the least."

I remember Sr. Chr. Wren told me, 1667, that winds might alter, as the apogæum: e.g. no raine in Egypt heretofore; now common: Spaine barren; Palseston sun-dried, &c. Quaere, Mr. Hook de hoc.

A proverbial rithme observed as infallible by the inhabitants on the Severne-side:-

"If it raineth when it doth flow,
Then yoke your oxe, and goe to plough;
But if it raineth when it doth ebb,
Then unyoke your oxe, and goe to bed."

——

It oftentimes snowes on the hill at Bowden-parke, when no snow falles at Lacock below it. This hill is higher than Lacock steeple three or four times, and it is a good place to try experiments. On this parke is a seate of my worthy friend George Johnson, Esqr., councillor at lawe, from whence is a large and most delightfull prospect over the vale of North Wiltshire.

Old Wiltshire country prognosticks of the weather:-

"When the hen doth moult before the cock,
The winter will be as hard as a rock;
But if the cock moults before the hen,
The winter will not wett your shoes seame."

In South Wiltshire the constant observation is that if droppes doe hang upon the hedges on Candlemas-day that it will be a good pease yeare. It is generally agreed on to be matter of fact; the reason perhaps may be that there may rise certain unctuous vapours which may cause that fertility. [This is a general observation: we have it in Essex. I reject as superstitious all prognosticks from the weather on particular days.-JOHN RAY.] ——

At Hullavington, about 1649, there happened a strange wind, which did not onely lay down flatt the corne and grasse as if a huge roller had been drawn over it, but it flatted also the quickset hedges of two or three grounds of George Joe, Esq.-It was a hurricane.

Anno 1660, I being then at dinner with Mr. Stokes at Titherton, news was brought in to us that a whirlewind had carried some of the hay- cocks over high elmes by the house: which bringes to my mind a story that is credibly related of one Mr. J. Parsons, a kinsman of ours, who, being a little child, was sett on a hay-cock, and a whirlewind took him up with half the hay-cock and carried him over high elmes, and layd him down safe, without any hurt, in the next ground.

——

Anno 1581, there fell hail-stones at Dogdeane, near Salisbury, as big as a child's fist of three or four yeares old; which is mentioned in the Preface of an Almanack by John Securis, Maister of Arts and Physick, dedicated to ..... Lord High Chancellor. He lived at Salisbury. "Tis pitty such accidents are not recorded in other Almanacks in order for a history of the weather. ——

Edward Saintlow, of Knighton, Esq. was buried in the church of Broad Chalk, May the 6th, 1578, as appeares by the Register booke. The snow did then lie so thick on the ground that the bearers carried his body over the gate in Knighton field, and the company went over the hedges, and they digged a way to the church porch. I knew some ancient people of the parish that did remember it. On a May day, 1655 or 1656, being then in Glamorganshire, at Mr. Jo. Aubrey's at Llanchrechid, I saw the mountaines of Devonshire all white with snow. There fell but little in Glamorganshire. ——

From the private Chronologicall Notes of the learned Edward Davenant, of Gillingham, D.D.:- "On the 25th of July 1670, there was a rupture in the steeple of Steeple Ashton by lightning. The steeple was ninety- three feet high above the tower; which was much about that height. This being mending, and the last stone goeing to be putt in by the two master workemen, on the 15th day of October following, a sudden storme with a clap of thunder tooke up the steeple from the tower, and killed both the workmen in nictu oculi. The stones fell in and broke part of the church, but never hurt the font. This account I had from Mr. Walter Sloper, attorney, of Clement's Inne, and it is registred on the church wall." [The inscription will be found in the Beauties of Wiltshire, vol. iii. page 205. It fully details the above circumstances.-J. B.]

Whilst the breaches were mending and the thunder showr arose, one standing in the church-yard observed a black cloud to come sayling along towards the steeple, and called to the workman as he was on the scaffold; and wisht him to beware of it and to make hast. But before he went off the clowd came to him, and with a terrible crack threw down the steeple, sc. about the middle, where he was at worke. Immediately they lookt up and their steeple was lost.

I doe well remember, when I was seaven yeares old, an oake in a ground called Rydens, in Kington St. Michael Parish, was struck with lightning, not in a strait but helical line, scil. once about the tree or once and a half, as a hop twists about the pole; and the stria remains now as if it had been made with a gouge. ——

On June 3rd, 1647, (the day that Cornet Joyce did carry King Charles prisoner to the Isle of Wight from Holdenby,) did appeare this phenomenon, [referring to a sketch in the margin which represents two luminous circles, intersecting each other; the sun being seen in the space formed by their intersection.-J. B.] which continued from about ten a clock in the morning till xii. It was a very cleare day, and few took notice of it because it was so near the sunbeams. It was seen at Broad Chalke by my mother, who espied it going to see what a clock it was at an horizontal dial, and then all the servants about the house sawe it Also Mr. Jo. Sloper the vicar here sawe it with his family, upon the like occasion looking on the diall. Some of Sr. George Vaughan of Falston's family who were hunting sawe it. The circles were of a rainbowe colour: the two filats, that crosse the circle (I presume they were segments of a third circle) were of a pale colour. ——

Ignis fatuus, called by the vulgar Kit of the Candlestick, is not very rare on our downes about Michaelmass. [These ignes fatui, or Jack-o'- lanthorns, as they are popularly called, are frequently seen in low boggy grounds. In my boyish days I was often terrified by stories of their leading travellers astray, and fascinating them.- J. B.]

Biding in the north lane of Broad Chalke in the harvest time in the twy-light, or scarce that, a point of light, by the hedge, expanded itselfe into a globe of about three inches diameter, or neer four, as boies blow bubbles with soape. It continued but while one could say one, two, three, or four at the most It was about a foot from my horse's eie; and it made him turn his head quick aside from it. It was a pale light as that of a glowe-worme: it may be this is that which they call a blast or blight in the country. ——

Colonel John Birch shewed me a letter from his bayliff, 166f, at Milsham, that advertised that as he was goeing to Warminster market early in the morning they did see fire fall from the sky, which did seem as big as a bushell I have forgot the day of the moneth. ——

From Meteors I will passe to the elevation of the poles. See "An Almanack, 1580, made for the Meridian of Salisbury, whose longitude is noted to bee ten degrees, and the latitude of the elevation of the Pole Arctick 51 degrees 47 minutes. By John Securis, Maister of Art and Physick". To which I will annexe the title of another old almanack, both which were collected by Mr. Will. Lilly. "Almanack, 1580, compiled and written in the City of Winchester, by Humphrey Norton, Student in Astronomic, gathered and made for the Pole Arctik of the said city, where the pole is elevated 51 degrees 42 minutes". ——

I come now to speak of ECHOS:-

"Vocalis Nymphe; quæ nec reticere loquenti
Nec prior ipsa loqui didicit, resonabilis Echo.
Ille fugit; fugiensque manus complexibus aufert."
- OVID, METAMORPH. lib. iii.

But this coy nymph does not onely escape our hands, but our sight, and wee doe understand her onely by induction and analogic. As the motion caused by a stone lett fall into the water is by circles, so sounds move by spheres in the same manner, which, though obvious enough, I doe not remember to have seen in any booke.

None of our ecchos in this country that I hear of are polysyllabicall. When the Gospels or Chapters are read over the choire dore of Our Lady Church in Salisbury, there is a quick and strong monosyllabicall echo, which comes presently on the reader's voice: but when the prayers are read in the choire, there is no echo at all. This reading place is 15 or 16 foot above the levell of the pavement: and the echo does more especially make its returnes from Our Ladies ChappelL

So in my kitchin-garden at the plain at Chalke is a monosyllabicall Echo; but it is sullen and mute till you advance .... paces on the easie ascent, at which place one's mouth is opposite to the middle of the heighth of the house at right angles; and then, - to use the expression of the Emperor Nero,-

"— reparabilis adsonat Echo."-PERSIUS.

——

Why may I not take the libertie to subject to this discourse of echos some remarks of SOUNDS? The top of one of the niches in the grot in Wilton gardens, as one sings there, doth return the note A "re", lowder, and clearer, but it doth not the like to the eighth of it. The diameter is 22 inches. But the first time I happened on this kind of experiment was when I was a scholar in Oxford, walking and singing under Merton-Colledge gate, which is a Gothique irregular vaulting, I perceived that one certain note could be returned with a lowd humme, which was C. "fa", "ut", or D. "sol", "re"; I doe not now well remember which. I have often observed in quires that at certain notes of the organ the deske would have a tremulation under my hand. So will timber; so will one's hat, though a spongie thing, as one holds it under one's arm at a musique meeting. These accidents doe make me reflect on the brazen or copper Tympana, mentioned by Vitruvius, for the clearer and farther conveying the sound of the recitatores and musicians to the auditors. I am from hence induc't to be of opinion that these tympana were made according to such and such proportions, suitable to such and such notes.

Mersennus, or Kircher, sayes, that one may know what quantity of liquor is in the vessel by the sound of it, knowing before the empty note. I have severall times heard great brasse pannes ring by the barking of a hound; and also by the loud voice of a strong man.-(The voice, if very strong and sharp, will crack a drinking glass.- J. EVELYN.)

[I have been favoured with a confirmation of this note of Evelyn from the personal experience of my old friend. Mr. Brayley, who was present at a party on Ludgate Hill, London, many years ago, when Mr. Broadhurst, the famed public vocalist, by singing a high note, caused a wine glass on the table to break, the bowl being separated from the stem.-J. B.] ——

After the echos I would have the draught of the house of John Hall, at Bradford, Esq., which is the best built house for the quality of a gentleman in Wilts. It was of the best architecture that was commonly used in King James the First's raigne. It is built all of freestone, full of windowes, hath two wings: the top of the house adorned with railes and baristers. There are two if not three elevations or ascents to it: the uppermost is adorned with terrasses, on which are railes and baristers of freestone. It faceth the river Avon, which lies south of it, about two furlongs distant: on the north side is a high hill. Now, a priori, I doe conclude that if one were on the south side of the river opposite to this elegant house, that there must of necessity be a good echo returned from the house; and probably if one stand east or west from the house at a due distance, the wings will afford a double echo.

[Part of this once fine and interesting mansion still remains, but wofully degraded and mutilated. It is called Kingston House, having been formerly the residence of a Duke of Kingston. It appears to have been built by the same architect as the mansion of Longleat, which was erected between the years 1567 and 1579, and for which, it is believed, John of Padua was employed to make designs.-J. B.]

CHAPTER II

SPRINGS MEDICINALL.

[IN Aubrey's time the mineral waters of Bath, Tonbridge, and other places, were very extensively resorted to for medical purposes, and great importance was attached to them in a sanatory point of view. The extracts which have been selected from this chapter sufficiently shew the limited extent of the author's chemical knowledge, in the analysis of waters; which he appears to have seldom carried beyond precipitation or evaporation. He mentions several other springs in Wiltshire and elsewhere, attributing various healing properties to some of them; but of others merely observing, with great simplicity, whether or not their water was adapted to wash linen, boil pease, or affect the fermentation of beer. The chapter comprises a few remarks on droughts; and particularly mentions a remarkable cure of cancer by an "emplaster" or "cataplasme" of a kind of unctuous earth found in Bradon forest.- J. B.]

HOLY-WELL, in the parish of Chippenham, near Sheldon, by precipitation of one-third of a pint with a strong lixivium, by the space of twenty- four houres I found a sediment of the quantity of neer a small hazell nut-shell of a kind of nitre; sc. a kind of flower of that colour (or lime stone inclining to yellow); the particles as big as grosse sand. Upon evaporation of the sayd water, which was a pottle or better, I found two sorts of sediment, perhaps by reason of the oblique hanging of the kettle: viz. one sort of a deep soot colour; the other of the colour of cullom earth. It changed not colour by infusion of powder of galles. Try it with syrup of violettes.

Hancock's well at Luckington is so extremely cold that in summer one cannot long endure one's hand in it. It does much good to the eies. It cures the itch, &c. By precipitation it yields a white sediment, inclining to yellow; sc. a kind of fine flower. I believe it is much impregnated with nitre. In the lane that leads from hence to Sapperton the earth is very nitrous, which proceeds from the rich deep blew marle, which I discovered in the lane which leads to Sapworth.

Biddle-well lies between Kington St. Michael and Swinley; it turnes milke. In the well of the mannour house (Mr. Thorn. Stokes) of Kington St. Michael is found talc, as also at the well at Priory St. Maries, in this parish; and I thinke common enough in these parts.

In Kington St. Michael parish is a well called Mayden-well, which I find mentioned in the Legeir-booke of the Lord Abbot of Glaston, called Secretum Domini [or Secretum Abbatis.] Let it be tryed. Alice Grig knows where about it is.

In the park at Kington St. Michael is a well called Marian's-well, mentioned in the same Legeir-book.

In the parish of North Wraxhall, at the upper end of ye orchard of Duncomb-mill at ye foot of ye hill ye water petrifies in some degree; which is the onely petrifying water that I know in this countie. [In subsequent pages Aubrey refers to other petrifying waters near Calne, Devizes, and elsewhere.-J. B.]

At Draycott Cerne (the seate of my ever honoured friend Sir James Long, Baronet, whom I name for honour's sake) the waters of the wells are vitriolate, and with powder of galles doe turne of a purple colour.-[I have a delicate, cleare, and plentifull spring at Upper Deptford, never dry, and very neer the river Ravens-born; the water famous for ye eyes, and many other medicinal purposes. Sr Rich. Browne, my father-in-lawe, immur'd it, wth a chaine and iron dish for travellers to drink, and has sett up an inscription in white marble.- JOHN EVELYN.] ——

Stock-well, at Rowd, is in the highway, which is between two gravelly cliffs, which in warm weather are candied. It changed not colour with powder of galles; perhaps it may have the effect of Epsham water. The sediment by precipitation is a perfect white flower, Mice nitre. The inhabitants told me that it is good for the eies, and that it washes very well. It is used for the making of medicines. ——

At Polshutt rises a spring in a ditch neer Sommerham-bridge, at Seenes townes-end, in a ground of Sir Walter Long, Baronet, which with galles does presently become a deepe claret colour. ——

At Polshutt are brackish wells; but especiall that of Rich. Bolwell, two quarts whereof did yield by evaporation two good spoonfulls heapt of a very tart salt. Dr. Meret believes it to be vitriolish.

Neer to which is Send (vulgo Seene), a very well built village on a sandy hill, from whence it has its name; sand being in the old English called send (for so I find writ in the records of the Tower); as also Send, in Surrey, is called for the same reason. Underneath this sand (not very deep), in some place of the highway not above a yard or yard and a half, I discovered the richest iron oare that ever I sawe or heard of. Come there on a certain occasion,* it rained at twelve or one of the clock very impetuously, so that it had washed away the sand from the oare; and walking out to see the country, about 3 p.m., the sun shining bright reflected itself from the oare to my eies. Being surprised at so many spangles, I took up the stones with a great deale of admiration. I went to the smyth, Geo. Newton, an ingeniose man, who from a blacksmith turned clock maker and fiddle maker, and he assured me that he has melted of this oare in his forge, which the oare of the forest of Deane, &c. will not doe.

* At the Revell there, An°. D. 1666.

The reader is to be advertised that the forest of Milsham did extende itselfe to the foot of this hill. It was full of goodly oakes, and so neer together that they say a squirrill might have leaped from tree to tree. It was disafforested about 1635, and the oakes were sold for 1s. or 2s. per boord at the most; and then nobody ever tooke notice of this iron-oare, which, as I sayd before, every sun-shine day, after a rousing shower, glistered in their eies. Now there is scarce an oake left in the whole parish, and oakes are very rare all hereabout, so that this rich mine cannot be melted and turned to profit. Finding this plenty of rich iron-oare, I was confident that I should find in the village some spring or springs impregnated with its vertue; so I sent my servant to the Devizes for some galles to try it; and first began at Mr. J. Sumner's, where I lay, with the water of the draught- well in the court within his house, which by infusion of a little of the powder of the galles became immediately as black as inke; that one may write letters visible with it; sc. as with inke diluted with water, which the water of Tunbridge will not doe, nor any other iron water that ever I met with or heard of. I tryed it by evaporation and it did yield an umberlike sediment: I have forgot the proportion. I gave it to the Royall Society.

In June 1667,1 sent for three bottles of this well water to London, and experimented it before the Royall Society at Gresham Colledge, at which, time there was a frequent assembly, and many of the Physitians of the Colledge of London. Now, whereas the water of Tunbridge, and others of that kind, being carried but few miles loose their spirits, and doe not alter their colour at all with powder of galles, these bottles, being brought by the carrier eighty odd miles, and in so hot weather, did turn, upon the infusion of the powder, as deep as the deepest claret; to the admiration of the physitians then present, who unanimously declared that this water might doe much good: and Dr. Piers sayd that in some cases such waters were good to begin with, and to end with the Bath; and in some "è contra". This place is but 9 or 10 miles from Bath.

The Drs. then spake to me, to write to some physitians at Bath, and to recommend it to them, whom I knew; which I did. But my endeavours were without effect till August 1684. But they doe so much good that they now speake aloud their own prayses. They were satisfied (I understood at last) of ye goodnesse and usefulnesse of these waters, but they did not desire to have patients to be drawn from ye Bath. Now, whereas one person is grieved with aches, or bruises, or dead palseys, for which diseases the Bath is chiefly proper, ten or more are ill of chronicall diseases and obstructions, for the curing whereof these chalybiate waters are the most soveraigne remedie.

This advertisement I desired Dr. Rich. Blackburne to word. He is one of the College of Physitians, and practiseth yearly at Tunbridge- wells. It was printed in an Almanack of Hen. Coley about 1681, but it tooke no effect.

"Advertisement.- At Seen (neer ye Devizes in Wiltshire) are springs discovered to be of the nature and vertue of those at Tunbridge, and altogether as good. They are approved of by severall of ye physitians of the Colledge in London, and have donne great cures, viz. particularly in the spleen, the reines, and bladder, affected with heat, stone, or gravell; or restoring hectick persons to health and strength, and wonderfully conducing in all cases of obstructions."

I proceeded and tryed other wells, but my ingeniose faithfull servant Robert Wiseman (Prudhome) tryed all the wells in the village, and found that all the wells of the south side doe turne with galles more or lesse, but the wells of the north side turne not with them at all. This hill lies eastward and westward; quod N.B.

The water of Jo. Sumner's well was so bad for household use that they could not brew nor boyle with it, and used it only to wash the house, &c.; so that they were necessitated to sinke a well in the common, which is walled, about a bow shott or more from his dwelling house, where is fresh and wholsome water. Memorandum. Dr. Grew in his [Catalogue] of the Royall Society has mistaken this well in the common for the medicinall well of J. Sumner. But, mem., there is another well that turnes, I thinke, as deep as J. Sumner's. [On the subject of this discovery by Aubrey, to which he attached great importance, the reader is referred to Britton's "Memoir of Aubrey", published by the Wiltshire Topographical Society, p. 17. As there stated, most of the property about Seend now belongs to W. H. Ludlow Bruges, Esq. M.P., who preserves the well; but its waters are not resorted to for sanatory purposes. - J. B.] ——

Memorandum. That Dudley, Lord North, grandfather to Sir Francis North, Lord Keeper, and Baron of Guildford, returning from his travells from the Spaw, &c. making a visit to the Earle of Leicester at Penshurst, his relation, as he was riding thereabout made observation of the earth where the water run, the colour whereof gave him an indication of its vertue. He sent for galles, and tryed it by evaporation, &c. and found out the vertue, which hath ever since continued and donne much good to the drinkers, and the inhabitants thereabout* This discovery was this year (1685), about seventy-five years since, and 'tis pitty it should be buried in oblivion. My Lord Keeper North told me of this himselfe.

*At Tunbridge and Epsom Wells, where were only wild commons, now are abundance of well-built houses. [The changes and improvements at Tunbridge Wells have been very great since Aubrey wrote. In 1832 I wrote and published an octavo volume- " Descriptive Sketches of Tunbridge Wells and the Calverley Estate", with maps and prints. Since that time the railroad has been opened to that place, which will increase its popularity. Epsom Wells are now deserted. At Melksham, in the vicinity of Seend, a pump-room, baths, and lodging-houses were erected about twenty-five years ago; but fashion has not favoured the place with her sanction. See Beauties of Wiltshire, vol. iii.- J. B.]

——

When the springs doe breake in Morecombe-bottom, in the north side of the parish of Broad Chalke, which is seldome, 'tis observed that it foretells a deer yeare for corne. It hath discontinued these forty yeares. ——

At Crudwell, neer to the mannour house, is a fine spring in the street called Bery-well. Labourers say it quenches thirst better than the other waters; as to my tast, it seemed to have aliquantulum aciditatis; and perhaps is vitriolate. The towne, a mannour of the Lord Lucas, hath its denomination from this well; perhaps it is called Crudwell from its turning of milke into cruds.

At Wotton Basset, in the parke, is a petrifying water, which petrifies very quickly.

At Huntsmill, in this parish, is a well where the water turnes leaves,
&c. of a red colour.

——

Below the Devises, the water in all the ditches, at the fall of the leafe, lookes blewish, which I could not but take notice of when I was a schoole boy. ——

In the parish of Lydyard-Tregoz is a well called by the country people Antedocks-well (perhaps here was the cell of some anchorete or hermite); the water whereof they say was famous heretofore in the old time for working miracles and curing many diseases. ——

As I rode from Bristoll to Welles downe Dundery-hill, in the moneth of June, 1663, walking down the hill on foot, presently after a fine shower I sawe a little thinne mist arise out of the ditch on the right hand by the highwayes side. But when I came neer to the place I could not discern it: so I went back a convenient distance and saw it again; and then tooke notice of some flower or weed that grew in the ditch whence the vapour came. I came againe to the marke, and could see nothing of a mist, as before; but my nose was affected with a smell which I knew; but immediately it came not to my mind; which was the smell of the canales that come from the bathes at Bath. By this time my groom was come to me, who, though of a dull understanding, his senses were very quick; I asked him if he smelt nothing, and after a sniff or two, he answered me, he smelt the smell of the Bath. This place is about two parts of three of the descent of Dundery-hill, ——

I doe believe the water of the fountaine that serves Lacock abbey is impregnated with {symbol for mars}[iron]. That at Crokerton, near Warminster, I thinke not at all inferior to those of Colbec in France. The best felt hatts are made at both places. ——

At or near Lavington is a good salt spring. (From ye Earl of Abingdon.)

The North Wilts horses, and other stranger horses, when they come to drinke of the water of Chalke-river, they will sniff and snort, it is so cold and tort I suppose being so much impregnated with {alchemical sign for nitre} [nitre]. ——

Advise my countrymen to try the rest of the waters as the Sieur Du Clos, Physitian to his most Christian Majestie, has donne, and hath directed in his booke called " Observations of the Minerall Waters of France made in ye Academy of Sciences."- I did it transient, and full of businesse, and "aliud agens tanquam canis e Nilo". ——

The freestone fountaine above Lacock, neer Bowdon, in the rode-way, is higher than the toppe of Lacock steeple. Sir J. Talbot might have for a small matter the highest and noblest Jeddeau [jet-d'eau] in England. ——

It is at the foot of St. Anne's-hill, or else Martinsoll-hill, {that} three springs have their source and origen; viz. the south Avon, which runnes to Sarum, and disembogues at Christes Church in Hants; the river Kynet, which runnes to Morlebrugh, Hungerford, and disembogues into the Thames about Reading; and on the foote of the north side arises another that runnes to Calne, which disembogues into the north Avon about Titherton, and runnes to Bristowe into the Severne. [See also Chap. III. Rivers.-J. B.] ——

In the parish of....... is a spring dedicated to St. Winifred, formerly of great account for its soveraigne vertues. What they were I cannot learne; neither can I thinke the spring to be of less vertue now than in the time of Harry the Eight; in which age I am informed it was of great esteeme: and I am apt to conjecture that the reason why the spring grew out of fame was because S*. Winifred grew out of favour. ——

At the Devizes, on the north side of the castle, there is a rivulet of water which doth petrifie leafes, sticks, plants, and other things that grow by it; which doth seem to prove that stones grow not by apposition only, as the Aristotelians assert, but by susception also; for if the stick did not suscept some vertue by which it is transmuted we may admire what doth become of the matter of the stick ——

At Knahill [Knoyle] is a minerall water, which Dr. Toop and Dr. Chamberlayn have tryed. It is neer Mr. Willoughby's house: it workes very kindly, and without any gripeing; it hath been used ever since about 1672. ——

Dr. Guydot sayes the white sediment in the water of North Wiltshire is powder of freestone; and he also tells me that there is a medicinall well in the street at Box, near Bathe, which hath been used ever since about 1670. ——

Mr. Nich. Mercator told me that water may be found by a divining rod made of willowe; whiche he hath read somewhere; he thinks in Vitruvius. Quaere Sir John Hoskins de hoc. ——

In Poulshott parish the spring was first taken notice of about thirty yeares since by S. Pierse, M.D. of Bathe, and some few made use of it Some of the Devises, who dranke thereof, told me that it does good for the spleen, &c., and that a hectick and emaciated person, by drinking this water, did in the space of three weekes encrease in flesh, and gott a quick appetite.

Memorandum. In this village are severall springs, which tast brackish; which I had not the leisure to try, but onely by præcipitation, and they yield a great quantity of the white flower-like sediment. ——

Bitteston.- At the George Inne, the beere that is brewed of the well there is diuretique. I knew some that were troubled with the stone and gravell goe often thither for that reason. The woman of the house was very much troubled with fitts of the mother; and having lived here but a quarter of a yeare, found herself much mended; as also her mother, troubled with the same disease. I observed in the bottome of the well deep blew marle.

[The hysterical paroxysms to which females are peculiarly subject were in Aubrey's time commonly termed "the mother", or "fits of the mother". Dr. Edward Jorden published a "Discourse on the Suffocation of the Mother", (4to.) in 1603.- J. B.] ——

Alderton. - Mr. Gore's well is a hard water, which, when one washes one's hands will make them dry, as if it were allume water. I tryed it by præcipitation, and the sediment was the colour of barme, white and yellow, and fell in a kind of flakes, as snow sometimes will fall, whereas all the other sediments were like fine flower or powder. ——

In Minety Common in Bradon forest, neer the rode which leadeth to Ashton Caynes, is a boggy place called the Gogges, where is a spring, or springs, rising up out of fuller's earth. This puddle in hot and dry weather is candid like a hoar frost; which to the tast seemes nitrous. I have seen this salt incrustation, even 14th September, four foot round the edges. With half a pound of this earth I made a lixivium. Near half a pint did yield upon evaporation a quarter of an ounce wanting two graines. Of the remainder of the lixivium, which was more than a pint, I evaporated almost all to crystallize in a cellar. The liquor turned very red, and the crystalls being putt on a red hott iron flew away immediately, like saltpetre, leaving behind a very little quantity of something that look'd like burnt allum. Now it is certain that salts doe many times mixe; and Mr. Robert Boyle tells me hee believes it is sea-salt mix't with {nitre}, and there is a way to separate them. After a shower this spring will smoake. The mudd or earth cleanses and scowres incomparably. A pike of eighteen foot long will not reach to the bottome.

My Lady Cocks of Dumbleton told me that ladies did send ten miles and more for water from a spring on Malverne hill in Worcestershire to wash their faces and make 'em faire. I believe it was such a nitrous spring as this. ——

The fuller's earth which they use at Wilton is brought from Woburne in Bedfordshire; and sold for ten groates a bushell. ——

The Baths may have its tinging vertue from the antimonie in Mendip. Quaere Mr. Kenrick, that when he changed a sixpence holding it in his hand it turned yellow, and a woman refused it for bad silver. I thinke he had been making crocus of antimonie. The chymists doe call antimony Proteus, from its various colouring. ——

Mr. T. Hanson, of Magd. Coll. Oxon, acquaints me in a letter of May 18, 1691, that he observes that almost all the well-waters about the north part of Wiltshire were very brackish. At High-worth, Mr. Alhnon, apothecary, told him he had often seen a quantity of milke coagulated with it: and yet the common people brew with it, which gives their beer an ungratefull tast. At Cricklad their water is so very salt that the whole town are obliged to have recourse to a river hard by for their necessary uses. At Wootton Basset, at some small distance from the town, they have a medicinall spring, which a neighbouring divine told him Dr. Willis had given his judgment of, viz. that it was the same with that of Astrop. They have also a petrifying spring. At the Devizes, about a quarter of a mile from the towne, a petrifying spring shewn me by Dr. Merriweather, a physitian there. At Bagshot, near Hungerford, is a chalybiate, dranke by some gentlemen with good successe. ——

Mdm. In my journey to Oxford, comeing through Bagley-wood, on St. Mark's day, 1695,1 discovered two chalybiate springs there, in the highway; which On May the 10th I tryed with powder of galles, and they give as black a tincture as ever I saw such waters: one may write with it as legibly as with black lead.

At the gate at Wotton Common, near Cumnor in Berkshire, is a spring which I have great reason to believe is such another: and also at the foot of Shotover-hill, near the upping-stock, I am confident by the clay, is such another spring. Deo gratias. ——

Quæres for the Tryall of Minerall Waters; by the Honourable Sir William Petty, Kt.:-

1. How much heavier 'tis than brandy ?
2. How much common water will extinguish its tast ?
3. What quantity of salt upon its evaporation ?
4. How much sugar, allum, vitriol, nitre, will dissolve in a pint of
it ?

5. Whether any animalcule will breed in it, and in how long time ?
6. Whether fish, viz. trout, eeles, &c. will live in it, and how long?
7. Whether 'twill hinder or promote the curdling of milk, and fermentation ?
8. Whether soape will mingle with it ?
9. Whether 'twill extract the dissolvable parts of herbes, rootes, seedes, &c. more or less than other waters; (i. e.) whether it be a more powerful menstruum ?
10. How galles will change its colour ?
11. How 'twill change the colour of syrup of violets ?
12. How it differs from other waters in receiving colours, cochineel, saffron, violets &c.?
13. How it boyles dry pease?
14. How it colours fresh beefe, or other flesh in boyling ?
15. How it washes hands, beards, linnen, SEC. ?
16. How it extracts mault in brewing ?
17. How it quenches thirst, with meat or otherwise ?
8. Whether it purges; in what quantity, time, and with what symptomes?
19. Whether it promotes urine, sweat, or sleep ?
20. In what time it passeth, and how afterwards ?
21. Whether it sharpens or flattens the appetite to meate ?
22. Whether it vomits, causes coughs, &c. ?
23. Whether it swell the belly, legges; and how, in what time, and quantity &c. ?
24. How it affects sucking children, and (if tryed) foetus in the wombe ?
25. Whether it damps or excites venerie ?
26. How blood lett whilest the waters are dranke lookes, and how it changes ?
27. In what degrees it purges, in different degrees of evaporation, and brewed ?
28. Whether it breakes away by eructation and downwards ?
29. Whether it kills the asparagus in the urine?
30. What quantity may be taken of it in prime ?
31. Whether a sprig of mint or willow growes equally as out of other waters?
32. In what time they putrify and stink ?

CHAPTER III.

RIVERS.

[THE following extracts include the whole of this chapter, with the exception of a few extraneous passages.-J. B.]

I SHALL begin with the river of Wyley-bourn, which gives name to Wilton, the shire town. The mappe-makers write it Wyley fulvous, and joiner a British and a Saxon word together: but that is a received error. I doe believe that the ancient and true name was Twy, as the river Twy in Herefordshire, which signifies vagary: and so this river Wye, which is fed with the Deverill springs, in its mandrels winding, watering the meadows, gives the name to the village called Wyley, as also Wilton (Wyley-ton); where, meeting with the upper Avon and the river Adder, it runnes to Downtown and Fording bridge, visiting the New Forest, and disembogues into the sea at Christ Church in Hampshire. On Monday morning, the 20th of September, [1669] was begun a well intended designe for cutting the river [Avon] below Salisbury to make it navigable to carry boats of burthen to and from Christ Church. This work was principally encouraged by the Right Reverend Father in God, Seth, Lord Bishop of Salisbury, his Lordship digging the first spit of earth, and driving the first wheeled barrow. Col. John Wyndham was also a generous benefactor and encourager of this undertaking. He gave to this designe an hundred pounds. He tells me that the Bishop of Salisbury gave, he thinks, an hundred and fifty pounds: he is sure a hundred was the least. The engineer was one Mr. Far trey, but it seems not his craft's-master; for through want of skill all this charge and paines came to nothing: but An° Done 16. . .it was more auspiciously undertaken and perfected; and now boats passe between Salisbury and Christ Church, and carry wood and corne from the New Forest, the cartage whereof was very dearer; but as yet they want a haven at Christ Church, which will require time and charge.

[Of the numerous rivers in Wiltshire only a few are navigable, and those only for a short distance in the county. This is the consequence of its inland position and comparative elevation; whence it results that the principal streams have little more than their sources within its limits. The project of rendering the Avon navigable from Salisbury to Christ Church appears to have been first promulgated by John Taylor, the Water Poet, who, in 1625, made an excursion in his own sherry, with five companions, from London to Christ Church, and thence up the Avon to Salisbury. He published an account of his voyage, under the title of " A Discovery by sea, from London to Salisbury." Francis Mathew also suggested the improvement of the navigation of the river in 1655; and an Act of Parliament for that purpose was obtained in 1664. Bishop Ward was translated to the see of Salisbury in 1667, but the commencement of the works, as described by Aubrey, was probably delayed till 1669, in August of which year the Mayor of Salisbury and others were constituted a Committee "to consult and treat with such persons as will undertake to render the Avon navigable." Two other pamphlets urging the importance of the project were published in 1672 and 1675 (see Gough's Topography, vol. ii. p. 366); and in 1687 a series of regulations was compiled "for the good and orderly government and usage of the New Haven and Pier now made near Christchurch, and of the passages made navigable from thence to the city of New Sarum." (See Hatcher's History of Salisbury, pp. 460, 497.) The works thus made were afterwards destroyed by a flood, and remained in ruins till 1771. Some repairs were then executed, but they were inefficient; and the navigation is now given up, except at the mouth of the river; and even there the bar of Christchurch is an insurmountable obstacle except at spring tides.-(Penny Cyclopædia, art. Wiltshire.) As the Bishop dug the first spitt, or spadeful of earth, and drove the first wheelbarrow, that necessary process was no doubt made a matter of much ceremony. The laying the "first stone" of an important building has always been an event duly celebrated; and the practice of some distinguished individual "digging the first spitt" of earth has lately been revived with much pomp and parade, in connection with the great railway undertakings of the present age.- J. B.] ——

The river Adder riseth about Motcomb, neer Shaftesbury. In the Legeir booke of Wilton Abbey it is wrott Noþþre, "a Nodderi fluvii ripa", (hodie Adder-bourn, Naþþre}, "serpens, anguis", Saxonicè, Addar, in Welsh, signifies a bird.*) This river runnes through the magnificent garden of the Earle of Pembroke at Wilton, and so beyond to Christ Church. It hath in it a rare fish, called an umber, which are sent from Salisbury to London. They are about the bignesse of a trowt, but preferred before a trowt This kind of fish is in no other river in England, except the river Humber in Yorkeshire. [The umber is perhaps more generally known as the grayling. See Chap. XL Fishes.-J. B.]

* [Adar is the plural of Aderyn, a bird, and therefore signifies birds.-J. B.]

——

The rivulet that gives the name to Chalke-bourn,† and running through Chalke, rises at a place called Naule, belonging to the farme of Broad Chalke, where are a great many springs that issue out of the chalkie ground. It makes a kind of lake of the quantity of about three acres. There are not better trouts (two foot long) in the kingdom of England than here; I was thinking to have made a trout pond of it. The water of this streame washes well, and is good for brewing. I did putt in craw-fish, but they would not live here: the water is too cold for them. This river water is so acrimonious, that strange horses when they are watered here will snuff and snort, and cannot well drinke of it till they have been for some time used to it. Methinks this water should bee admirably good for whitening clothes for cloathiers, because it is impregnated so much with nitre, which is abstersive.

† Bourna, fluvius. (Vener. Bed. Hist. Eceles.) As in some counties they say, In such or such a vale or dale; so in South Wilts they say, such or such a bourn: meaning a valley by such a river. ——

The river Stour hath its source in Sturton Parke, and gives the name [Stourhead.-J. B.] to that ancient seat of the Lord Sturtons. Three of the springs are within the park pale and in Wiltshire; the other three are without the pale in

Somersetshire. The fountaines within the parke pale are curbed with pierced cylinders of free stone, like tunnes of chimneys; the diameter of them is eighteen inches. The coate armour of the Lord Sturton is, Sable, a bend or, between six fountaines; which doe allude to these springs. Stour is a British word, and signifies a great water: sc. "dwr" is water; "ysdwr" is a considerable, or great water: "ys", is "particula augens". [The Stour rises near the junction of the three counties, Wiltshire, Somersetshire, and Dorsetshire. Its course is chiefly through the last mentioned county, after leaving which it enters Hampshire, and flows into the South Avon near Christchurch.- J. B.] ——

Deverill hath its denomination from the diving of the rill, and its rising again. Mr. Cambden saieth, In this shire is a small rill called Deverill, which runneth a mile under ground,* like as also doth the little river Mole in Surry, and the river Anas [Guadiana ?-J. B.] in Spain, and the Niger in Africk. Polybius speakes the like of the river Oxus, "which, falling with its force into great ditches, which she makes hollow, and opens the bottome by the violence of her course, and by this meanes takes its course under ground for a small space, and then riseth again." (lib. x.)

* I am informed by the minister of Deverill Longbridge, and another gentleman that lived at Maiden Bradley thirty years, that they never knew or heard of this river Deverall that runs underground.-(BISHOP TANNER.) [Yet Selden, in his "Notes to Drayton's Poly-Olbion", makes the same statement as Aubrey does respecting the Deverill.- J. B.]

"Sic ubi terreno Lycus est epotus hiatu,
Existit procul hinc, alioq{ue} renascitur ore.
Sic modò combibitur, tecto modò gurgite lapsus
Redditur Argolicis ingens Erasinus in arvis:
Et Mysum capitisq{ue} sui ripaq{ue} prioris
Pœnituisse ferunt, aliò nunc ire, Calcum."
- OVID, METAMORPH. lib. xv.

In Grittleton field is a swallow-hole, where sometimes foxes, &c. doe take sanctuary; there are severall such in North Wiltshire, made by flouds, &c.; but neer Deene is a rivulet that runnes into Emmes-poole, and nobody knowes what becomes of it after it is swallowed by the earth.

[The reader will find a full account of the remarkable "swallows", or "swallow holes", in the course of the river Mole, in Brayley's History of Surrey, vol. i. p. 171-185, with a map, and some geological comments by Dr. Mantell. The river, or stream designated by Aubrey as the Deverill, is probably the principal of several streams which rise near the villages of Longbridge Deverill, Hill Deverill, Brixton Deverill, Monkton Deverill, and Kingston Deverill (in the south west part of Wiltshire), and, after running through Maiden Bradley, flow into the Wyley near Warminster.-J. B.] ——

At the foot of Martinsoll-hill doe issue forth three springs, which are the sources of three rivers; they divide like the parting of the haire on the crowne of the head, and take their courses three severall wayes: viz. one on the south side of the hill, which is the beginning of the upper Avon,† which runnes to Salisbury; on the other side springes the river Kynet, which runnes eastward to Marleborough;‡ from thence passing by Hungerford, Newbury, &c. it looses itselfe and name in the river of Thames, near Reading. The third spring is the beginning of the stream that runnes to Caln, called Marden,§ and driving several mills, both for corne and fulling, is swallowed up by the North Avon at Peckingill-meadow near Tytherington. [See also Aubrey's description of these three springs, ante, page 24.- J. B.]

† Avon, a river, in the British language. ‡ Cynetium, Marleborough, hath its name from the river. The Welsh pronounce y as wee doe u. § Quaere, if it is called Marden, or Marlen? [Marden is the present name.- J. B.]

The North Avon riseth toward Tedbury in Gloucestershire, and runnes to Malmesbury, where it takes in a good streame, that comes from Hankerton, and also a rivulet that comes from Sherston,* which inriching the meadows as it runnes to Chippenham, Lacock, Bradford, Bath, Kainsham, and the city of Bristowe, disembogues into the Severne at Kingrode.

* [The Sheraton rivulet, and not that which rises near Tetbury, is generally regarded as the source of the North, or Bristol Avon.-J. B.] ——

The silver Thames takes some part of this county in its journey to Oxford. The source of it is in Gloucestershire, neer Cubberley (in the rode from Oxford to Gloucester), where there are severall springs. In our county it visits Cricklad, a market towne, and gives name to Isey, a village neer; and with its fertile overflowing makes a most glorious verdure in the spring season. In the old deeds of lands at and about Cricklad they find this river by the name of Thamissis fluvius and the Thames. The towne in Oxfordshire is writt Tame and not Thame; and I believe that Mr. Cambden's marriage of Thame and Isis, in his elegant Latin poem, is but a poeticall fiction: I meane as to the name of Thamisis, which he would not have till it comes to meet the river Thame at Dorchester.

[The true source of the river Thames has been much disputed. A spring which rises near the village of Kemble, at the north-western extremity of Wiltshire, has been commonly regarded, during the last century, as the real "Thames head". It flows thence to Ashton Keynes, and onward to Cricklade. At the latter place it is joined by the river Churn, which comes from Coberly, about 20 miles to the northward, in Gloucestershire. Aubrey refers to the latter stream as the source of the Thames; and, on the principle of tracing the origin of a river to its most remote source, the same view has been taken by some other writers, who consequently dispute the claims of the Kemble spring. - J. B.] ——

The river Thames, as it runnes to Cricklad, passes by Ashton Kaynes;† from whence to Charleton, where the North Avon runnes, is about three miles. Mr. Henry Brigges (Savilian professor of Geometrie at Oxford) observing in the mappe the nearnesse of these two streames, and reflecting on the great use that might accrue if a cutt were made from the one to the other (of which there are many examples in the Low Countreys), tooke a journey from Oxford to view it, and found the ground levell and sappable and was very well pleased with his notion; for that if these two rivers were maried by a canal between them, then might goods be brought from London to Bristow by water, which would be an extraordinary convenience both for safety and to avoid overturning. This was about the yeare 1626. But there had been a long calme of peace, and men minded nothing but pleasure and luxury.

"Jam patimur longæ pacis mala, sævior armis Luxuria incumbit."- LUCAN.

+ [If Aubrey was right in the preceding paragraph in regarding the stream which rises at "Cubberley" in Gloucestershire as the source of the Thames, he is wrong in stating that "the Thames" passes by Ashton Keynes. It is the other brook, from Kemble, which runs through that village; and the two streams only become united at Cricklade, which is some distance lower down, to the eastward of Ashton Keynes.- J. B.]

Knowledge of this kind was not at all in fashion, so that he had no encouragement to prosecute this noble designe: and no more done but the meer discovery: and not long after he died, scilicet Anno Domini 1631, January 31st.; and this ingeniose notion had died too and beene forgotten, but that Mr. Francis Mathew, (formerly of the county of Dorset, a captain in his majestie King Charles I. service), who was acquainted with him, and had the hint from him, and after the wars ceased revived this designe. Hee tooke much paines about it; went into the countrey and made a mappe of it, and wrote a treatise of it, and addressed himselfe to Oliver the Protector, and the Parliament. Oliver was exceedingly pleased with the designe; and, had he lived but a little longer, he would have had it perfected: but upon his death it sank.

After his Majesties restauration, I recommended Captain Mathew to the Lord Wm. Brouncker, then President of the Royall Societie, who introduced him to his Majestie; who did much approve of the designe; but money was wanting, and publick-spirited contributions; and the Captain had no purse (undonn by the warres), and the heads of the Parliament and Counsell were filled with other things.- Thus the poor old gentleman's project came to nothing.

He died about 1676, and left many good papers behind him concerning this matter, in the hands of his daughters; of which I acquainted Mr. John Collins, R.S.S. in An°. 1682, who tooke a journey to Oxford (which journey cost him his life, by a cold), and first discoursed with the barge-men there concerning their trade and way: then he went to Lechlade, and discoursed with the bargemen there; who all approved of the designe. Then he took a particular view of the ground to be cutt between Ashton-kaynes and Charleton. From Malmesbury he went to Bristoll. Then he returned to Malmesbury again and went to Wotton Bassett, and took a view of that way. Sir Jonas Moore told me he liked that way, but J. Collins was clearly for the cutt between Ashton-Kayns and Charleton.

At his return to London I went with him to the daughters of Mr. Mathew, who shewed him their father's papers; sc. draughts, modells, copper-plate of the mappe of the Thames, Acts of Parliament, and Bills prepared to be enacted, &c.; as many as did fill a big portmantue. He proposed the buying of them to the R. Societie, and tooke the heads of them, and gave them an abstract of them. The papers, &c. were afterwards brought to. the R. Societie; the price demanded for all was but five pounds (the plate of the mappe did cost 8li.) The R. Societie liked the designe; but they would neither undertake the businesse nor buy the papers. So that noble knight, Sir James Shaen, R.S.S., who was then present, slipt five guineas into J. Collins's hand to give to the poor gentlewomen, and so immediately became master of these rarities. There were at the Societie at the same time three aldermen of the city of London (Sir Jo. Laurence, Sir Patient Ward, and ....), fellows of the Society, who when they heard that Sir James Shaen had gott the possession of them were extremely vex't; and repented (when 'twas too late) that they had overslipped such an opportunity: then they would have given 30li. This undertaking had been indeed most proper for the hon{oura}ble city of London.

Jo. Collins writt a good discourse of this journey, and of the feazability, and a computation of the chardge. Quaere, whether he left a copie with the R. Society. Mr. Win, mathematicall instrument maker in Chancery-lane, had all his papers, and amongst many others is to be found this.

I have been the more full in this account, because if ever it shall happen that any publick-spirited men shall arise to carry on such a usefull work, they may know in whose hands the papers that were so well considered heretofore are now lodged.

Sir Jonas Moore, Surveyor of the Ordinance, told me that when the Duke of York sent him to survey the manor of Dauntesey, formerly belonging to Sir Jo. Danvers, he did then take a survey of this designe, and said that it is feazable; but his opinion was that the best way would be to make a cutt by Wotton Bassett, and that the King himselfe should undertake it, for they must cutt through a hill by Wotton-Basset; and that in time it might quit cost. As I remember, he told me that forty thousand pounds would doe it.

But I thinke, Jo. Collins sayes in his papers, that the cutt from Ashton-Kains to Charleton may bee made for three thousand pounds.

[Some of the above facts are more briefly stated by Aubrey in his "Description of North Wiltshire" (printed by Sir Thomas Phillipps, Bart.) They are however sufficiently interesting to be inserted here; and they clearly shew that, notwithstanding Aubrey's credulity and love of theory, he was fully sensible of the beneficial results to be expected from increased facilities of conveyance and locomotion. On this point indeed he and his friends, Mr. Mathew and Mr. Collins, were more than a century in advance of their contemporaries, for it was not till after the year 1783 that Wiltshire began to profit by the formation of canals.

Sanctioned by the approval of King Charles the Second, for which, as above stated, he was indebted to Aubrey, Francis Mathew published an explanation of his project for the junction of the Thames with the Bristol Avon. This work, which advocated similar canals in other parts of the country, bears the following title: "A Mediterranean Passage by water from London to Bristol, and from Lynn to Yarmouth, and so consequently to the city of York, for the great advancement of trade." (Lond. 1670, 4to.) An extract from this scarce volume is transcribed by Aubrey into the Royal Society's MS. of his own work; and a copy of Mr. Mathew's map, which illustrated it, is also there inserted.

The liberality of Sir James Shaen in the purchase of Mathew's papers, and the apathy of the London aldermen, until too late to secure them, are amusingly described. Similar instances of civic meanness are not wanting in the present day; indeed the indifference of corporate authorities to scientific topics is strikingly illustrated by the fact that the Royal Society has not at present enrolled upon its list of Fellows a single member of the corporation of London; whereas in Aubrey's time there were no less than three.

The short canal projected in the seventeenth century to connect the Thames and Avon has never been executed: subsequent speculators having found that the wants and necessities of the country could be better supplied by other and longer lines of water communication. Hence we have the Thames and Severn Canal, from Lechlade to Stroud, commenced in 1783; the Kennet and Avon Canal, from Newbury to Bath, begun in 1796; and the Wilts and Berks Canal (1801), from Abingdon to a point on the last mentioned canal between Devizes and Bradford.- J. B.] ——

Mdm.-The best and cheapest way of making a canal is by ploughing; which method ought to be applied for the cheaper making the cutt between the two rivers of Thames and Avon. The same way serves for making descents in a garden on the side of a hill.- See ...... Castello della Currenti del Acquo, 4to; which may be of use for this undertaking.

Consider the scheme in Captain Yarrington's book, entitled "England's Improvement", as to the establishing of granaries at severall townes on the Thames and Avon; e. g. at Lechlade, Cricklade, &c. See also Plin. Nat. Hist. lib. vi. c. 11.

At Funthill Episcopi, higher towards Hindon, water riseth and makes a streame before a dearth of corne, that is to say, without raine; and is commonly look't upon by the neighbourhood as a certain presage of a dearth; as, for example, the dearness of corne in 1678.

So at Morecomb-bottome, in the parish of Broad Chalke, on the north side of the river, it has been observed time out of mind, that, when the water breaketh out there, that it foreshewes a deare yeare of corne; and I remember it did so in the yeare 1648. Plinie saieth (lib. ii. Nat. Hist.) that the breaking forth of some rivers "annonæ mutationem significant".

[At Weston-Birt, in Gloucestershire, near the borders of Wiltshire, water gushes from the ground in spring and autumn, and at other times, in many hundred places at once, and continues to flow with great rapidity for several days, when the whole valley, in which the houses are placed, is completely filled. The street of the village is provided with numerous rude bridges, which on these occasions become available for purposes of communication.-J. B.] ——

'Tis a saying in the West, that a dry yeare does never cause a dearth.

Anno 1669, at Yatton Keynel, and at Broomfield in that parish, they went a great way to water their cattle; and about 1640 the springs in these parts did not breake till neer Christmas.

CHAPTER IV.

SOILES.

[THIS and the three succeeding chapters, on "Mineralls and Fossills," "Stones," and "Formed Stones", comprise the Geological portions of Aubrey's work. In a scientific view, these chapters may be regarded as of little value; though creditable to their author as a minute observer, and enthusiastic lover of science. It has been necessary to omit much which the progress of scientific knowledge has rendered obsolete; and in the passages quoted, the object has been to select such as possessed the most general interest, as well as having direct application to Wiltshire. A good summary of the Geological characteristics of the county will be found in the article "Wiltshire," in the Penny Cyclopædia. Mr. John Provis, of Chippenham, contributed a similar sketch to the third volume of the Beauties of Wiltshire; and the geology of Salisbury and its vicinity is described in Hatcher's History of Salisbury, by the son of the historian, Mr. W. H. Hatcher.-J. B.]

THIS county hath great variety of earth. It is divided, neer about the middle, from east to west into the dowries; commonly called Salisbury- plaine, which are the greatest plaines in Europe: and into the vale; which is the west end of the vale of Whitehorse.

The vale is the northern part; the soile whereof is what wee call a stone-brash; sc. red earth, full of a kind of tile-stone, in some places good tiles. It beareth good barley. In the west places of the soile, wormewood growes very plentifully; whereas in the south part they plant it in their garden.

The soile of Malmesbury hundred, which is stone-brash and clay, and the earth vitriolish, produces excellent okes, which seem to delight in a vitriolate soile, and where iron oare is. The clay and stones doe hinder the water from sinking down, whereby the surface of the earth becomes dropsicall, and beares mosse and herbs naturall to such moist ground. In the ploughed fields is plenty of yarrow; in the pasture grounds plenty of wood wax; and in many grounds plenty of centaury, wood sorrell, ladies' bed-straw, &c., sowre herbes.

I never saw in England so much blew clay as in the northern part of this county, and it continues from the west part to Oxfordshire. Under the planke-stones is often found blew marle, which is the best. ——

In Vernknoll, a ground belonging to Fowles-wick, adjoyning to the lands of Easton-Pierse, neer the brooke and in it, I bored clay as blew as ultra-marine, and incomparably fine, without anything of sand, &c., which perhaps might be proper for Mr. Dwight for his making of porcilaine. It is also at other places hereabout, but 'tis rare.

[It is not very clear that "blew clay," however fine, could be "proper for the making of porcilane," the chief characteristic of which is its transparent whiteness. Apart from this however, Aubrey's remark is curious; as it intimates that the manufacture of it was attempted in this country at an earlier period than is generally believed. The famous porcelain works at Chelsea were not established till long afterwards; and according to Dr. Plott, whose "Natural

History of Staffordshire" was published in 1686, the only kinds of pottery then made in this country were the coarse yellow, red, black, and mottled wares; and of those the chief sale was to "poor crate-men, who carried them on their backs all over the country", I have not found any account of the Mr. Dwight mentioned by Aubrey, or of his attempts to improve the art of pottery.- J. B.] —
—

Clay abounds, particularly about Malmesbury, Kington St. Michael, Allington, Easton Piers (as also a hungry marle), Dracott-Cerne, Yatton-Keynell, Minty, and Bradon-forest.

At Minty, and at a place called Woburn, in the parish of Hankerton, is very good fullers'-earth. The fullers'-earth at Minty-common, at the place called the Gogges, when I tooke it up, was as black as black polished marble; but, having carryed it in my pocket five or six dayes, it became gray.

At Hedington, at the foot of the hill, is a kind of white fullers'- earth which the cloth-workers doe use; and on the north side of the river at Broad Chalke, by a poole where are fine springs (where the hermitage is), is a kind of fullers'-earth which the weavers doe use for their chaines: 'tis good Tripoly, or "lac lunæ". Lac lunæ is the mother of silver, and is a cosmetick.

In Boudon-parke, fifteen foot deep under the barren sand, is a great plenty of blew marle, with which George Johnson, Esq., councellor-at- law, hath much improved his estate there. The soile of the parke was so exceedingly barren, that it did beare a gray mosse, like that of an old park pale, which skreeks as one walkes on it, and putts ones teeth on edge. Furzes did peep a little above the ground, but were dwarfes and did not thrive.

At Bitteston, in the highway, blew marle appears. Mr. Montjoy hath drawn the water that runnes through it, and is impregnated with its nitre, into his pasture grounds, by which meanes they are improved from —— to —— per annum. ——

In Bradon-forest, and at Ashton Kaynes, is a pottery. There is potters' clay also at . .. . Deverell, on the common towards Frome, and potts are made there.
——

At Clarendon-parke is lately discovered (1684) an earth that cleanseth better than Woburne earthe in Bedfordshire; and Mr. Cutler, the cloathier of Wilton, tells me he now makes only use of it. There is at Burton-hill, juxta Malmesbury, fullers' earth, as also about Westport, and elsewhere thereabout, which the cloathiers use.

Tobacco-pipe-clay excellent, or the best in England, at Chittern, of which the Gauntlet pipes at Amesbury are made, by one of that name. They are the best tobacco pipes in England. [See a curious paragraph on the subject of Gauntlet-pipes in Fuller's Worthies,- Wiltshire.-J. B.] ——

The earth about Malmesbury hundred and Chippenham hundred, especially about Pewsham-forest, is vitriolate, or aluminous and vitriolate; which in hot weather the sun does make manifest on the banks of the ditches.

At Bradfield and Dracot Cerne is such vitriolate earth; which with galles will make inke. This makes the land so soure, it beares sowre and austere plants: it is a proper soile for dayries. At summer it hunger-banes the sheep; and in winter it rotts them.

These clayy and marly lands are wett and dirty; so that to poore people, who have not change of shoes, the cold is very incommodious, which hurts their nerves exceedingly. Salts, as the Lord Chancellor Bacon sayes, doe exert (irradiate) raies of cold. Elias Ashmole, Esq. got a dangerous cold by sitting by the salt sacks in a salter's shop, which was like to have cost him his life. And some salts will corrode papers, that were three or four inches from it. The same may be sayd of marble pavements, which have cost some great persons their lives. ——

The soil of South Wilts is chalke and white marle, which abounds with nitre; and is inimique to the nerves by the nitre that irradiates from it. 'Tis that gives the dampishnesse to the flowres and walles of Salisbury and Chalke, &c. E contra, Herefordshire, Salop, Montgomeryshire, &c. the soile is clear of any salt; which, besides the goodnesse of the air, conduces much to their longævitas: e. g., 100 yeares of age in those parts as common as 80 in Wilts, &c.

The walles of the church of Broad Chalke, and of the buttery at the farme there, doe shoot out, besides nitre, a beautifull red, lighter than scarlet; an oriental horse-flesh colour.

The soile of Savernake forest is great gravelle: and (as I remember) pebbley, as on the sea side. At Alderbury, by Ivy Church, is great plenty of fine gravelle; which is sent for all over the south parts of the countrey.

At Sutton Benger eastward is a gravelly field called Barrets, which is sown every year onely with barley: it hath not lain fallow in the memory of the oldest man's grandfather there. About 1665 Mr. Leonard Atkins did sow his part of it with wheat for a triall. It came up wonderfully thick and high; but it proved but faire strawe, and had little or nothing in the eare. This land was heretofore the vineyard belonging to the abbey of Malmesbury; of which there is a recitall in the grant of this manner by K. Henry VIII. to Sir —— Long. This fruitfull ground is within a foot or lesse of the gravell. ——

The soil of Christian Malford, a parish adjoyning to Sutton, is very rich, and underneath is gravell in many parts. ——

The first ascent from Chippenham, sc. above the Deny hill, is sandy: e. g. Bowdon-parke, Spy-parke, Sandy-lane, great clear sand, of which I believe good glasse might be made; but it is a little too far from a navigable river. They are ye biggest graines of sand that ever I saw, and very transparent: some where thereabout is sand quite white.

At Burbidge the soile is an ash-coloured gray sand, and very naturall for the production of good turnips. They are the best that ever I did eate, and are sent for far and neere: they are not tough and stringy like other turnips, but cutt like marmalad.

Quaere, how long the trade of turnips has been here? For it is certain that all the turnips that were brought to Bristoll eighty years since [now 1680] were from Wales; and now none come from thence, for they have found out that the red sand about Bristoll doth breed a better and a bigger turnip.

Burbidge is also remarqueable for excellent pease. ——

The turf of our downes, and so east and west, is the best in the world for gardens and bowling- greens; for more southward it is burnt, and more north it is course.

Temple downe in Preshut parish, belonging to the right honble Charles Lord Seymour, worth xxs. per acre, and better, a great quantity of it.

As to the green circles on the downes, vulgarly called faiery circles (dances), I presume they are generated from the breathing out of a fertile subterraneous vapour. (The ring-worme on a man's flesh is circular. Excogitate a paralolisme between the cordial heat and ye subterranean heat, to elucidate this phenomenon.) Every tobacco-taker knowes that 'tis no strange thing for a circle of smoke to be whiff'd out of the bowle of the pipe; but 'tis donne by chance. If you digge under the turfe of this circle, you will find at the rootes of the grasse a hoare or mouldinesse. But as there are fertile steames, so contrary wise there are noxious ones, which proceed from some mineralls, iron, &c.; which also as the others, cæteris paribus, appear in a circular forme. ——

In the common field of Winterbourn ...... is the celebrated path called St. Thomas Becket's path. It leads from the village up to Clarendon Parke. Whether this field be sown or lies fallow, the path is visible to one that lookes on it from the hill, and it is wonderfull. But I can add yet farther the testimonies of two that I very well know (one of them my servant, and of an excellent sight) that will attest that, riding in the rode from London one morning in a great snow, they did see this path visible on the snow. St. Thomas Becket, they say, was sometime a cure priest at Winter-bourn, and did use to goe along this path up to a chapell in Clarendon Parke, to say masse, and very likely 'tis true: but I have a conceit that this path is caused by a warme subterraneous steame from a long crack in the earth, which may cause snow to dissolve sooner there than elsewhere: and consequently gives the dissolving snow a darker colour, just as wee see the difference of whites in damask linnen.

The right reverend father in God, Seth, Lord Bishop of Salisbury, averres to me that at Silchester in Hampshire, which was a Roman citie, one may discerne in the corne ground the signe of the streetes; nay, passages and hearthes: which also Dr. Jo. Wilkins (since Lord Bishop of Chester) did see with him, and has affirm'd the same thing to me. They were there, and saw it in the spring.

—— "ita res accendunt lumina rebus".- LUCRETIUS. ——

The pastures of the vale of White Horse, sc. the first ascent below the plaines, are as rich a turfe as any in the kingdom of England: e. g. the Idovers at Dauntesey, of good note in Smithfield, which sends as fatt cattle to Smythfield as any place in this nation; as also Tytherton, Queenfield, Wroughton, Tokenham, Mudgelt, Lydyard Tregoz, and about Cricklad, are fatting grounds, the garden of Wiltshire. ——

In a little meadow called Mill-mead, belonging to the farme of Broad Chalke, is good peate, which in my father's time was digged and made use of; and no doubt it is to be found in many other places of this country, if it were search't after. But I name it onely to bring in a discovery that Sr Christopher Wren made of it, sc. that 'tis a vegetable, which was not known before. One of the pipes at Hampton Court being stop't, Sr Christopher commanded to have it opened (I think he say'd 'twas an earthen pipe), and they found it choak't with peate,* which consists of a coagmentation of small fibrous vegetables. These pipes were layd in Cardinal Wolsey's time, who built the house.

* I believe that in ye pipes was nothing else but Alga fontalis trichodes, (C. B.) which is often found in conduit pipes. See my Synopsis.-[JOHN RAY.]

———

Earth growing. - In the court of Mrs. Sadler's, the great house in the close in Salisbury, the pitched causeway lay neglected in the late troubles, and not weeded: so at lengthe it became overgrown and lost: and I remember about 1656, goeing to pave it, they found,.... inches deep, a good pavement to their hands.

In the court of my honoured friend Edm. Wyld Esq., at Houghton in Bedfordshire, in twenty-four yeares, viz. from 1656 to 1680, the ground increased nine inches, only by rotting grasse upon grasse. 'Tis a rich soile, and reddish; worth xxs. per acre. ——

The spring after the conflagration at London all the ruines were overgrown with an herbe or two; but especially one with a yellow flower: and on the south side of St. Paul's Church it grew as thick as could be; nay, on the very top of the tower. The herbalists call it Ericolevis Neapolitana, small bank cresses of Naples; which plant Tho. Willis told me he knew before but in one place* about the towne, and that was at Battle Bridge by the Pindar of Wakefield, and that in no great quantity. [The Pindar of Wakefield is still a public-house, under the same sign, in Gray's Inn Road, in the parish of St. Pancras, London.- J. B.]

*It growes abundantly by ye waysides between London and Kensington.- [J. RAY.]

———

Sir John Danvers, of Chelsey, did assure me to his knowledge that my Lord Chancellor Bacon was wont to compound severall sorts of earths, digged up very deep, to produce severall sorts of plants. This he did in the garden at Yorke House, where he lived when he was Lord Chancellor. (See Sir Ken. Digby, concerning his composition of earth of severall places.)

Edmund Wyld, Esq. R.S.S. hath had a pott of composition in his garden these seven yeares that beares nothing at all, not so much as grasse or mosse. He makes his challenge, if any man will give him xx li. he will give him an hundred if it doth not beare wheate spontaneously; and the party shall keep the key, and he shall sift the earth composition through a fine sieve, so that he may be sure there are no graines of wheat in it He hath also a composition for pease; but that he will not warrant, not having yet tryed it, ——

Pico's [Peaks.] - In this county are Clay-hill, near Warminster; the Castle-hill at Mere, and Knoll-hill, near Kilmanton, which is half in Wilts, and half in Somersetshire; all which seem to have been raised (like great blisters) by earthquakes. [Bishop TANNER adds in a note, "Suthbury hill, neer Collingburn, which I take to be the highest hill hi Wiltshire".] That great vertuoso, Mr.

Francis Potter, author of the "Interpretation of 666,"† Rector of Kilmanton, took great delight in this Knoll-hill. It gives an admirable prospect every way; from hence one may see the foss-way between Cyrencester and Glocester, which is fourty miles from this place. You may see the Isle of Wight, Salisbury steeple, the Severne sea, &c. It would be an admirable station for him that shall make a geographical description of Wilts, Somersett, &c.

†[The full title of the work referred to is a curiosity in literature. It exemplifies forcibly the abstruse and mystical researches in which the literati of the seventeenth century indulged.

"An Interpretation of the Number 666; wherein not only the manner how this Number ought to be interpreted is clearly proved and demonstrated; but it is also shewed that this Number is an exquisite and perfect character, truly, exactly, and essentially describing that state of government to which all other notes of Antichrist do agree; with all knowne objections solidly and fully answered that can be materially made against it". (Oxford, 1642, 4to.) So general were studies of this nature at the time, that Potter's volume was translated into French, Dutch, and Latin. The author, though somewhat visionary, was a profound mathematician, and invented several ingenious mechanical instruments. In Aubrey's "Lives", appended to the Letters from the Bodleian, 8vo. 1813, will be found an interesting biographical notice of him.-J. B.]

CHAPTER V.

MINERALLS AND FOSSILLS.

[IN its etymological sense the term fossil signifies that which may be dug out of the earth. It is strictly applicable therefore, not only to mineral bodies, and the petrified forms of plants and animals found in the substance of the earth, but even to antiquities and works of art, discovered in a similar situation. The chapter of Aubrey's work now under consideration mentions only mineralogical subjects; whence it would appear that he employed the term "mineralls" instead of "metals", including such mineral substances as were not metals under the general term "fossills".

At present the term fossil is restricted to antediluvian organic remains; which are considered by Aubrey, in Chapter VII. under the name of "Formed Stones".- J. B.]

THIS county cannot boast much of mineralls: it is more celebrated for superficiall treasure.

At Dracot Cerne and at Easton Piers doe appeare at the surface of the earth frequently a kind of bastard iron oare, which seems to be a vancourier of iron oare, but it is in small quantity and course.

At Send, vulgarly called Seen, the hill whereon it stands is iron- oare, and the richest that ever I saw. (See Chap. II.)

About Hedington fields, Whetham, Bromham, Bowdon Parke, &c. are still ploughed up cindres; sc. the scoria of melted iron, which must have been smelted by the Romans (for the Saxons were no artists), who used only foot-blasts, and so left the best part of the metall behind. These cinders would be of great use for the fluxing of the iron-oare at Send. ——

At Redhill, in the parish of..... (I thinke Calne) they digge plenty of ruddle, which is a bolus, and with which they drench their sheep and cattle for .... and poor people use it with good successe for ...... This is a red sandy hill, tinged by {iron}, and is a soile that bears very good carrets. ——

Mr. John Power of Kington St. Michael (an emperick) told me heretofore that in Pewsham Forest is vitriol; which information he had from his uncle Mr. .... Perm, who was an ingeniose and learned man in those daies, and a chymist, which was then rare. ——

At Dracot Cerne is good quantity of vitriol-oare, which with galles turnes as black as inke.

About the beginning of the raigne of King James the First, Sir Walter Long [of Dracot] digged for silver, a deep pitt, through blew clay, and gott five pounds worth, for sixty pounds charges or more. It was on the west end of the stable: but I doubt there was a cheat put upon him. Here are great indications of iron, and it may be of coale; but what hopes he should have to discover silver does passe my understanding. There was a great friendship between Sir Walter Raleigh and Sir Walter Long, and they were allied: and the pitt was sunk in Sir W. Raleigh's time, so that he must certainly have been consulted with. I have here annexed Sir James Long's letter.

"Mr. Aubrey, I cannot obey your commands concerning my grandfather's sinking of pitts for metalls here at Draycott, there being no person alive hereabouts who was born at that time. What I have heard was so long since, and I then so young, that there is little heed to be taken of what I can say; but in generall I can say that I doe believe here are many metalls and mineralls in these parts; particularly silver- oare of the blew sort, of which there are many stones in the bottome of the river Avon, which are extremely heavy, and have the hardnesse of a file, by reason of the many minerall and metalline veines. I have consulted many bookes treating of minerall matters, and find them suite exactly with the Hungarian blew silver oare. Some sixteen or eighteen yeares ago in digging a well neer my house, many stones very weighty where digged out of the rocks, which also slaked with long lyeing in the weather. I shewed some to Monsieur Cock, since Baron of Crownstronie in Sweden, who had travelled ten yeares to all the mines in North Europe, and was recommended to me by a London merchant, in his journey to Mindip, and staied with me here about three weekes. He told me the grains in that oare seemed to be gold rather than copper; they resembled small pinnes heads. Wee pounded some of it, and tried to melt the dust unwashed in a crucible; but the sulphur carried the metall away, if there was any, as he said. He has been in England since, by the name of Baron Crownstrome, to treat from his master the King of Sweden, over whose mines he is superintendant, as his father was before him. The vitriol-oare we find here is like suckwood, which being layd in a dry place slakes itself into graine of blew vitriol, calcines red, and with a small quantitie of galles makes our water very black inke. It is acid tasted as other vitriol, and apt to raise a flux in the mouth. Sir, yours, &c.
August 12, 1689. J. L".

——

"In the parish of Great Badminton, in a field called Twelve Acres, the husbandmen doe often times plough up and find iron bulletts, as big as pistoll bulletts; sometimes almost as big as muskett bulletts". Dr. Childrey's Britannia Baconica, p. 80. ["Britannia Baconica, or the Natural Rarities of England, Scotland, and Wales, historically related, according to the precepts of Lord Bacon". By Joshua Childrey, D.D. 1661. 8°.]

These bulletts are Dr. Th. Willises aperitive pills; sc. he putts a barre of iron into the smith's forge, and gives it a sparkling heat; then thrusts it against a roll of brimstone, and the barre will melt down into these bulletts; of which he made his aperitive pills. In this region is a great deale of iron, and the Bath waters give sufficient evidence that there is store of sulphur; so that heretofore when the earthquakes were hereabouts, store of such bulletts must necessarily be made and vomited up. [Dr. Willis was one of the most eminent physicians of his age, and author of numerous Latin works on medical subjects. The above extract is a curious illustration of the state of professional knowledge at the time. - J. B.] —

—

Copperas. - Thunder-stones, as the vulgar call them, are a pyrites; their fibres doe all tend to the centre. They are found at Broad Chalke frequently, and particularly in the earth pitts belonging to the parsonage shares, below Bury Hill, next Knighton hedge; but wee are too fare from a navigable river to make profit by them; but at the Isle of Wight they are gathered .from the chalkie rocks, and carried by boates to Deptford, to make copperas; where they doe first expose them to the aire

and raine, which makes them slake, and fall to pieces from the centre, and shoot out a pale blewish salt; and then they boile the salt with pieces of old rusty iron. ——

In the chalkie rocks at Lavington is umber, which painters have used, and Dr. Chr. Meret hath inserted it in his Pinax. ["Pinax Rerum Naturalium Britannicarum, continens Vegetabilia, Animalia, et Fossilia in hac Insula reperta". By Christopher Merret, M.D., 1666, 12mo.] ——

In the parish of Steeple Ashton, at West Ashton, in the grounds of Mr. Tho. Beech, is found plenty of a very ponderous marchasite, of which Prince Rupert made tryall, but without effect. It flieth away in sulphur, and the fumes are extreme unwholsom: it is full of (as it were) brasse, and strikes fire very well. It is mundick, or mock-oare. The Earle of Pembroke hath a way to analyse it: not by fire, but by corroding waters.

Anno Domini, 1685, in Chilmark, was found by digging of a well a blewish oare, with brasse-like veines in it; it runnes two foot thick. I had this oare tryed, and it flew away in sulphur, like that of Steeple Ashton. ——

On Flamstone downe (in the parish of Bishopston) neer the Race-way a quarrie of sparre exerts itselfe to the surface of the turfe. It is the finest sparre that ever I beheld. I have made as good glasse of this sparre as the Venice glasse. It is of a bright colour with a very little tincture of yellow; transparent; and runnes in stirias, like nitre; it is extraordinary hard till it is broken, and then it breakes into very minute pieces. ——

We have no mines of lead; nor can I well suspect where we should find any: but not far off in Glocestershire, at Sodbury, there is. Capt. Ralph Greatorex, the mathematical instrument maker, sayes that it is good lead, and that it was a Roman lead-worke. ——

Tis some satisfaction to know where a minerall is not. Iron or coale is not to be look't for in a chalky country. As yet we have not discovered any coale in this county; but are supplied with it from Glocestershire adjoyning, where the forest of Kingswood (near Bristowe) aboundeth most with coale of any place in the west of England: all that tract under ground full of this fossill. It is very observable that here are the most holly trees of any place in the west. It seemes to me that the holly tree delights in the effluvium of this fossil, which may serve as a guide to find it. I was curious to be satisfied whether holly trees were also common about the collieries at Newcastle, and Dr.. .. . , Deane of Durham, affirmes they are. These indications induce me to thinke it probable that coale may be found in Dracot Parke. The Earledomes, near Downton, (woods so called belonging to the Earledome of Pembroke,) for the same reason, not unlike ground for coale.

They have tryed for coale at Alderbery Common, but was baffled in it. (I have heard it credibly reported that coale has been found in Urchfont parish, about fifty or sixty yeares since; but upon account of the scarcity of workmen, depth of the coale, and the then plenty of firing out of ye great wood called Crookwood, it did not quit the cost, and so the mines were stop'd up. There hath been great talk several times of searching after coale here again. Crookwood, once full of sturdy oakes, is now destroyed, and all sort of fuel very dear in all the circumjacent country. It lies very commodious, being situate about the middle of the whole county; three miles from the populous town of the Devises, two miles from Lavington, &c.-BISHOP TANNER.)

[Several abortive attempts have been made at different periods to find coal on Malmesbury Common.-J. B.]

CHAPTER VI.

STONES.

I WILL begin with freestone (lapis arenarius), as the best kind of stone that this country doth afford.

The quarre at Haselbury [near Box] was most eminent for freestone in the western parts, before the discovery of the Portland quarrie, which was but about anno 1600. The church of Portland, which stands by the sea side upon the quarrie, (which lies not very deep, sc. ten foot), is of Cane stone, from Normandie. Malmesbury Abbey and the other Wiltshire religious houses are of Haselbury stone. The old tradition is that St. Adelm, Abbot of Malmesbury, riding over the ground at Haselbury, did throw down his glove, and bad them dig there, and they should find great treasure, meaning the quarre. ——

AT Chilmarke is a very great quarrie of freestone, whereof the religious houses of the south part of Wiltshire and Dorset were built. [The walls, buttresses, and other substantial parts of Salisbury Cathedral are constructed of the Chilmarke stone. - J. B.]

At Teffont Ewyas is a quarrie of very good white freestone, not long since discovered.

At Compton Basset is a quarrie of soft white stone betwixt chalke and freestone: it endures fire admirably well, and would be good for reverbatory furnaces: it is much used for ovens and hearth-stones: it is as white as chalke. At my Lord Stowell's house at Aubury is a chimney piece carved of it in figures; but it doth not endure the weather, and therefore it ought not to be exposed to sun and raine.

At Yatton Keynel, in Longdean, is a freestone quarrie, but it doth not endure the weather well.

In Alderton-field is a freestone quarrie, discovered a little before the civill-warres broke forth.

In Bower Chalke field, in the land that belongs to the farme of Broad Chalke, is a quarrie of freestone of a dirty greenish colour, very soft, but endures the weather well. The church and houses there are built with it, and the barne of the farme, w{hi}ch is of great antiquity. ——

The common stone in Malmesbury hundred and thereabout is oftentimes blewish in the inside, and full of very small cockles, as at Easton Piers. These stones are dampish and sweate, and doe emitt a cold and unwholsome dampe, sc. the vitriolate petrified salt in it exerts itselfe.

——

I know no where in this county that lime is made, unlesse it be made of Chalke stones: whereas between Bath and Bristoll all the stone is lime-stone. If lime were at xs. or xxs. per lib. it would be valued above all other drugges. ——

At Swindon is a quarrie of stones, excellent for paveing halls, staire-cases, &c; it being pretty white and smooth, and of such a texture as not to be moist or wett in damp weather. It is used at London in Montagu-house, and in Barkeley-house &c. (and at Cornberry, Oxon. JOHN EVELYN). This stone is not inferior to Purbac grubbes, but whiter. It takes a little polish, and is a dry stone. It was discovered but about 1640, yet it lies not above four or five foot deep. It is near the towne, and not above [ten] miles from the river of Thames at Lechlade. [The Wilts and Berks Canal and the Great Western Railway now pass close to the town of Swindon, and afford great faculties for the conveyance of this stone, which is now in consequence very extensively used.- J. B.] ——

If Chalk may be numbred among stones, we have great plenty of it. I doe believe that all chalke was once marle; that is, that chalke has undergone subterraneous bakeings, and is become hard: e. g, as wee make tobacco-pipes. ——

Pebbles. - The millers in our country use to putt a black pebble under the pinne of ye axis of the mill-wheele, to keep the brasse underneath from wearing; and they doe find by experience, that nothing doth weare so long as that. The bakers take a certain pebble, which they putt in the vaulture of their oven, which they call the warning-stone: for when that is white the oven is hot.

In the river Avon at Lacock are large round pebbles. I have not seen the like elsewhere. Quaere, if any transparent ones? From Merton, southward to the sea, is pebbly.

There was a time when all pebbles were liquid. Wee find them all ovalish. How should this come to passe? As for salts, some shoot cubicall, some hexagonall. Why might there not be a time, when these pebbles were making in embryone (in fieri), for such a shooting as falls into an ovalish figure?

Pebbles doe breake according to the length of the greatest diameter: but those wee doe find broken in the earth are broken according to their shortest diameter. I have broken above an hundred of them, to try to have one broken at the shortest diameter, to save the charge and paines of grinding them for molers to grind colours for limming; and they all brake the long way as aforsayd. ——

Black flints are found in great plenty in the chalkie country. They are a kind of pyrites, and are as regular; 'tis certain they have been "in fluore".

Excellent fire-flints are digged up at Dun's Pit in Groveley, and fitted for gunnes by Mr. Th. Sadler of Steeple Langford. ——

Anno 1655, I desired Dr. W. Harvey to tell me how flints were generated. He sayd to me that the black of the flint is but a natural vitrification of the chalke: and added that the medicine of the flint is excellent for the stone, and I thinke he said for the greene sicknesse; and that in some flints are found stones in next degree to a diamond. The doctor had his armes and his wife's cutt in such a one, which was bigger than the naile of my middle finger; found at Folkston in Kent, where he told me he was borne.

In the stone-brash country in North Wilts flints are very rare, and those that are found are but little. I once found one, when I was a little boy learning to read, in the west field by Easton Piers, as big as one's fist, and of a kind of liver colour. Such coloured flints are very common in and about Long Lane near Stuston, [Sherston ?-J. B.] and no where else that I ever heard of.

It is reported that at Tydworth a diamond was found in a flint, which the Countess of Marleborough had set in a ring. I have seen small fluores in flints (sparkles in the hollow of flints) like diamonds; but when they are applied to the diamond mill they are so soft that they come to nothing. But, had he that first found out the way of cutting transparent pebbles (which was not long before the late civill warres) kept it a secret, he might have got thousands of pounds by it; for there is no way to distinguish it from a diamond but by the mill. ——

I shall conclude with the stones called the Grey Wethers; which lye scattered all over the downes about Marleborough, and incumber the ground for at least seven miles diameter; and in many places they are, as it were, sown so thick, that travellers in the twylight at a distance take them to be flocks of sheep (wethers) from whence they have their name. So that this tract of ground looks as if it had been the scene where the giants had fought with huge stones against the Gods, as is described by Hesiod in his {Gk: theogonia}.

They are also (far from the rode) commonly called Sarsdens, or Sarsdon stones. About two or three miles from Andover is a village called Sersden, i. e. Csars dene, perhaps don: Cæsar's dene, Cæsar's plains; now Salisbury plaine. (So Salisbury, Cæsaris Burgus.) But I have mett with this kind of stones sometimes as far as from Christian Malford in Wilts to Abington; and on the downes about Royston, &c. as far as Huntington, are here and there those Sarsden-stones. They peep above the ground a yard and more high, bigger and lesser. Those that lie in the weather are so hard that no toole can touch them. They take a good polish. As for their colour, some are a kind of dirty red, towards porphyry; some perfect white; some dusky white; some blew, like deep blew marle; some of a kind of olive greenish colour; but generally they are whitish. Many of them are mighty great ones, and particularly those in Overton Wood. Of these kind of stones are framed the two stupendous antiquities of Aubury and Stone-heng. I have heard the minister of Aubury say those huge stones may be broken in what part of them you please without any great trouble. The manner is thus: they make a fire on that line of the stone where they would have it to crack; and, after the stone is well heated, draw over a line with cold water, and immediately give a smart knock with a smyth's sledge, and it will breake like the collets at the glasse-house. [This system of destruction is still adopted on the downs in the neighbourhood of Avebury. Many of the upright stones of the great Celtic Temple in that parish have been thus destroyed in my time.- J. B.]

Sir Christopher Wren sayes they doe pitch (incline) all one way, like arrowes shot. Quaere de hoc, and if so to what part of the heavens they point? Sir Christopher thinks they were cast up by a vulcano.

CHAPTER VII.

OF FORMED STONES.

[AUBREY, and other writers of his time, designated by this term the fossil remains of antediluvian animals and vegetables. This Chapter is very brief in the manuscript; and the following are the only passages adapted for this publication.

The numerous excavations which have been made in the county since Aubrey's time have led to the discovery of a great abundance of organic remains; especially in the northern part of the county, from Swindon to Chippenham and Box. Large collections have been made by Mr. John Provis and Mr. Lowe, of Chippenham, which it is hoped will be preserved in some public museum, for the advantage of future geologists.-J. B.]

THE stones at Easton-Piers are full of small cockles no bigger than silver half-pennies. The stones at Kington St. Michael and Dracot Cerne are also cockley, but the cockles at Dracot bigger. Cockleborough, near Chippenham, hath its denomination from the petrified cockles found there in great plenty, and as big as cockles. Sheldon, in the parish of Chippenham, hath its denomination from the petrified shells in the stones there.

At Dracot Cerne there is belemnites, as also at Tytherington Lucas.
They are like hafts of knives, dimly transparent, having a seame on one side.

——

West from Highworth, towards Cricklad, are stones as big, or bigger than one's head, that lie common even in the highway, which are petrified sea-mushromes. They looke like honeycombs, but the holes are not hexagons, but round. They are found from Lydiard Tregoze to Cumnor in Barkshire, in which field I have also seen them. [See page 9.-J. B.] ——

At Steeple Ashton are frequently found stones resembling the picture of the unicorne's horn, but not tapering. They are about the bignesse of a cart-rope, and are of a reddish gray colour.

In the vicaridge garden at Bower Chalke are found petrified oyster shells; which the learned Mr. Lancelot Morehouse, who lived there some yeares, assured me: and I am informed since that there are also cockle shells and scalop shells. Also in the parish of Wotton Basset are found petrified oyster shells; and there are also found cornua ammonis of a reddish gray, but not very large.

About two or three miles from the Devises are found in a pitt snake-stones (cornua ammonis) no bigger than a sixpence, of a black colour. Mr. John Beaumont, Junr., of Somersetshire, a great naturalist, tells me that some-where by Chilmarke lies in the chalke a bed of stones called "echini marini". He also enformes me that, east of Bitteston, in the estate of Mr. Montjoy, is a spring,- they call it a holy well,-where five-pointed stones doe bubble up (Astreites) which doe move in vinegar.

At Broad Chalke are sometimes found cornua ammonis of chalke. I doe believe that they might be heretofore in as great abundance hereabout as they are about Caynsham and Burnet in Somersetshire; but being soft, the plough teares them in pieces; and the sun and the frost does slake them like lime. They are very common about West Lavington, with which the right honourable James, Earle of Abington, has adorned his grotto's there. There are also some of these stones about Calne.

CHAPTER VIII.

AN HYPOTHESIS OF THE TERRAQUEOUS GLOBE. A DIGRESSION.

[THE seventeenth century was peculiarly an age of scientific research and investigation. The substantial and brilliant discoveries of Newton induced many of his less gifted contemporaries to pursue inquiries into the arcana and profound mysteries of science; but where rational inferences and deductions failed, they too frequently had recourse to mere unsupported theory and conjectural speculation.

The stratification of the crust of our globe, and the division of its surface into land and water, was a fertile theme for conjecture; and many learned and otherwise sagacious writers, assigned imaginary causes for the results which they attempted to explain.

The chapter of Aubrey's work which bears the above title is, to some extent, of this nature. It consists chiefly of speculative opinions extracted from other works, with a few conjectures of his own, which, though based upon the clear and judicious views of his friend Robert Hooke, do not, upon the whole, deserve much consideration; although to the curious in the history of Geological science they may appear interesting. Its author had sufficient diffidence as to the merits of this chapter to describe it as "a digression; ad mentem Mr. R. Hook, R.S.S."; and his friend Ray, in a letter already quoted, observes, after commending other portions of the present work, "I find but one thing that may give any just offence; and that is, the Hypothesis of the Terraqueous Globe; wherewith I must confess myself not to be satisfied: but that is but a digression, and aliene from your subject; and so may very well be left out". Ray's work on "Chaos and Creation" published in 1692, a year after the date of this letter, was a valuable contribution to the geological knowledge of the time. Some notes by

Evelyn, on Aubrey's original MS., shew that he was at least equally credulous with the author.

Aubrey concludes that the universal occurrence of "petrified fishes' shells gives clear evidence that the earth hath been all covered over with water". He assumes that the irregularities and changes in the earth's surface were occasioned by earthquakes; and has inserted in his manuscript, from the London Gazette, accounts of three earthquakes, in different parts of Italy, in the years 1688 and 1690. A small 4to pamphlet, being "A true relation of the terrible Earthquake which happened at Ragusa, and several other cities in Dalmatia and Albania, the 6th of April 1667", is also inserted in the MS. Aubrey observes: "As the world was torne by earthquakes, as also the vaulture by time foundred and fell in, so the water subsided and the dry land appeared. Then, why might not that change alter the center of gravity of the earth? Before this the pole of the ecliptique perhaps was the pole of the world". And in confirmation of these views he quotes several passages from Ovid's Metamorphoses, book i. fab. 7. 8. He also cites the scheme of Father Kircher, of the Society of Jesus, which, in a section of the globe, represents it as "full of cavities, and resembling the inside of a pomegranade", the centre being marked with a blazing fire, or "ignis centralis". "But now", writes Aubrey in 1691, "Mr. Edmund Halley, R.S.S., hath an hypothesis that the earth is hollow, about five hundred miles thick; and that a terella moves within it, which causes the variation of the needle; and in the center a sun". Further on he says, "that the centre of this globe is like the heart that warmes the body, is now the most commonly received opinion". On the subject of subterranean heats and fires the author quotes several pages from Dr. Edward Jorden's "Discourse of Natural Baths and Mineral Waters; wherein the original of fountains, the nature and differences of water, and particularly those of the Bathe, are declared". (4to. 1632.) He also extracts a passage from Lemery's "Course of Chymistry", (8vo. 1686,) as the foundation of a theory to explain the heat of the Bath waters.

The difficulty of reconciling the various opinions that were advanced with the Mosaic account of the Creation, was a great stumbling-block to the progress of geological science at the time when Aubrey wrote. He was not however inclined to read the sacred writings too literally on this subject, for after giving a part of the first chapter of Genesis, he quotes (from Timothy, ch. iii. v. 15) the words, "from a child thou hast known the Holy Scriptures, which are able to make thee wise unto salvation:" upon which he observes, "the Apostle doth not say, to teach natural philosophy: and see Pere Symond, where he says that the scriptures in some places may be erroneous as to philosophy, but the doctrine of the church is right". It is presumed that the above passages, which indicate the general nature of Aubrey's theory, will be sufficient, without further quotations from this chapter. - J. B.]

CHAPTER IX.

OF PLANTS.

Præsentemq{ue} refert quaelibet herba Deum.- OVID.

[THIS is one of the most copious chapters in Aubrey's work. Ray has appended a number of valuable notes to it, several of which are here printed. Dr. Maton has quoted from this chapter, which he mentions in terms of commendation, in his "Notices of animals and plants of that part of the county of Wilts within 10 miles round Salisbury", appended to Hatcher's History of Salisbury, folio, 1843.-J. B.]

IT were to be wish't that we had a survey or inventory of the plants of every county in England and Wales, as there is of Cambridgeshire by Mr. John Ray; that we might know our own store, and whither to repaire for them for medicinall uses. God Almighty hath furnished us with plants to cure us, that grow perhaps within five or ten miles of our abodes, and we know it not.

Experience hath taught us that some plants have wonderful vertues; and no doubt all have so, if we knew it or could discover it. Homer writes sublimely, and calls them {Gk: Cheires Theion}, the hands of the gods: and we ought to reach them religiously, with praise and thanksgiving.

I am no botanist myselfe, and I thinke we have very few in our countrey that are; the more is the pity. But had Tho. Willisel* lived, and been in England, I would have employed him in this search.

* THOMAS WILLISEL was a Northamptonshire man (Lancashire - J. RAY), a very poor fellow, and was a foot soldier in ye army of Oliver Cromwell. Lying at St. James's (a garrison then I thinke), he happened to go along with some simplers. He liked it so well that he desired to goe with them as often as they went, and tooke such a fancy to it that in a short time he became a good botanist. He was a lusty fellow, and had an admirable sight, which is of great use for a simpler; was as hardy as a Highlander; all the clothes on his back not worth ten groates, an excellent marksman, and would maintain himselfe with his dog and his gun, and his fishing-line. The botanists of London did much encourage him, and employed (sent) him all over England, Scotland, and good part of Ireland, if not all; where he made brave discoveries, for which his name will ever be remembred in herballs. If he saw a strange fowle or bird, or a fish, he would have it and case it. When ye Lord John Vaughan, now Earle of Carbery, was made Governour of Jamaica, 167-, I did recommend him to his Excellency, who made him his gardiner there. He dyed within a yeare after his being there, but had made a fine collection of plants and shells, which the Earle of Carbery hath by him; and had he lived he would have given the world an account of the plants, animals, and fishes of that island. He could write a hand indifferent legible, and had made himself master of all the Latine names: he pourtrayed but untowardly. All the profession he had was to make pegges for shoes.

Sir William Petty surveyed the kingdome of Ireland geographically, by those that knew not what they did. Why were it impossible to procure a botanique survey of Wiltshire by apothecaries of severall quarters of the county? Their profession leadeth them to an acquaintance of herbes, and the taske being divided, would not be very troublesome; and, besides the pleasure, would be of great use. The apothecaries of Highworth, Malmesbury, Calne, and Bath (which is within three miles of Wilts) might give an account of the northern part of Wiltshire, which abounds with rare simples: the apothecaries of Warminster, the Devises, and Marleborough, the midland part; and the apothecaries of Salisbury the south part, towards the New Forest.

Mr. Hayward, the apothecary of Calne, is an ingenious person and a good botanist; and there-about is great variety of earths and plants. He is my friend, and eagerly espouses this designe. He was bred in Salisbury, and hath an interest with the apothecaries there, and very likely at Bath also. I had a good interest with two very able apothecaries in Salisbury: Hen. Denny (Mr. Hayward's master), and Mr. Eires; but they are not long since dead. But Mr. Andrewes, on the ditch there, hath assured a friend of mine, Robt. Good, M.A. that he will preserve the herbes the herbe-women shall bring him, for my use.

If such an inventory were made it would sett our countrey-men a worke, to make 'em love this knowledge, and to make additions.

In the meantime, that this necessary topick be not altogether void, I will sett down such plants as I remember to have seen in my frequent journeys. 'Twas pleasant to behold how every ten or twenty miles yield a new entertainment in this kind.

I will begin in the north part, towardes Coteswold in Gloucestershire.

In Bradon Forest growes very plentifully rank wood-wax; and a blew grasse they call July-flower grasse, which cutts the sheepes mouthes; except in the spring. (I suppose it is that sort of Cyperus grasse which some herbarists call "gramen caryophylleu{s}".- J. RAY.) Wood- wax growes also plentifully between Easton-Piers and Yatton Keynel; but not so rank as at Bradon Forest.

———

At Mintie is an abundance of wild mint, from whence the village is denominated.

———

Argentina (wild tansey) growes the most in the fallowes in Coteswold, and North Wilts adjoyning, that I ever saw. It growes also in the fallowes in South Wiltshire, but not so much. (Argentina grows for ye most part in places that are moist underneath, or where water stagnates in winter time. - J. RAY.) ——

About Priory St. Maries, and in the Minchin-meadowes* there, but especially at Brown's-hill, which is opposite to the house where, in an unfortunate hour,† I drew my first breath, there is infinite variety of plants; and it would have tempted me to have been a botanist had I had leisure, which is a jewell I could be never master of. In the banks of the rivulet growes abundantly maiden-haire (adiantum capillas veneris), harts-tongue, phyllitis, brooke-lime (anagallis aquatica), &c. cowslip (arthritica) and primroses (primula veris) not inferior to Primrose Hills. In this ground calver-keys, hare-parsely, wild vetch, maiden's-honesty, polypodium, fox-gloves, wild-vine, bayle. Here is wonderfull plenty of wild saffron, carthamus, and many vulnerary plants, now by me forgott. There growes also adder's-tongue, plenty - q. if it is not the same with viper's-tongue? (We have no true black mayden-hair growing in England. That which passeth under that name in our apothecaries' shops, and is used as its succeedaneum, is trichomores. Calver-keys, hare's-parseley, mayden's-honesty, are countrey names unknown to me. Carthamus growes no where wild with us. It may possibly be sown in ye fields, as I have seen it in Germany.-J. RAY.)

* Minchin is an old word for a nunne.

† Vide my Villa. "Quoque loco primum tibi sum male cognitus infans". In Natalem, Ovid. Trist. lib. iii.

This north part of the shire is very naturall for barley. Till the beginning of the civill warrs wheat was rarely sown hereabout; and the brown bread was barley: now all the servants and poor people eat wheaten bread. ——

Strawberries (fragaria), in Colern woods, exceeding plentifull; the earth is not above two inches above the free-stone. The poor children gather them, and sell them to Bathe; but they kill the young ashes, by barking them to make boxes to put them in.

Strawberries have a most delicious taste, and are so innocent that a woman in childbed, or one in a feaver, may safely eate them: but I have heard Sir Christopher Wren affirm, that if one that has a wound in his head eates them, they are mortall. Methinks 'tis very strange. Quaere, the learned of this? ——
About Totnam-well is a world of yellow weed (q. nomen) which the diers use for the first tinge for scarlet; and afterwards they use cutchonele.

——

Bitter-sweet (dulcamara), with a small blew flower, plenty at Box. (And Market Lavington, in the withy-bed belonging to the vicarage.- BISHOP TANNER.)

Ferne (filix); the largest and rankest growes in Malmesbury hundred: but the biggest and tallest that ever I saw is in the parke at Draycot Cerne, as high almost as a man on horseback, on an ordinary horse.

"The forest of Savernake is of great note for plenty of game, and for a kind of ferne there that yieldeth a most pleasant savour".-(Fuller's Worthies: Wilts, Hen. Sturmy.)

This ferne is mentioned by Dr. Peter Heylin in his Church History, in the Pedegre of Seymour. The vicar of Great Bedwin told me that he hath seen and smelt the ferne, and that it is like other ferne, but not so big. He knowes not where it growes, but promised to make enquirie. Now Mr. Perkins sayes that this is sweet cis, and that it is also found in the New Forest; but me thinkes the word Savernake seems to be a sweet- oke-ferne: - oke, is oake; verne is ferne; perhaps sa, or sav, is sweet or savorous. - (Vide Phytologia Britannic., where this fern is taken notice of. Sweet fern is the vulgar name, for sweet chervill or cicely; but I never found that plant wild in England.-J. RAY.)

Danes-blood (ebulis) about Slaughtonford is plenty. There was heretofore (vide J. Milton) a great fight with the Danes, which made the inhabitants give it that name.

Wormewood exceedingly plentifull in all the wast grounds in and about Kington St. Michael, Hullavington, and so to Colerne, and great part of the hundred of Malmesbury.

Horse-taile (equisetum). Watchmakers and fine workers in brasse use it after smooth filing. They have it from Holland; but about Dracot Cerne and Kington St. Michael, in the minchin-meadow of Priory St. Maries, is great quantity of the same. It growes four and five foot high.

Coleworts, or kale, the common western dish, was the Saxon physic. In the east it is so little esteemed that the poor people will not eate it.

About Malmesbury "ros solis", which the strong-water men there doe distill, and make good quantitys of it. In the woods about the Devises growes Solomon's-seale; also goates-rue (gallega); as also that admirable plant, lilly-convally. Mr. Meverell says the flowers of the lilly-convally about Mosco are little white flowers.-(Goat's-rue:- I suspect this to be a mistake; for I never yet heard that goat's-rue was found by any man growing wild in England.-J. RAY.)

The middle part of Wilts.- Naked-boys (q. if not wild saffron) about Stocton. (Naked-boys is, I suppose, meadow saffron, or colchicum, for I doe not remember ever to have seen any other sort of saffron growing wild in England. - J. RAY.) ——

The watered meadows all along from Marleborough to Hungerford, Ramesbury, and Littlecot, at the later end of Aprill, are yellow with butter flowers. When you come to Twyford the floted meadowes there are all white with little flowers, which I believe are ladysmocks (cardamine): quaere of some herbalist the right name of that plant. (Ranunculus aquaticus folio integro et multum diviso, C. Bankini.- J. RAY.) The graziers told me that the yellow meadowes are by much the better, and those white flowers are produc't by a cold hungry water. ——

South part. - At the east end of Ebbesbourne Wake is a meadowe called Ebbesbourne, that beareth grasse eighteen foot long. I myself have seen it of thirteen foot long; it is watered with the washing of the village. Upon a wager in King James the First's time, with washing it more than usuall, the grasse was eighteen foot long. It is so sweet that the pigges will eate it; it growes no higher than other grasse, but with knotts and harles, like a skeen of silke (or setts together). They cannot mowe it with a sythe, but they cutt it with such a hooke as they bagge pease with.

At Orston [Orcheston] St. Maries is a meadowe of the nature of that at Ebbesbourne aforesayd, which beares a sort of very long grasse. Of this grasse there was presented to King James the First some that were seventeen foot long: here is only one acre and a half of it. In common yeares it is 12 or 13 foot long. It is a sort of knott grasse, and the pigges will eate it.

[The "Orcheston Grass" has long been famous as one of the most singular vegetable products of this country. From the time of Fuller, who particularly mentions it in his "Worthies of England", many varying and exaggerated accounts of it have been published; but in the year 1798 Dr. Maton carefully examined the grass, and fully investigated the peculiar circumstances of soil and locality which tend to its production. He contributed the result of his inquiries to the Linnæan Society, in a paper which is printed in the fifth volume of their Transactions. Some comments on that paper, and on the subject generally, by Mr. Davis, of Longleat, will be found in the second volume of the Beauties of Wiltshire, p. 79. That gentleman states that "its extraordinary length is produced by the overflowing of the river on a warm gravelly bed, which disposes the grass to take root and shoot out from the joints, and then root again, and thus again and again; so that it is frequently of the length of ten or twelve feet and the quantity on the land immense, although it does not stand above two feet high from the ground". Although the meadow at Orcheston St. Mary in which this grass grows is only two acres and a half in extent, its produce in a favourable season, is said to have exceeded twelve tons of hay. Shakspere, to whom all natural and rural objects were familiar, alludes to the "hindering knot-grass", in A Midsummer Night's Dream, Act iii. sc. 2. ——

Ramsons (allium ursinum, fl. albo): tast like garlick: they grow much in Cranbourn Chace. A proverb: -

"Eate leekes in Lide,* and ramsins in May, And all the yeare after physitians may play".

* March.

[I have seen this old proverb printed, "Eat leekes in Lent, and raisins in May, &c." - J. B.]

No wild oates in Wiltshire, or rarely. In Somersetshire, common. (There is abundance of wild oats in the middle part of Wiltsh., especially in the west clay of Market Lavington field, when the crop is barley. - BISHOP TANNER.) ——

Thorowax beares a pretty little yellow flower, not much unlike the blowing of a furze that growes so common on the downes, close to the ground: the bees love it extremely. (There is a mistake in thorowax, or perfoliata; for that rises to a good stature, and hath no such flower. I suppose the plant you mean is trifolium corniculatum, or bird's-foot trefoil.-J. RAY.) ——

The right honorable James, Earle of Abingdon, tells me that there are plenty of morillons about Lavingtons, which he eates, and sends to London. Methinkes 'tis a kind of ugly mushroom. Morillons we have from Germany and other places beyond sea, which are sold here at a deare rate; the outer side is like a honeycombe. I have seen them of nine inches about They grow near the rootes of elmes.

Poppy (papaver) is common in the corn fields; but the hill above Harnham, by Salisbury, appeares a most glorious scarlet, it is so thick there.

"Ilia soporiferum, parvas initura penates,
Colligit agresti lene papaver humo.
Dum legit oblito fertur gustàsse palato,
Longamq{ue} imprudens exsoluisse famem". - OVID. FAST. lib. iv.

——

In a ground of mine called Swices (which is a neck of land at the upper end of the field called Shatcomb) growes abundantly a plant called by the people hereabout crow-bells, which I never saw any where but there. "Swice", in the old English, signifies a neck. ——

Dwarfe-elder (ebulus) at Box, &c. common enough: at Falston and Stoke Verdon, in the high waies. The juice of ebulus turnes haire black; and being mingled with bull's fatt is Dr. Buller's remedie for the gowte.

The best way to dye haire browne is to take alhanna in powder, mix't with fair water as thick as mustard: lay it on the haire, and so tye it up in a napkin for twelve houres time. Doe thus for six dayes together, putting on fresh every day for that time. This will keep the haire browne for one whole yeares time after it. The alhanna does prepare the hair and makes it of a darke red or tawny colour. Then they take "takout", which is like a small gall, and boyle it in oyle till it hath drunk up all the oyle; then pulverize it, and mix it with water and putt it on the haire. Grind a very little of alkohol, which they use in glazeing of their earthen vessels, in a mortar with the takout, and this turnes the haire to a perfect black. This receipt I had from my worthy and obligeing friend Mr. Wyld Clarke, merchant, of London, who was factour many yeares at S{an}cta-Cruce, in Barberie, and brought over a quantity of these leaves for his own use and his friends. 'Tis pity it is not more known. 'Tis leaves of a tree like a berbery leafe. Mr. Clarke hath yet by him (1690) above half a peck of the alhanna.

Dr. Edw. Brown, M.D. in his Travells, sc. description of Larissa and Thessalie, speakes of alhanna. Mr. Wyld Clarke assures me that juice of lemons mixt with alhanna strikes a deeper and more durable colour either in the hands or nailes. ——

Tobacco. - We have it onely in gardens for medicine; but in the neighbouring county of Gloucester it is a great commodity. Mdm. "Tobacco was first brought into England by Ralph Lane in the eight and twentieth yeare of Queen Elizabeth's raigne". - Sir Richard Baker's Chronicle. Rider's Almanack (1682) sayes since tobacco was first brought into England by Sir Walter Raleigh, 99 yeares. Mr. Michael Weekes, of the custome house, assures me that the custom of tobacco is the greatest of all other, and amounts now (1688) to four hundred thousand pounds per annum. [Now (1847) about three millions and a half.- J. B.] ——

Broome keeps sheep from the rott, and is a medicine not long since found out by physitians for the dropsy. In some places I knew carefull husbandmen that quite destroyed their broome (as at Lanford), and afterwards their sheep died of the rott, from which they were free before the broom was cutt down; so ever since they doe leave a border of broome about their grounds for their sheep to browze on, to keep them sound. ——

Furzes (genista spinosa).-I never saw taller or more flourishing English furzes than at Chalke. The Great Duke of Thuscany carried furzes out of England for a rarity in his magnificent garden. I never saw such dwarft furzes as at Bowdon parke; they did but just peep above the ground. ——

Oakes (the best of trees).-We had great plenty before the disafforestations. We had in North Wiltshire, and yet have, though not in the former plenty, as good oakes as any in England. The best that we have now (1670) are at Okesey Parke, Sir Edward Poole's, in Malmesbury hundred; and the oakes at Easton Piers (once mine) were, for the number, not inferior to them. In my great-grandfather Lite's time (15—) one might have driv'n a plough over every oake in the oak- close, which are now grown stately trees. The great oake by the day-house [dairy house - J. B.] is the biggest oake now, I believe, in all the countie. There is a common wealth of rookes there. When I was a boy the two greatest oakes were, one on the hill at the parke at Dracot Cerne; the other at Mr. Sadler's, at Longley Burrell. 'Twas of one of these trees, I remember, that the trough of the paper mill at Long-deane, in the parish of Yatton Keynell, anno 1636, was made. In Garsden Parke (now the Lord Ferrars) is perhaps the finest hollow oake in England; it is not high, but very capacious, and well wainscotted; with a little table, which I thinke eight may sitt round. When an oake is felling, before it falles, it gives a kind of shreikes or groanes, that may be heard a mile off, as if it were the genius of the oake lamenting. E. Wyld, Esq. hath heard it severall times. This gave the occasion of that expression in Ovid's Metamorph. lib. viii. fab. ii. about Erisichthon's felling of the oake sacred to Ceres:- "gemitumq{ue} dedit decidua quercus".

In a progresse of K. Charles I. in time of peace, three score and ten carts stood under the great oake by Woodhouse. It stands in Sir James Thinne's land. On this oake Sir Fr. D—— hung up thirteen, after quarter. Woodhouse was a garrison for the Parliament. He made a sonn hang his father, or è contra. From the body of this tree to the extreme branches is nineteen paces of Captain Hamden, who cannot pace less than a yard. (Of prodigious trees of this kind you will see many instances in my Sylva, which Mr. Ray has translated and inserted in his Herbal.- J. EVELYN.) ——

In the New Forest, within the trenches of the castle of Molwood (a Roman camp) is an old oake, which is a pollard and short It putteth forth young leaves on Christmas day, for about a week at that time of the yeare. Old Mr. Hastings, of Woodlands, was wont to send a basket full of them every yeare to King Charles I. I have seen of them severall Christmasses brought to my father.

But Mr. Perkins, who lives in the New Forest, sayes that there are two other oakes besides that which breed green buddes about Christmas day (pollards also), but not constantly. One is within two leagges of the King's-oake, the other a mile and a halfe off. [Leagges, probably lugs: a lug being "a measure of land, called otherwise a pole or perch". (Bailey's Dictionary.) The context renders leagues improbable.-J. B.] ——

Elmes.-I never did see an elme that grew spontaneously in a wood, as oakes, ashes, beeches, &c.; which consideration made me reflect that they are exotique; but by whom were they brought into this island? Not by the Saxons; for upon enquiry I am enformed that there are none in Saxony, nor in Denmarke, nor yet in France, spontaneous; but in Italy they are naturall; e. g. in Lombardie, &c. Wherefore I am induced to believe that they were brought hither out of Italy by the Romans, who were cultivators of their colonies. The Saxons understood not nor cared for such improvements, nor had hardly leisure if they would.

Anno 1687 I travelled from London as far as the Bishoprick of Durham. From Stamford to the bishoprick I sawe not one elme on the roade, whereas from London to Stamford they are in every hedge almost. In Yorkshire is plenty of trees, which they call elmes; but they are wich-hazells, as wee call them in Wilts (in some counties wich- elmes). I acquainted Mr. Jo. Ray of this, and he told me when he travelled into the north he minded it not, being chiefly intent on herbes; but he writes the contrary to what I doe here: but it is matter of fact, and therefore easily to bee prov'd. [See Ray's Letter to Aubrey, ante, p. 8.] "Omnesq{ue}, radicum plantis proveniunt". - Plin. lib. xvi. cap. 17.

In the Villare Anglicanum are a great many towns, called Ash-ton, Willough-by, &c. but not above three or four Elme-tons.

In the common at Urshfont was a mighty elme, which was blown down by the great wind when Ol. Cromwell died. I sawe it as it lay along, and I could but just looke over it. [See note in page 14.-J. B.] ——

Since the writing this of elmes, Edmund Wyld, Esq. of Houghton Conquest in Bedfordshire, R.S.S. assures me that in Bedfordshire, in severall woods, e. g. about Wotton, &c. that elmes doe grow naturally, as ashes, beeches, &c.; but quaere, what kind of elm it is? ——

Beeches.-None in Wilts except at Groveley. (In the wood belonging to Mr. Samwell's farm at Market Lavington are three very large beeches.- BISHOP TANNER.) I have a conceit that long time ago Salisbury plaines might have woods of them, but that they cut them down as an incumbrance to the ground, which would turn to better profit by pasture and arable. The Chiltern of Buckinghamshire is much of the like soile; and there the neernesse of Bucks to London, with the benefit of the Thames, makes their woods a very profitable commodity. ——

About the middle of Groveley Forest was a fair wood of oakes, which was called Sturton's Hatt. It appeared a good deale higher than the rest of the forest (which was most coppice wood), and was seen over all Salisbury plaines. In the middle of this hatt of trees (it resembled a hatt) there was a tall beech, which overtopt all the rest. The hatt was cutt down by Philip II. Earle of Pembroke, 1654; and Thomas, Earle of Pembroke, disafforested it, an°. 1684. ——

Birch. - Wee have none in North Wilts, but some (no great plenty) in South Wilts: most by the New Forest (In the parish of Market Lavington is a pretty large coppice, which consists for the most part of birch; and from thence it is well known by the name of the Birchen coppice.- BISHOP TANNER.) ——

In the parish of Hilmerton, in the way from Calne, eastward, leaving Hilmerton on the left hand, grows a red withy on the ditch side by the gate, 10 feet 6 inches about; and the spreading of the boughs is seaven yards round from the body of the tree. ——

Wich-hazel in the hundred of Malmesbury and thereabout, spontaneous. There are two vast wich-hazel trees in Okesey Parke, not much lesse than one of the best oakes there.

At Dunhed St. Maries, at the crosse, is a wich-hazell not lesse worthy of remarque than Magdalene-College oake (mentioned by Dr. Rob. Plott), for the large circumference of the shadowe that it causeth. When I was a boy the bowyers did use them to make bowes, and they are next best to yew. ——

Hornbeam we have none; neither did I ever see but one in the west of England, and that at Bathwick, juxta Bath, in the court yard of Hen. Nevill, Esq. ——

Yew trees naturally grow in chalkie countrys. The greatest plenty of them, as I believe, in the west of England is at Nunton Ewetrees. Between Knighton Ashes and Downton the ground produces them all along; but at Nunton they are a wood. At Ewridge, in the parish of Colern, in North Wilts (a stone brash and a free stone), they also grow indifferently plentifull; and in the parish of Kington St Michael I remember three or four in the stone brash and red earth.

When I learnt my accidents, 1633, at Yatton Keynel, there was a fair and spreading ewe-tree in the churchyard, as was common heretofore. The boyes tooke much delight in its shade, and it furnish't them with their scoopes and nutt-crackers. The clarke lop't it to make money of it to some bowyer or fletcher, and that lopping kill'd it: the dead trunke remaines there still. (Eugh-trees grow wild about Winterslow. A great eugh-tree in North Bradley churchyard, planted, as the tradition goes, in the time of ye Conquest. Another in .... Cannings churchyard. Leland (Itinerary) observes that in his time there was thirty-nine vast eugh-trees in the churchyard belonging to Stratfleur Abbey, in Wales.-BISHOP TANNER. Abundance of ewgh-trees in Surrey, upon the downes, heretofore, thô now much diminished.-J. EVELYN.) ——

Box, a parish so called in North Wilts, neer Bathe, in which parish is our famous freestone quarre of Haselbery: in all probability tooke its name from the box-trees which grew there naturally, but now worne out.

Not far off on Coteswold in Gloucestershire is a village called Boxwell, where is a great wood of it, which once in .... yeares Mr. Huntley fells, and sells to the combe-makers in London. At Boxley in Kent, and at Boxhill in Surrey, bothe chalkie soiles, are great box woods, to which the combe-makers resort. ——

Holy is indifferently common in Malmesbury hundred, and also on the borders of the New Forest: it seemes to indicate pitt-coale. In Wardour Parke are holy-trees that beare yellow berries. I think I have seen the like in Cranborne Chase. ——

Hazel.- Wee have two sorts of them. In the south part, and particularly Cranbourn Chase, the hazells are white and tough; with which there are made the best hurdles of England. The nutts of the chase are of great note, and are sold yearly beyond sea. They sell them at Woodbery Hill Faire, &c.; and the price of them is the price of a buschell of wheate. The hazell-trees in North Wilts are red, and not so tough, more brittle. ——

Coven-tree common about Chalke and Cranbourn Chase: the carters doe make their whippes of it. It growes no higher than a cherry-tree. ——

Buckthorne very common in South Wiltshire. The apothecaries make great use of the berries, and the glovers use it to colour their leather yellow.

——

Prick-timber (euonymus).- This tree is common, especially in North Wilts. The butchers doe make skewers of it, because it doth not taint the meate as other wood will doe: from whence it hath the name of prick-timber. ——

Osiers.- Wee have great plenty of them about Bemarton, &c. near Salisbury, where the osier beds doe yield four pounds per acre. ——

Service-trees grow naturally in Grettwood, in the parish of Gretenham, belonging to George Ayliffe, Esq. In the parke of Kington St. Michel is onely one. At the foot of Hedington Hill, and also at the bottome of the hill at Whitesheet, which is the same range of hill, doe growe at least twenty cervise-trees. They operate as medlars, but less effectually.

Pliny, lib. xv. c. 21. "De Sorbis. Quartum genus torminale appellatur, remedio tantum probabile, assiduum proventu minimumq{ue} pomo, arbore dissimili foliis plane platani". Lib. xvi. cap. 18.- "Gaudet frigidis Sorbus sed magis betulla". Dr. Gale, R.S.S. tells me that "Sorbiodunum", now Old Sarum, has its denomination from "sorbes"; but the ground now below the castle is all turned to arable. ——

Elders grow every where. At Bradford the side of the high hill which faces the south, about Mr. Paul Methwin's house, is covered with them. I fancy that that pent might be turned to better profit, for it is situated as well for a vinyard as any place can be, and is on a rocky gravelly ground. The apothecaries well know the use of the berries, and so doe the vintners, who buy vast quantities of them in London, and some doe make no inconsiderable profit by the sale of them. ——

At the parsonage house at Wyley growes an ash out of the mortar of the wall of the house, and it flourishes very well and is verdant. It was nine yeares old in 1686. I doe not insert this as a rarity; but 'tis strange to consider that it hath its growth and nourishment from the aire, for from the lime it can receive none. [In August 1847, I observed a large and venerable ash tree growing out of and united with the ancient Roman walls of Caistor, near Norwich. The whole of the base of the trunk was incorporated with bricks, rubble, and mortar; but the roots no doubt extended many yards into the adjacent soil.- J. B.] ——

Whitty-tree, or wayfaring-tree, is rare in this country; some few in Cranbourn Chace, and three or four on the south downe of the farme of Broad Chalke. In Herefordshire they are not uncommon; and they used, when I was a boy, to make pinnes for the yoakes of their oxen of them, believing it had vertue to preserve them from being forespoken, as they call it; and they use to plant one by their dwelling-house, believing it to preserve from witches and evill eyes.

——

Mr. Anthony Hinton, one of the officers of the Earle of Pembroke, did inoculate, not long before the late civill warres (ten yeares or more), a bud of Glastonbury Thorne, on a thorne at his farm-house at Wilton, which blossomes at Christmas as the other did. My mother has had branches of them for a flower-pott severall Christmasses, which I have seen. Elias Ashmole, Esq., in his notes upon "Theatrum Chymicum", saies that in the churchyard at Glastonbury grew a wallnutt tree that did putt out young leaves at Christmas, as doth the king's oake in the New Forest. In Parham Parke, in Suffolk (Mr. Boutele's), is a pretty ancient thorne that blossomes like that at Glastonbury; the people flock thither to see it on Christmas-day. But in the rode that leades from Worcester to Droitwiche is a blackthorne hedge at Clayn, halfe a mile long or more, that blossomes about Christmas-day for a week or more together. The ground is called Longland. Dr. Ezerel Tong sayd that about Runnly-marsh, in Kent, [Romney-marsh?] are thornes naturally like that at Glastonbury. The souldiers did cutt downe that neer Glastonbury: the stump remaines. ——

In the parish of Calne, at a pleasant seat of the Blakes, called Pinhill, was a grove of pines, which gives the name to the seate. About 1656 there were remaining about four or five: they made fine shew on the hill. ——

In the old hedges which are the boundes between the lands of Priory St. Marie, juxta Kington St. Michael, and the west field, which belonged to the Lord Abbot of Glastonbury, are yet remaining a great number of berberry-trees, which I suppose the nunnes made use of for confections, and they taught the young ladies that were educated there such arts. In those days there were not schooles for young ladies as now, but they were educated at religious houses.

CHAPTER X.

BEASTES.

[THIS Chapter, with the three which follow it, on "Fishes", "Birds", and "Reptils and Insects", constitute a principal branch of the work. On these topics Aubrey was assisted by his friend Sir James Long, of Draycot, Bart., whose letters to him are inserted in the original manuscript. Besides the passages here given, the chapter on "Beastes" comprises some extracts from Dame Juliana Berners' famous "Treatyse on Hawkynge, Hunting, and Fisshynge" (1481); together with a minute account of a sculptured representation of hunting the wild boar, over a Norman doorway at Little Langford Church. This bas-relief is engraved in Hoare's Modern Wiltshire. - J. B.]

I WILL first begin with beastes of venerie, whereof there hath been great plenty in this countie, and as good as any in England. Mr. J. Speed, who wrote the description of Wiltshire, anno Domini [1611], reckons nine forests, one chace, and twenty-nine parkes.

This whole island was anciently one great forest. A stagge might have raunged from Bradon Forest to the New Forest; sc. from forest to forest, and not above four or five miles intervall (sc. from Bradon Forest to Grettenham and Clockwoods; thence to the forest by Boughwood-parke, by Calne and Pewsham Forest, Blackmore Forest, Gillingham Forest, Cranbourn Chase, Holt Forest, to the New Forest.) Most of those forests were given away by King James the First. Pewsham Forest was given to the Duke of Buckingham, who gave it, I thinke, to his brother, the Earle of Anglesey. Upon the disafforesting of it, the poor people made this rhythme:-

"When Chipnam stood in Pewsham's wood,
Before it was destroy'd,
A cow might have gone for a groat a yeare-
but now it is denyed".

The metre is lamentable; but the cry of the poor was more lamentable. I knew severall that did remember the going of a cowe for 4d. per annum. The order was, how many they could winter they might summer: and pigges did cost nothing the going. Now the highwayes are encombred with cottages, and the travellers with the beggars that dwell in them. ——

The deer of the forest of Groveley were the largest of fallow deer in England, but some doe affirm the deer of Cranborne Chase to be larger than Groveley. Quaere Mr. Francis Wroughton of Wilton concerning the weight of the deer; as also Jack Harris, now keeper of Bere Forest, can tell the weight of the best deere of Verneditch and Groveley: he uses to come to the inne at Sutton. Verneditch is in the parish of Broad Chalke. 'Tis agreed that Groveley deer were generally the heaviest; but there was one, a buck, killed at Verneditch about an°. 165-, that out-weighed Groveley by two pounds. Dr. Randal Caldicot told me that it was weighed at his house, and it weighed eight score pounds.

About the yeare 1650 there were in Verneditch-walke, which is a part of Cranborne Chase, a thousand or twelve hundred fallow deere; and now, 1689, there are not above five hundred. A glover at Tysbury will give sixpence more for a buckskin of Cranborne Chase than of Groveley; and he saies that he can afford it. ——

Clarendon Parke was the best parke in the King's dominions. Hunt and Palmer, keepers there, did averre that they knew seven thousand head of deere in that parke; all fallow deere. This parke was seven miles about. Here were twenty coppices, and every one a mile round. ——

Upon these disafforestations the marterns were utterly destroyed in North Wilts. It is a pretty little beast and of a deep chesnutt colour, a kind of polecat, lesse than a fox; and the furre is much esteemed: not much inferior to sables. It is the richest furre of our nation. Martial saies of it -

"Venator capta marte superbus adest". - Epigr.

In Cranborn Chase and at Vernditch are some marterns still remaining. ——

In Wiley river are otters, and perhaps in others. The otter is our English bever; and Mr. Meredith Lloyd saies that in the river Tivy in Carmarthenshire there were real bevers heretofore - now extinct. Dr. Powell, in his History of Wales, speakes of it. They are both alike; fine furred, and their tayles like a fish. (The otter hath a hairy round tail, not like the beavers. - J. RAY.) ——

I come now to warrens. That at Auburn is our famous coney-warren; and the conies there are the best, sweetest, and fattest of any in England; a short, thick coney, and exceeding fatt The grasse there is very short, and burnt up in the hot weather. 'Tis a saying, that conies doe love rost-meat. ——

Mr. Wace's notes, p. 62.- "We have no wild boares in England: yet it may be thought that heretofore we had, and did not think it convenient to preserve this game". But King Charles I. sent for some out of France, and putt them in the New Forest, where they much encreased, and became terrible to the travellers. In the civill warres they were destroyed, but they have tainted all the breed of the pigges of the neighbouring partes, which are of their colour; a kind of soot colour.

(There were wild boars in a forest in Essex formerly. I sent a Portugal boar and sow to Wotton in Surrey, which greatly increased; but they digged the earth so up, and did such spoyle, that the country would not endure it: but they made incomparable bacon.- J. EVELYN.) ——

In warrens are found, but rarely, some old stotes, quite white: that is, they are ermins. My keeper of Vernditch warren hath shewn two or three of them to me.

At Everley is a great warren for hares; and also in Bishopston parish neer Wilton is another, where the standing is to see the race; and an°. 1682 the Right Honble James, Earle of Abingdon, made another at West Lavington. ——

Having done now with beastes of venerum, I will come to dogges. The British dogges were in great esteeme in the time of the Romans; as appeares by Gratius, who lived in Augustus Caesar's time, and Oppian, who wrote about two ages after Gratius, in imitation of him. "Gratii Cynegeticon", translated by Mr. Chr. Wace, 1654:-

"What if the Belgique current you should view,
And steer your course to Britain's utmost shore'!
Though not for shape, and much deceiving show,
The British hounds no other blemish know:
When fierce work comes, and courage must he shown,
And Mars to extreme combat leads them on,
Then stout Molossians you will lesse commend;
With Athemaneans these in craft contend."

——

It is certain that no county of England had greater variety of game, &c. than Wiltshire, and our county hounds were as good, or rather the best of England; but within this last century the breed is much mix't with northern hounds. Sir Charles Snell, of Kington St. Michael, who was my honoured friend and neighbour, had till the civill warrs as good hounds for the hare as any were in England, for handsomenesse and mouth (deep-mouthed) and goodnesse, and suited one another admirably well. But it was the Right Hon. Philip I. Earle of Pembroke, that was the great hunter. It was in his lordship's time, sc. tempore Jacobi I. and Caroli I. a serene calme of peace, that hunting was at its greatest heighth that ever was in this nation. The Roman governours had not, I thinke, that leisure. The Saxons were never at quiet; and the barons' warres, and those of York and Lancaster, took up the greatest part of the time since the Conquest: so that the glory of the English hunting breath'd its last with this Earle, who deceased about 1644, and shortly after the forests and parkes were sold and converted into arable, &c. 'Twas after his lordship's decease [1650] that I was a hunter; that is to say, with the Right Honourable William, Lord Herbert, of Cardiff, the aforesaid Philip's grandson. Mr. Chr. Wace then taught him Latin, and hunted with him; and 'twas then that he translated Gratii Cynegeticon, and dedicated it to his lordship, which will be a lasting monument for him. Sir Jo. Denham was at Wilton at that time about a twelve moneth. ——

The Wiltshire greyhounds were also the best of England, and are still; and my father and I have had as good as any were in our times in Wiltshire. They are generally of a fallow colour, or black; but Mr. Button's, of Shirburn in Glocestershire, are some white and some black. But Gratius, in his Cynegeticon, adviseth:-

"And chuse the grayhound py'd with black and white,
He runs more swift than thought, or winged flight;
But courseth yet in view, not hunts in traile,
In which the quick Petronians never faile."

We also had in this county as good tumblers as anywhere in the nation. Martial speakes of the tumblers:-

"Non sibi sed domino venatur vertagus acer, Illæsum leporem qui tibi dente feret" -

Turnebus, Young, Gerard, Vossius, and Janus Ulitius, all consenting that the name and dog came together from Gallia Belgica. Dr. Caldicot told me that in Wilton library there was a Latine poeme (a manuscript), wrote about Julius Caesar's time, where was mention of tumblers, and that they were found no where but in Britaine. I ask'd him if 'twas not Gratius; he told me no. Quaere, Mr. Chr. Wace, if he remembers any such thing? The books are now most lost and gonne: perhaps 'twas Martial.

Very good horses for the coach are bought out of the teemes in our hill-countrey. Warminster market is much used upon this account. ——

I have not seen so many pied cattle any where as in North Wiltshire. The country hereabout is much inclined to pied cattle, but commonly the colour is black or brown, or deep red. Some cow-stealers will make a hole in a hott lofe newly drawn out of the oven, and putt it on an oxes horn for a convenient tune, and then they can turn their softned homes the contrary way, so that the owner cannot swear to his own beast. Not long before the King's restauration a fellow was hanged at Tyburn for this, and say'd that he had never come thither if he had not heard it spoken of in a sermon. Thought he, I will try this trick.

CHAPTER XI

FISHES.

HUNGERFORD trowtes are very much celebrated, and there are also good ones at Marleborough and at Ramesbury. In the gravelly stream at Slaughtenford are excellent troutes; but, though I say it, there are none better in England than at Nawle, which is the source of the streame of Broad Chalke, a mile above it; but half a mile below Chalke, they are not so good. King Charles I. loved a trout above all fresh fish; and when he came to Wilton, as he commonly did every summer, the Earle of Pembroke was wont to send for these trowtes for his majesties eating. ——

The eeles at Marleborough are incomparable; silver eeles, truly almost as good as a trout. In ye last great frost, 168-, when the Thames was frozen over, there were as many eeles killed by frost at the poole at the hermitage at Broad Chalke as would fill a coule; and when they were found dead, they were all curled up like cables. ["Coul, a tub or vessel with two ears." Bailey's Dictionary.- J. B.] ——

Umbers are in the river Nadder, and so to Christ Church; but the late improvement of drowning the meadowes hath made them scarce. They are only in the river Humber besides. [Aubrey's friend, Sir James Long, mentions these fish as "graylings, or umbers". They are best known by the former name. Dr. Maton states that they are still to be found in the Avon, at Downton, where Walton speaks of them as being caught in his time. Mr. Hatcher says that "the umber abounds in the waters between Wilton and Salisbury". (History of Salisbury, p. 689.)-J. B.] ——

Crafish are very plenty at Salisbury; but the chiefest places for them Hungerford and Newbury: they are also at Ramesbury, and in the Avon at Chippenham.

"Greeke, carps, turkey-cocks, and beere,
Came into England all in a yeare."

In the North Avon are sometimes taken carpes which are extraordinary good. [Besides giving "the best way of dressing a carpe", Aubrey has annexed to his original manuscript a piece of paper, within the folds of which is inclosed a small bone. The paper bears the following inscription: "1660. The bone found in the head of a carpe. Vide Schroderi. It is a good medicine for the apoplexie or falling sickness; I forget whether." Aubrey's reference is to "Zoology; or the History of Animals, as they are useful in Physic and Chirurgery"; by John Schroderus, M.D. of Francfort Done into English by T. Bateson. London, 1659, 8vo.

When a boy I caught many of these fish in the pond at Kington St. Michael, both by angling and by baiting three or four hooks at the end of a piece of string and leaving them in the water all night. In the morning I have found two, and sometimes three, large fish captured. On one occasion "Squire White", the proprietor of the estate, discharged his gun, apparently at me, to deter me from this act of poaching and trespassing. - J. B.] ——

As for ponds, we cannot boast much of them; the biggest is that in Bradon Forest. There is a fair pond at West Lavington which was made by Sir John Danvers. At Draycot Cerne the ponds are not great, but the carpes very good, and free from muddinesse. In Wardour Parke is a stately pond; at Wilton and Longleat two noble canals and severall small ponds; and in the parke at Kington St. Michael are several ponds in traine. [The latter ponds are supplied by two springs in the immediate vicinity, forming one of the tributaries of the Avon. The stream abounds with trout, many of which I have caught at the end of the summer season, by laving out the water from the deeper holes. - J. B.] ——

Tenches are common. Loches are in the Upper Avon at Amesbury. Very good perches in the North Avon, but none in the Upper Avon. Salmons are sometimes taken in the Upper Avon, rarely, at Harnham Bridge juxta Sarum. [On the authority of this passage, Dr. Maton includes the salmon among the Wiltshire fish; but he adds, "I know no person now living who has ascertained its having ascended the Avon so far as Salisbury." Hatcher's Hist, of Salisbury, p. 689.-J. B.] ——

Good pikes, roches, and daces in both the Avons. In the river Avon at Malmesbury are lamprills (resembling lampreis) in knotts: they are but..... inches long. They use them for baytes; and they squeeze these knotts together and make little kind of cheeses of them for eating.

CHAPTER XII.

BIRDS.

WE have great plenty of larkes, and very good ones, especially in Golem-fields and those parts adjoyning to Coteswold. They take them by alluring them with a dareing-glasse,* which is whirled about in a sun- shining day, and the larkes are pleased at it, and strike at it, as at a sheepe's eye, and at that time the nett is drawn over them. While he playes with his glasse he whistles with his larke-call of silver, a tympanum of about the diameter of a threepence. In the south part of Wiltshire they doe not use dareing-glasses but catch these pretty ætheriall birds with trammolls.

* ["Let his grace go forward, and dare us with his cap like larks." - Shakspere, Henry VIII. Act iii. sc. 2.]

The buntings doe accompany the larkes. Linnets on the downes. Woodpeckers severall sorts: many in North Wilts.

Sir Bennet Hoskins, Baronet, told me that his keeper at his parke at Morehampton in Hereford-shire, did, for experiment sake, drive an iron naile thwert the hole of the woodpecker's nest, there being a tradition that the damme will bring some leafe to open it. He layed at the bottome of the tree a cleane sheet, and before many houres passed the naile came out, and he found a leafe lying by it on the sheete. Quaere the shape or figure of the leafe. They say the moone-wort will doe such things. This experiment may easily be tryed again. As Sir Walter Raleigh saies, there are stranger things to be seen in the world than are between London and Stanes. [This is the "story" which Ray, in the letter printed in page 8, justly describes as, "without doubt, a fable." - J. B.]

In Sir James Long's parke at Draycot Cerne are some wheat-eares; and on come warrens and downes, but not in great plenty. Sussex doth most abound with these. It is a great delicacie, and they are little lumps of fatt.

On Salisbury plaines, especially about Stonehenge, are bustards. They are also in the fields above Lavington: they doe not often come to Chalke. (Many about Newmarket, and sometimes cranes. J. EVELYN.) [In the "Penny Cyclopaedia" are many interesting particulars of the bustard, and in Hoare's "Ancient Wiltshire, vol. i. p. 94, there is an account of two of these birds which were seen near Warminster in the summer of 1801; since when the bustard has not been seen in the county.-J. B.]

On Salisbury plaines are gray crowes, as at Royston. [These are now met with on the Marlborough downs.- J. B.]

" Like Royston crowes, where, as a man may say,
Are friars of both the orders, black and gray."
- J. CLEVELAND'S POEMS.

'Tis certain that the rookes of the Inner Temple did not build their nests in the garden to breed in the spring before the plague, 1665; but in the spring following they did.

Feasants were brought Into Europe from about the Caspian sea. There are no pheasants in Spaine, nor doe I heare of any in Italy. Capt. Hen. Bertie, the Earle of Abingdon's brother, when he was in Italy, was at the great Duke of Tuscany's court entertained with all the rarities that the country afforded, but he sawe no pheasants. Mr. Wyld Clarke, factor fifteen yeares in Barberie, affirmes there are none there. Sir John Mordaunt, who had a command at Tangier twenty-five yeares, and had been some time governour there, a great lover of field sports, affirmes that there are no pheasants in Africa or Spaine. [See Ray's Letter to Aubrey, ante, page 8.] ——

Bitterns in the breaches at Allington, &c. Herons bred heretofore, sc. about 1580, at Easton- Piers, before the great oakes were felled down neer the mannour-house; and they doe still breed in Farleigh Parke. An eirie of sparrow-hawkes at the parke at Kington St. Michael. The hobbies doe goe away at..... and return at the spring. Quære Sir James Long, if any other hawkes doe the like? —

—

Ganders are vivacious animals. Farmer Ady of Segary had a gander that was fifty yeares old, which the soldiers killed. He and his gander were both of the same age. (A goose is now living, anno 1757, at Hagley hall in Worcestershire, full fifty yeares old. MS. NOTE.)

Sea-mewes. Plentie of them at Colern-downe; elsewhere in Wiltshire I doe not remember any. There are presages of weather made by them. [Instead of "presages of weather," the writer would have been more accurate if he had said that when "sea-mewes," or other birds of the ocean, are seen so far inland as Colern, at least twenty miles from the sea, they indicate stormy weather in their natural element. - J. B.]-Virgil's Georgics, lib. i. Englished by Mr. T. May:-

"The seas are ill to sailors evermore
When cormorants fly crying to the shore;
From the mid-sea when sea-fowl pastime make
Upon dry land; when herns the ponds forsake,
And, mounted on their wings, doe fly aloft."

CHAPTER XIII
REPTILS AND INSECTS.

[THIS Chapter contains several extraordinary recipes for medicines to be compounded in various ways from insects and reptiles. As a specimen one of them may he referred to which begins as follows:-"Calcinatio Bufonum. R. Twenty great fatt toades; in May they are the best; putt them alive in a pipkin; cover it, make a fire round it to the top; let them stay on the fire till they make no noise," &c. &c. Aubrey says that Dr. Thomas Willis mentions this medicine in his tractat De Febribus, and describes it as a special remedy for the plague and other diseases.-J. B.]

No snakes or adders at Chalke, and toades very few: the nitre in the chalke is inimique to them. No snakes or adders at Harcot-woods belonging to — Gawen, Esq.; but in the woods of Compton Chamberleyn adjoyning they are plenty. At South Wraxhall and at Colern Parke, and so to Mouncton-Farley, are adders.

In Sir James Long's parke at Draycot-Cerne are grey lizards; and no question in other places if they were look't after; but people take them for newts. They are of that family. About anno 1686 a boy lyeing asleep in a garden felt something dart down his throat, which killed him: 'tis probable 'twas a little newt. They are exceeding nimble: they call them swifts at Newmarket Heath. When I was a boy a young fellow slept on the grasse: after he awak't, happening to putt his hand in his pocket, something bitt him by the top of his finger: he shak't it suddenly off so that he could not perfectly discerne it. The biteing was so venomous that it overcame all help, and he died in a few hours:-

"Virus edax superabat opera: penituaq{ue} receptum Ossibus, et toto corpore pestis erat."- OVID. FASTOR.

Sir George Ent, M.D. had a tenant neer Cambridge that was stung with an adder. He happened not to dye, but was spotted all over. One at Knahill in Wilts, a neighbour of Dr. Wren's, was stung, and it turned to a leprosy. (From Sr. Chr. Wren.)

At Neston Parke (Col. W. Eire's) in Cosham parish are huge snakes, an ell long; and about the Devises snakes doe abound.

Toades are plentifull in North Wiltshire: but few in the chalkie countreys. In sawing of an ash 2 foot + square, of Mr. Saintlowe's, at Knighton in Chalke parish, was found a live toade about 1656; the sawe cutt him asunder, and the bloud came on the under-sawyer's hand: he thought at first the upper-sawyer had cutt his hand. Toades are oftentimes found in the milstones of Darbyshire.

——

Snailes are everywhere; but upon our downes, and so in Dorset, and I believe in Hampshire, at such degree east and west, in the summer time are abundance of very small snailes on the grasse and come, not much bigger, or no bigger than small pinnes heads. Though this is no strange thing among us, yet they are not to be found in the north part of Wilts, nor on any northern wolds. When I had the honour to waite on King Charles I.* and the Duke of York to the top of Silbury hill, his Royal Highnesse happened to cast his eye on some of these small snailes on the turfe of the hill. He was surprised with the novelty, and commanded me to pick some up, which I did, about a dozen or more, immediately; for they are in great abundance. The next morning as he was abed with his Dutches at Bath he told her of it, and sent Dr. Charleton to me for them, to shew her as a rarity.

* [This should be "Charles II." who visited Avebury and Silbury Hill, in company with his brother, afterwards James II., in the autumn of the year 1663, when Aubrey attended them by the King's command. See his account of the royal visit, in the Memoir of Aubrey, 4to. 1845. - J. B.] ——

In the peacefull raigne of King James I. the Parliament made an act for provision of rooke-netts and catching crows to be given in charge of court-barons, which is by the stewards observed, but I never knew the execution of it. I have heard knowing countreymen affirme that rooke-wormes, which the crows and rookes doe devour at sowing time, doe turne to chafers, which I think are our English locusts: and some yeares wee have such fearfull armies of them that they devour all manner of green things; and if the crowes did not destroy these wormes, it would oftentimes happen. Parliaments are not infallible, and some thinke they were out in this bill. ——

Bees. Hampshire has the name for the best honey of England, and also the worst; sc. the forest honey: but the south part of Wiltshire having much the like turfe must afford as good, or little inferiour to it. 'Tis pitty these profitable insects should loose their lives for their industry.

"Flebat Aristæus, quod Apes cum stirpe necatas Viderat incoeptos destituisse favos."-OVID. FAST. lib. i.

A plaster of honey effectually helpeth a bruise. (From Mr. Francis Potter, B. D., of Kilmanton.) It seemes to be a rational medicine: for honey is the extraction of the choicest medicinal flowers.

Mr. Butler of Basingstoke, in Hampshire, who wrote a booke of Bees, had a daughter he called his honey-girle; to whom, when she was born, he gave certain stocks of bees; the product of which when she came to be married, was 400li. portion. (From — Boreman, of Kingston-upon- Thames, D.D.)

Mr. Harvey, at Newcastle, gott 80li. per annum by bees. (I thinke Varro somewhere writes that in Spaine two brothers got almost as much yearly by them.- J. EVELYN.) Desire of Mr. Hook, R.S.S. a copie of the modelle of his excellent bee-hive, March 1684-5; better than any yet known. See Mr. J. Houghton's Collections, No. 1683, June, where he hath a good modelle of a bee-hive, pag. 166. Mr. Paschal hath an ingeniouse contrivance for bees at Chedsey; sc. they are brought into his house. Bee-hive at Wadham College, Oxon; see Dr. Plott's Oxfordshire, p. 263.

Heretofore, before our plantations in America, and consequently before the use of sugar, they sweetened their [drink, &c.] with honey; as wee doe now with sugar. The name of honey-soppes yet remaines, but the use is almost worne out. (At Queen's College, Oxon, the cook treats the whole hall with honey-sops on Good Friday at dinner. - BISHOP TANNER.) Now, 1686, since the great increase of planting of sugar-canes in the Barbados, &c. sugar is but one third of the price it was at thirty yeares since. In the time of the Roman Catholique religion, when a world of wax candles were used in the churches, bees-wax was a considerable commodity.

To make Metheglyn:-(from Mistress Hatchman. This receipt makes good Metheglyn; I thinke as good as the Devises). Allow to every quart of honey a gallon of water; and when the honey is dissolved, trie if it will beare an egg to the breadth of three pence above the liquor; or if you will have it stronger putt in more honey. Then set it on the fire, and when the froth comes on the toppe of it, skimme it cleane; then crack eight or ten hen-egges and putt in the liquor to cleare it: two or three handfulls of sweet bryar, and so much of muscovie, and sweet marjoram the like quantity; some doe put sweet cis, or if you please put in a little of orris root. Boyle all these untill the egges begin to look black, (these egges may be enough for a hoggeshead,) then straine it forth through a fine sieve into a vessell to coole; the next day tunne it up in a barrell, and when it hath workt itself cleare, which will be in about a weeke's time, stop it up very close, and if you make it strong enough, sc. to carry the breadth of a sixpence, it will keep a yeare. This receipt is something neer that of Mr. Thorn. Piers of the Devises, the great Metheglyn-maker. Metheglyn is a pretty considerable manufacture in this towne time out of mind. I doe believe that a quantity of mountain thyme would be a very proper ingredient; for it is most wholesome and fragrant [Aubrey also gives another "receipt to make white metheglyn," which he obtained "from old Sir Edward Baynton, 1640." I have seen this old English beverage made by my grandmother, as here described.-J. B.]

Mr. Francis Potter, Rector of Kilmanton, did sett a hive of bees in one of the lances of a paire of scales in a little closet, and found that in summer dayes they gathered about halfe a pound a day; and one day, which he conceived was a honey-dew, they gathered three pounds wanting a quarter. The hive would be something lighter in the morning than at night. Also he tooke five live bees and putt them in a paper, which he did cutt like a grate, and weighed them, and in an hower or two they would wast the weight of three or four wheatcornes. He bids me observe their thighes in a microscope. (Upon the Brenta river, by Padua in Italy, they have hives of bees in open boates; the bees goe out to feed and gather till the honey-dews are spent neer the boate; and then the bee master rows the boate to a fresh place, and by the sinking of the boate knows when to take the honey, &c.- J. EVELYN.)

CHAPTER XIV.

OF MEN AND WOEMEN.

[THE following instances of remarkable longevity, monstrous births, &c. will suffice to shew the nature of this Chapter. It must be admitted that its contents are unimportant except as matters of curious speculation, and as connected with the several localities referred to.-J. B.]

A PROVERB: -•

'Salisbury Plain
Never without a thief or twain.'

As to the temper and complexion of the men and woemen, I have spoken before in the Prolegomena.

As to longævity, good aire and water doe conduce to it: but the inhabitants are also to tread on dry earth; not nitrous or vitriolate, that hurts the nerves. South and North Wiltshire are wett and dampish soiles. The stone walles in the vale here doe also cast a great and unwholsome dampe. Eighty-four or eighty-five is the age the inhabitants doe rarely exceed. But I have heard my worthy friend George Johnson of Bowdon, Esq., one of the judges in North Wales, say that he did observe in his circuit, sc. Montgomery, Flint, and Denbigh, that men lived there as commonly to an hundred yeares as with us to eighty. Mr. Meredith Lloyd hath seen at Dolkelly, a great parish in Merionithshire, an hundred or more of poore people at eighty yeares of age at church in a morning, who came thither bare-foot and bare-legged a good way. In the chancell of Winterborn Basset lies interred Mr. Ambrose Brown, who died 166-,aged 103 yeares. Old goodwife Dew of Broad Chalke died about 1649, aged 103. She told me she was, I thinke, sixteen yeares old when King Edward the sixth was in this countrie, and that he lost his courtiers, or his courtiers him, a hunting, and found him again in Falston-lane. In the parish of Stanton St. Quintin are but twenty- three houses, and when Mr. Byron was inducted, 167-, here were eight persons of 80 yeares of age. Mr. Thorn. Lyte of Easton-Piers, my mother's grand- father, died 1626, aged 96; and about 1674 died there old William Kington, a tenant of mine, about 90 yeares of age. A poore woman of Chippenham died about 1684, aged 108 yeares.

Part of an Epitaph at Colinbourne-Kinston in Wiltshire, communicated to the Philosophicall Conventus at the Musæum at Oxford, by Mr. Arthur Charlett, Fellow of Trinity College, Oxford:- "Pray for the soule of Constantine Darrel, Esq. who died Anno Dni. 1400, and....... his wife, who died A°. Dni. 1495." See it. I doe believe the dates in the inscription are in numerical letters. [In this case the former date was probably left unfinished, when the husband placed the inscription to his wife, and after his death it was neglected to be filled up, as in many other instances. The numerals would be in black letter.- J. B.]

In the chancel at Milsham is an inscription of Isaac Self, a wealthy cloathiers of that place, who died in the 92nd yeare of his age, leaving behind him a numerous offspring; viz. eighty and three in number.

Ella, Countesse of Salisbury, daughter to [William] Longespe, was foundress of Lacock Abbey; where she ended her days, being above a hundred yeares old; she outlived her understanding. This I found in an old MS. called Chronicon de Lacock in Bibliotheca Cottoniana. [The chronicle referred to was destroyed by the fire which so seriously injured the Cotton MSS. in 1731. The extracts preserved from it do not confirm Aubrey's statements, but place the Countess Ela's death on the ix kal. Sept. 1261, in the 74th year of her age. See Bowles's History of Lacock, Appendix, p. v. - J. B.]

Dame Olave, a daughter and coheire of Sir [Henry] Sharington of Lacock, being in love with [John] Talbot, a younger brother of the Earle of Shrewsbury, and her father not consenting that she should marry him; discoursing with him one night from the battlements of the Abbey Church, said shee, "I will leap downe to you:" her sweet heart replied he would catch her then; but he did not believe she would have done it. She leap't downe, and the wind, which was then high, came under her coates and did something breake the fall. Mr. Talbot caught her in his armes, but she struck him dead: she cried out for help, and he was with great difficulty brought to life again. Her father told her that since she had made such a leap she should e'en marrie him. She was my honoured friend Col. Sharington Talbot's grandmother, and died at her house at Lacock about 1651, being about an hundred yeares old. Quaere, Sir Jo. Talbot?

[This romantic story seems to have escaped the attention of the venerable historian of Lacock, the Rev. Canon Bowles. The late John Carter mentions a tradition of which he was informed on visiting Lacock in 1801, to the effect that "one of the nuns jumped from a gallery on the top of a turret there into the arms of her lover." He observes, as impugning the truth of the story, that the gallery "appears to have been the work of James or Charles the First's time." Aubrey's anecdote has an appearance of authenticity. Its heroine, Olave, or Olivia Sherington, married John Talbot, Esq. of Salwarpe, in the county of Worcester, fourth in descent from John, second Earl of Shrews- bury. She inherited the Lacock estate from her father, and it has ever since^ remained the property of that branch of the Talbot family, now represented by the scientific Henry Fox Talbot, Esq. -J. B.] ——

The last Lady Prioresse of Priorie St Marie, juxta Kington St. Michael, was the Lady Mary Dennys, a daughter of the Dennys's of Pocklechurch in Gloucestershire; she lived a great while after the dissolution of the abbeys, and died in Somersetshire about the middle or latter end of the raigne of King James the first

The last Lady Abbese of Amesbury was a Kirton, who after the dissolution married to..... Appleton of Hampshire. She had during her life a pension from King Henry VIII.: she was 140 yeares old when she dyed. She was great-great-aunt to Mr. Child, Rector of Yatton Keynell; from whom I had this information. Mr. Child, the eminent banker in Fleet Street, is Parson Child's cosen-german. [The name of the last Abbess of Amesbury was Joan Darell, who surrendered to the King, 4 Dec. 1540. Hoare's Modern Wiltshire, Amesbury Hundred, p. 73. J. B.]

When King Charles II. was at Salisbury, 1665, a piper of Stratford sub Castro playd on his tabor and pipe before him, who was a piper in Queen Elizabeth's time, and aged then more than 100. ——

One goodwife Mills of Yatton Keynel, a tenant of my father's, did dentire in the 88 yeare of her age, which was about the yeare 1645. The Lord Chancellour Bacon speakes of the like of the old Countesse of Desmond, in Ireland. ——

Mr. William Gauntlett, of Netherhampton, born at Amesbury, told me that since his remembrance there were digged up in the churchyard at Amesbury, which is very spacious, a great number of huge bones, exceeding, as he sayes, the size of those of our dayes. At Highworth, at the signe of the Bull, at one Hartwells, I have been credibly enformed is to be seen a scull of-a vast bignesse, scilicet half as big again as an ordinary one. From Mr. Kich. Brown, Rector of Somerford Magna, (At Wotton in Surrey, where my brother enlarged the vault in which our family are buried, digging away the earth for the foundations, they found a complete skeleton neer nine foot in length, the skull of an extraordinary size. - J. EVELYN.)

George Johnson Esq. bencher of the Middle Temple, digging for marle at Bowdon Parke, Ano. 1666, the diggers found the bones of a man under a quarrie of planke stones: he told me he saw it. He was a serious person, and "fide dignus". ——

At Wishford Magna is the inscription, "Hic jacet Thomas Bonham, armiger, quondam Patronus istius Ecclesiæ, qui quidem Thomas obiit vicesimo nono die Maii, Anno Domini MCCCCLXXIII (1473); el Editha uxor ejus, quæ quidem Editha obiit vicesimo sexto die Aprilis, Anno D'ni MCCCCLXIX. (1469). Quorum animabus propitietur Deus.- Amen." They lye both buried under the great marble stone in the nave of this church, where is the above said inscription, above which are their pourtraictures in brasse, and an escucheon now illegible. Beneath this inscription are the small figures of nine young children in brasse. This Mr. Bonham's wife had two children at one birth, the first time: and he being troubled at it travelled, and was absent seven yeares. After his returne she was delivered of seven children at one birth. In this parish is a confident tradition that these seven children were all baptized at the font in this church, and that they were brought thither in a kind of chardger, which was dedicated to this church, and hung on two nailes, which are to be seen there yet, neer the bellfree on the south side. Some old men are yet living that doe remember the chardger. This tradition is entred into the register booke there, from whence I have taken this narrative (1659). [See the extract from the register, which is signed by "Roger Powell, Curate there," in Hoare's Modern Wilts. (Hundred of Branch and Dole) p. 49.-J. B.] ——

On Tuesday the 25th day of October, Anno Dni 1664, Mary, the wife of John Waterman, of Fisherton Anger, neer Salisbury, hostler, fell into travell, and on Wednesday, between one and two in the morning, was delivered of a female child, with all its parts duly formed. Aboute halfe an hour after she was delivered of a monstrous birth, having two heades, the one opposite to the other; the two shoulders had also [each] two armes, with the hands bearing respectively each against the other; two feet, &c. About four o'clock in the afternoon it was christened by the name of Martha and Mary, having two pretty faces, and lived till Fryday next. The female child first borne, whose name was Elselet, lived fourteen days, and died the 9th of November following: the mother then alive and in good health.

[This narrative is accompanied by a description of the internal structure of the lusus naturæ, as developed in a post mortem examination; which "accurate account," says Aubrey, "was made by my worthy and learned friend Thorn. Guidot, Dr. of Physick, who did kindly communicate it to me out of his collection of medicinall observations in Latin."]

Dr. Wm. Harvey, author of the Circulation of the Blood, told me that one Mr. Palmer's wife in Kent did beare a child every day for five daies together. — —

A wench being great with child drowned herself in the river Avon, where, haveing layn twenty-four houres, she was taken up and brought into the church at Sutton Benger, and layd upon the board, where the coroner did his office. Mris. Joane Sumner hath often assured me that the sayd wench did sweat a cold sweat when she lay dead; and that she severall times did wipe off the sweat from her body, and it would quickly returne again: and she would have had her opened, because she did believe that the child was alive within her and might bee saved. ——

In September 1661 a grave was digged in the church of Hedington for a widow, where her husband was buried in 1610. In this grave was a spring; the coffin was found firme; the bodie not rotten, but black; and in some places white spotts; the lumen was rotten. Mr. Wm. Scott's wife of this parish, from whom I have this, saw it, with severall of her neighbours.

Mrs. Mary Norborne, of Calne, a gentlewoman worthy of belief, told me that Mr.... White, Lord of Langley's grave was opened forty years after he was buried. He lay in water, and his body not perished, and some old people there remembred him and knew him. He was related to Mrs. Norborne, and her husband's brother was minister here, in whose time this happened. ——

Mrs. May of Calne, upon the generall fright in their church of the falling of the steeple, when the people ran out of the church, occasioned by the throwing of a stone by a boy, dyed of this fright in halfe an hour's time. Mrs. Dorothy Gardiner was frightened at Our Lady Church at Salisbury, by the false report of the falling of the steeple, and died in... houres space. The Lady Jordan being at Cirencester when it was beseiged (anno atatis 75) was so terrified with the shooting that her understanding was so spoyled that she became a child, that they made babies for her to play withall. ——

At Broad Chalke is a cottage family that the generation have two thumbes. A poor woman's daughter in Westminster being born so, the mother gott a carpenter to amputate one of them with his chizel and mallet. The girl was then about seven yeares old, and was a lively child, but immediately after the thumb was struck off, the fright and convulsion was so extreme, that she lost her understanding, even her speech. She lived till seventeen in that sad condition.

The Duke of Southampton, who was a most lovely youth, had two foreteeth that grew out, very unhandsome. His cruel mother caused him to be bound fast in a chaire, and had them drawn out; which has caused the want of his understanding.

[This refers to Charles Fitzroy, one of the natural sons of King Charles II. by his mistress, Barbara Villiers, Duchess of Cleveland. He was created Duke of Southampton in 1674; became Duke of Cleveland on the death of his "cruel mother "in 1709; and died in 1730.-J. B.] ——

Mdm. Dr. W. Harvey told me that the biteing of a man enraged is poysonous. He instanced one that was bitt in the hand in a quarrell, and it swoll up to his shoulder, and killed him in a short time. [That death, from nervous irritation, might follow such a wound is not improbable: but that it was caused by any "poison" infused into the system is an idea too absurd for refutation.- J. B.]

CHAPTER XV.

DISEASES AND CURES.

[SEVERAL passages may have been noticed in the preceding pages, calculated to shew the ignorance which prevailed in Aubrey's time on medical subjects, and the absurd remedies which were adopted for the cure of diseases. In the present chapter this topic is further illustrated. It contains a series of recipes of the rudest and most unscientific character, amongst which the following are the only parts suited to this publication. Aubrey describes in the manuscript an instrument made of whalebone, to be thrust down the throat into the stomach, so as to act as an emetic. He states that this contrivance was invented by "his counsel learned in the law," Judge Rumsey; and proceeds to quote several pages, with references to its advantages, from a work by W. Rumsey, of Gray's Inn, Esq., entitled, "Organon Salutis, an instrument to cleanse the stomach: with new experiments on Tobacco and Coffee." The work quoted seems to have been popular in its day, for there were three editions of it published. (London, 1657, 1659, 1664, 12mo.)-J. B.]

THE inscription over the chapell dore of St. Giles, juxta Wilton, sc. "1624. This hospitall of St. Giles was re-edified by John Towgood, Maior of Wilton, and his brethren, adopted patrons thereof, by the gift of Queen Adelicia, wife unto King Henry the first." This Adelicia was a leper. She had a windowe and a dore from her lodgeing into the chancell of the chapell, whence she heard prayers. She lieth buried under a plain marble gravestone; the brasse whereof (the figure and inscription) was remaining about 1684. Poore people told me that the faire was anciently kept here.

At Maiden Bradley, a maiden infected with the leprosie founded a house for maidens that were lepers. [See a similar statement in Camden's "Britannia," and Gough's comments thereon.-J. B.] ——

Ex Registro. Anno Domini 1582, May 4, the plague began in Kington St. Michaell, and lasted the 6th of August following; 13 died of it, most of them being of the family of the Kington's; which name was then common, as appeared by the register, but in 1672 quite extinct.

[The words "here the plague began," and "here the plague rested," appear in the parish register of Kington St. Michael, under the dates mentioned by Aubrey. Eight of the thirteen persons who died during its continuance were of the family of the Kingtons.-J. B.] ——

May-dewe is a very great dissolvent of many things with the sunne, that will not be dissolved any other way; which putts me in mind of the rationality of the method used by Wm. Gore of Clapton, Esq}. for his gout; which was, to walke in the dewe with his shoes pounced; he found benefit by it. I told Mr. Wm. Mullens, of Shoe Lane, Chirurgion, this story; and he sayd this was the very method and way of curing that was used in Oliver Cromwell, Protectour. [See "Observations and Experiments upon May-Dew," by Thomas Henshaw, in Philosophical Transactions, 1665. Abbr. i. 13.-J. B.] ——

For the gowte. Take the leaves of the wild vine (bryony, vitis alba); bruise them and boyle them, and apply it to the place grieved, lapd in a colewort-leafe. This cured an old man of 84 yeares of age, at Kilmanton, in 1669, and he was well since, to June 1670: which account I had from Mr. Francis Potter, the rector there.

Mr. Wm. Montjoy of Bitteston hath an admirable secret for the cure of the Ricketts, for which he was sent to far and neer; his sonne hath the same. Rickettie children (they say) are long before they breed teeth. I will, whilst 'tis in my mind, insert this remarque; viz. about 1620, one Ricketts of Newbery, perhaps corruptly from Ricards, a practitioner in physick, was excellent at the curing children with swoln heads and small legges; and the disease being new and without a name, he being so famous for the cure of it they called the disease the ricketts; as the King's evill from the King's curing of it with his touch; and now 'tis good sport to see how they vex their lexicons, and fetch it from the Greek {Gk: Rachis} the back bone. ——

For a pinne-and-webbe* in the eye, a pearle, or any humour that comes out of the head. My father laboured under this infirmity, and our learned men of Salisbury could doe him no good. At last one goodwife Holly, a poore woman of Chalke, cured him in a little time. My father gave her a broad piece of gold for the receipt, which is this:-Take about halfe a pint of the best white wine vinegar; put it in a pewter dish, which sett on a chafing dish of coales covered with another pewter dish; ever and anon wipe off the droppes on the upper dish till you have gott a little glassefull, which reserve in a cleane vessell; then take about half an ounce of white sugar candie, beaten and searcht very fine, and putt it in the glasse; so stoppe it, and let it stand. Drop one drop in the morning and evening into the eye, and let the patient lye still a quarter of an hour after it.

I told Mr. Robert Boyle this receipt, and he did much admire it, and tooke a copie of it, and sayd that he that was the inventor of it was a good chymist. If this medicine were donne in a golden dish or porcelane dish, &c. it would not doe this cure; but the vertue proceeds, sayd hee, from the pewter, which the vinegar does take off.

* [The following definitions are from Bailey's Dictionary (1728):-" Pin and Web, a horny induration of the membranes of the eye, not much unlike a Cataract." "Pearl (among oculists), a web on the eye."- J.B.] ——

In the city of Salisbury doe reigne the dropsy, consumption, scurvy, gowte; it is an exceeding dampish place.

At Poulshot, a village neer the Devises, in the spring time the inhabitants appeare of a primrose complexion; 'tis a wett, dirty place.

——

Mrs. Fr. Tyndale, of Priorie St. Maries, when a child, voyded a lumbricus biceps. Mr. Winceslaus Hollar, when he was at Mechlin, saw an amphisbæna, which he did very curiously delineate, and coloured it in water colours, of the very colour: it was exactly the colour of the inner peele of an onyon: it was about six inches long, but in its repture it made the figure of a semicircle; both the heads advancing equally. It was found under a piece of old timber, about 1661; under the jawes it had barbes like a barbel, which did strengthen his motion in running. This draught, amongst a world of others, Mr. Thorn. Chiffinch, of Whitehall, hath; for which Mr. Hollar protested to me he had no compensation. The diameter was about that of a slo-worme; and I guesse it was an amphisbænal slo-worme.

[The serpents called amphisbæna are so designated (from the Greek {Gk: amphisbaina}) in consequence of their ability to move backwards as well as forwards. The head and tail of the amphisbæna are very similar in form: whence the common belief that it possesses a head at each extremity. It was formerly supposed that cutting off one of its "heads" would fail to destroy this animal; and that its flesh, dried and pulverized, was an infallible remedy for dislocations and broken bones.-J. B.]

CHAPTER XVI.

OBSERVATIONS ON PARISH REGISTERS,
ACCORDING TO THE WAY PRESCRIBED BY THE HONBLE. SIR WM. PETTY, KNIGHT.

[THIS chapter consists merely of memoranda for the further examination of those valuable materials for local and general statistics - the parochial registers. Aubrey has inserted the number of baptisms, marriages, and burials, recorded in the registers of Broad Chalke, for each year, from 1630 to 1642, and from 1676 to 1684 inclusive; distinguishing the baptisms and burials of males and females in each year. The like particulars are given for a period of five years from the registers of Dunhead St. Mary. He adds, "In anno 1686 I made extracts out of the register bookes of half a dozen parishes in South Wiltshire, which I gave to Sir Wm. Petty." The following passages will suffice to indicate the nature of his remarks.- J. B.]

MR. ROBERT GOOD, M.A., of Bower Chalke, hath a method to calculate the provision that is spent in a yeare in their parish; and does find that one house with another spends six pounds per annum; which comes within an hundred pounds of the parish rate.

Sir "W. Petty observes, from the account of the people, that not above halfe teeming women are marryed; and that if the Government pleased there might be such a multiplication of mankind as in 1500 yeares would sufficiently plant every habitable acre in the world. ——

Mdm. The poore's rate of St. Giles-in-the-fields, London, comes to six thousand pounds per annum. [The sixth chapter of Mr. Rowland Dobie's "History of the United Parishes of St. Giles- in-the-Fields and St. George, Bloomsbury," (8vo. 1829) contains some curious and interesting "historical sketches of pauperism." Speaking of the parish workhouse, the author says, "It contains on an average from 800 to 900 inmates, which is however but a small proportion to the number constantly relieved, at an expense [annually] of nearly forty thousand pounds."-J. B.] ——

Dunhead St. Mary.-The reason why so few marriages are found in the register bookes of these parts is that the ordinary sort of people goe to Ansted to be married, which is a priviledged church; and they come 40 and 50 miles off to be married there. ——

Of periodicall small-poxes. - Small-pox in Sherborne dureing the year 1626, and dureing the yeare 1634; from Michaelmas 1642 to Michaelmas 1643; from Michaelmas 1649 to Michaelmas 1650; &c. Small-pox in Taunton all the year 1658; likewise in the yeare 1670, &c. I would I had the like observations made in great townes in Wiltshire; but few care for these things.

It hath been observed that the plague never fix't (encreased) in Bridgenorth in Salop. Also at Richmond it never did spread; but at Petersham, a small village a mile or more distant, the plague made so great a destruction that there survived only five of the inhabitants. 1638 was a sickly and feaverish autumne; there were three graves open at one time in the churchyard of Broad Chalke.

PART II.

CHAPTER I.

WORTHIES.

[IN this chapter Aubrey has transcribed that portion of Fuller's Worthies of England which relates to celebrated natives of the county of Wilts; but as Fuller's work is so well known, it is un- necessary to print Aubrey's extracts from it here. He has interspersed them with additional matter from which the following passages are selected. - J. B.]

PRINCES. - There is a tradition at Wootton Basset that King Richard the Third was born at Vasthorne [Fasterne], now the seate of the earle of Rochester. This I was told when I was there in 1648. Old Mr. Jacob, then tenant there to the Lady Inglefield, was then eighty yeares old, and the like other old people there did affirme.

[According to the best authorities, this tradition is incorrect: Richard was born in Fotheringhay Castle, Northamptonshire, on the 2d of October, 1452.-J. B.]

Anne, eldest daughter of Sir Edward Hyde, Knight, was born at Purton, in this county, and married to His Royal Highnesse James Duke of Yorke, [James II.] by whom she left issue Mary Queen of England, and Anne Princesse of Denmark [afterwards Queen]. ——

SAINTS. - St. Adelm. There was a great bell at Malmesbury Abbey, which they called St. Adelm's bell, which was accounted a telesman, and to have the power, when it was rang, to drive away the thunder and lightning. I remember there is such a great bell at St. Germain's Abbey at Paris, which they ring to the aforesayd purpose when it thunders and lightens. Old Bartlemew and other old people of Malmesbury had by tradition severall stories of miracles donn by St. Adelm some whereof I wrott down heretofore; now with Mr. Anth. Wood at Oxford. [St. Adelm, or more correctly Aldhelm, is mentioned in page 42, ante. His life was written by William of Malmesbury, and published by the Rev. Henry Wharton, in his "Anglia Sacra." (fol. 1691.)- J. B.]

Methinkes it is pitie that Ela, daughter of [William] Longespe Earl of Salisbury, should be here omitted. [See ante, p.70]

PRELATES.- Since the Reformation. - Alexander Hyde, LL.Dr., sonn of Sir Laurence Hyde, and brother to Sir Robert Hyde, Lord Cheif Justice of the King's Bench, was born, I believe, at Hele, in this county. He was made Bishop of Salisbury 1665.

STATESMEN. - William Earle of Pembroke [the second of that name]. In the east windowe of the south aisle of the church at Wilton is this following inscription in gothick black letter:-"... church was... by the vertuose..... wife to the right.... Sir Henry Sidney, Knight of the Garter and Lord President of the Marches of Wales, &c. In April 1580, the eight day of that moneth, was born William Lord Herbert of Cardif, the first-born child to the noble Henry Earle of Pembroke, by his most dear wife Mary the Countesse, daughter to the forenamed Sir Henry and Lady Mary, whose lives Almighty God long prosper in much happiness."* Memorandum, to insert his titles inscribed under his printed picture. As I remember he was Lord High Steward of his Majesties Household, Justice in Eire of all his Majesties Forrests, &c. on this side Trent, Chancellor of the University of Oxford, one of his Majesties Privy Councell, and Knight of the Garter. He was a most noble person, and the glory of the court in the reignes of King James and King Charles. He was handsome, and of an admirable presence-

* [This inscription is not mentioned in the account of Wilton Church in Hoare's Modern, Wiltshire, but the author notices a tablet recording the birth and baptism of the Earl "over the south entrance." He states that the side aisles were added to the church "within the last two centuries " - J. B.]

"Gratior et pulchro veniens a corpore virtus."

He was the greatest Mecænas to learned men of any peer of his time or since. He was very generous and open handed. He gave a noble collection of choice bookes and manuscripts to the Bodleian Library at Oxford, which remain there as an honourable monument of his munificence. 'Twas thought, had he not been suddenly snatch't away by death, to the grief of all learned and good men, that he would have been a great benefactor to Pembroke Colledge in Oxford, whereas there remains only from him a great piece of plate that he gave there. His lordship was learned, and a poet; there are yet remaining some of his lordship's poetry in a little book of poems writt by his Lordship and Sir Benjamin Ruddyer in 12o. ["Poems, written by William Earl of Pembroke, &c. many of which are answered by way of repartee, by Sir Benjamin Rudyard. With other poems by them occasionally and apart." Lond. 1660, 8vo.-J. B.] He had his nativity calculated by a learned astrologer, and died exactly according to the time predicted therein, at his house at Baynard's Castle in London. He was very well in health, but because of the fatal direction which he lay under, he made a great entertainment (a supper) for his friends, went well to bed, and died in his sleep, the [10th] day of [April] anno Domini 1630. His body lies in the vault belonging to his family in the quire of Our Ladies Church in Salisbury. At Wilton is his figure cast in brasse, designed, I suppose, for his monument. [See the notices of the Earls of Pembroke in the ensuing chapter. - J. B.]

Sir Edward Hyde, Earle of Clarendon, Lord Chancellour of England, was born at Dynton in Wiltshire. His father was the fourth and youngest sonn of..... Hyde, of Hatch, Esq. Sir Edward married [Frances] daughter of Sir Thomas Aylesbury, one of the clarks of the councell In his exile in France he wrote the History of the late Times, sc. from 1641 to 1660; near finished, but broken off by death, by whom he was attacked as he was writing; the penn fell out of his hand; he took it up again and tryed to write; and it fell out the second time. He then saw that it was time to leave off, and betooke himself to thinke about the other world. (From the Countess of Thanet.) He shortly after ended his dayes at [Rouen] Anno Domini 1674, and his body was brought over into England, and interred privately at Westminster Abbey. From the Earle of Clarendon. [Anthony Wood states (probably on the authority of Aubrey) that Clarendon was buried on the north side of Henry the Seventh's chapel in Westminster

Abbey; but the place of his interment is not marked by any monument or inscription.-J. B.] ——

SOLDIERS. - Sir Henry Danvers, Knight, Earle of Danby and Baron of Dauntesey, was born at Dauntesey, 28th day of June Ano. Dni. 1573. He was of a magnificent and munificall spirit, and made that noble physic-garden at Oxford, and endowed it with I thinke 30li. per annum. In the epistles of Degory Wheare, History Professor of Oxford, in Latin, are severall addressed to his lordship that doe recite his worth. He allowed three thousand pounds per annum only for his kitchin. He bred up severall brave young gentleman and preferred them; e. g. Colonell Leg, and severall others, of which enquire further of my Lady Viscountesse Purbec. The estate of Henry Earle of Danby was above eleven thousand pounds per annum; near twelve. He died January the 20th, 1643, and lies buried in a little chapell made for his monument on the north side of Dantesey-church, near to the vault where his father and ancesters lye. [Aubrey here transcribes his epitaph, which, with other particulars of his life, will be found in the Beauties of Wiltshire, vol. iii. p. 76.—J. B.]

Sir Michael Ernele, Knight, was second son of Sir John Ernele, of Whetham in the County of Wilts. After he had spent some time at the University of Oxford, he betooke himself to a militarie life in the Low Countries, where he became so good a proficient that at his return into England at the beginning of the Civill warres, King Charles the First gave him the commission of a Colonell in his service, and shortly after he was made Governour of Shrewsbury, and he was, or intended to bee, Major Generall. He did his Majesty good service in the warres, as doth appeare by the Mercurii Aulici. His garrison at Shrewsbury being weakened by drawing out great part of them before the battel at Marston Moore, the townesmen plotted and betrayed his garrison to the Parliament soldiers. He was slain then in the market- place, about the time of the battle of Marston Moore.*

* [It was the common belief that Sir Michael Erneley was killed, as here stated, by the Parlimentary soldiers at the time Shrewsbury was taken (Feb. 3,1644-5); but in Owen and Blakeway's Hist, of Shrewsbury, 4to. 1825, the time and manner of his death is left uncertain. His name is included in the list of those who were made prisoners when the town surrendered.-J. B.]

William Ludlow, Esq. sonn and heir of Sir [Henry] Ludlow, and Dame...... daughter of the Lord Viscount Bindon, in this county, was Governour of Wardour Castle in this county, for the Parliament, which he valiantly defended till part of the castle was blown up, 1644 or 1645. He was Major General, &c. See his life in Mr. Anth. Wood's Antiquities of Oxford. [This passage refers to Edward (not William) Ludlow; the famous Republican general. His "Memoirs" were printed in 1698-9, at Vevay in Switzerland, where he died about five years previous to their publication. They have gone through several editions, and constitute a valuable historical record of the times. - J. B.]

Sir John Ernele, great-grandson of Sir John Ernele above sayd, and eldest sonn of Sir John Ernele, late Chancellour of the Exchequer, had the command of a flag-ship, and was eminent in some sea services. He married the daughter and heir of Sir John Kerle of.... in Herefordshire. ——

A DIGRESSION. - Anno 1633, I entred into my grammar at the latin schoole at Yatton-Keynel, in the church, where the curate, Mr. Hart, taught the eldest boyes Virgil, Ovid, Cicero, &c. The fashion then was to save the forules of their bookes with a false cover of parchment, sc. old manuscript, which I [could not] was too young to understand; but I was pleased with the elegancy of the writing and the coloured initiall letters. I remember the rector here, Mr. Wm. Stump, great gr.-son of St. the cloathier of Malmesbury, had severall manuscripts of the abbey. He was a proper man and a good fellow; and, when he brewed a barrell of speciall ale, his use was to stop the bung- hole, under the clay, with a sheet of manuscript; he sayd nothing did it so well: which me thought did grieve me then to see. Afterwards I went to schoole to Mr. Latimer at Leigh-delamer, the next parish, where was the like use of covering of bookes. In my grandfather's dayes the manuscripts flew about like butterflies. All music bookes, account bookes, copie bookes, &c. were covered with old manuscripts, as wee cover them now with blew paper or marbled paper; and the glovers at Malmesbury made great havoc of them; and gloves were wrapt up no doubt in many good pieces of antiquity. Before the late warres a world of rare manuscripts perished hereabout; for within half a dozen miles of this place were the abbey of Malmesbury, where it may be presumed the library was as well furnished with choice copies as most libraries of England; and perhaps in this library we might have found a correct Pliny's Naturall History, which Cantus, a monk here, did abridge for King Henry the Second. Within the aforesaid compass was Broad stock Priory, Stan Leigh Abbey, Farleigh Abbey, Bath Abbey, eight miles, and Cirencester Abbey, twelve miles. Anno 1638 I was transplanted to Blandford-schoole, in Dorset, to Mr. Wm. Sutton. (In Mr. Wm. Gardner's time it was the most eminent schoole for the education of gentlemen in the West of England.) Here also was the use of covering of bookes with old parchments, sc. leases, &c., but I never saw any thing of a manuscript there. Hereabout were no abbeys or convents for men. One may also perceive by the binding of old bookes how the old manuscripts went to wrack in those dayes. Anno 1647 I went to Parson Stump out of curiosity, to see his manuscripts, whereof I had seen some in my childhood; but by that time they were lost and disperse. His sons were gunners and souldiers, and scoured their gunnies with them; but he shewed me severall old deeds granted by the Lords Abbots, with their scales annexed, which I suppose his sonn Capt. Tho. Stump of Malmesbury hath still. [I have quoted part of this curious paragraph in my Memoir of Aubrey, 4to. 1845.-J. B.] ——

WRITERS.- William of Malmesbury. He was the next historiographer of this nation to Venerable Bede, as he himself written; and was fain, he sayes, to pick out his history out of ballads and old rhythmes..... hundred yeares after Bede. He dedicates his history to [Robert, Earl of Gloucester] "filio naturali Henrici primi". He wrote also the history of the abbey of Glastonbury, which is in manuscript in the library of Trinity College in Cambridge, wherein are many good remarques to be found, as Dr. Thomas Gale of Paules schoole enformes me. [This was edited by Gale, and published at Oxford in 1691, 8vo. - J. B.]

Robertus Sarisburiensis wrote a good discourse, De Piscinis, mentioned and commended by Sir Henry Wotton in his Elements of Architecture. Q. Anth. Wood, de hoc.

Dr..... Forman, - Mr. Ashmole thinkes his name was John, [Simon.- J. B.]- physitian and astrologer, was born at Wilton, in Wilts. He was of the University of Oxford, but took his degree of Doctor in Cambridge, practised in Salisbury, where he was persecuted for his astrologie, which in those ignorant times was accounted conjuring. He then came to London, where he had very good practise, and did great cures; but the college hated him, and at last drove him out of London: so he lived and died at Lambeth, where he lies buried. Elias Ashmole, Esq. has severall bookes of his writing (never printed), as also his own life. There it may be seen whether he was not a favorite of Mary, Countesse of Pembroke. He was a chymist, as far as chymistry went in those dayes, and 'tis very likely he was a favorite of her honour's. Quaere Mr. Dennet, the Earl of Pembrock's steward, if he had not a pension from the Earl of Pembrock? Forman is a common name in Calne parish, Wilts, where there are still severall wealthy men, cloathiers, &c. of that name; but tempore Reginæ Elizabethæ there was a Forman of Calne, Lord Maior of London. My grandfather Lyte told me that at his Lord Maior's shew there was the representation of the creation of the world, and writt underneath, "and all for man." [Some interesting passages from Forman's MS. Diary have recently been brought forward by Mr. Collier in illustration of the history of Shakspere's works. They describe some very early performances of several of his plays, at which Forman was present. - J. B.]

Sr Johan Davys, Knight, was born at Tysbury; his father was a tanner. He wrote a poeme in English, called "Nosce Teipsum"*; also Reports. He was Lord Chief Justice in Ireland. His wife was sister to the Earle of Castle-Haven that was beheaded; she had also aliquid dementiæ, and was a prophetesse, for which she was confined in the Tower, before the late troubles, for her predictions. His onely daughter and heire was married to [Ferdinando] Earle of Huntingdon.

[*"Nosce Teipsum: this oracle expounded in two elegies. 1st. Of Human knowledge. 2nd. Of the soule of man, and the immortality thereof;" with acrostics on Queen Elizabeth. (London, 1609, small 8vo.) The works of the above named Lady Eleanor Davies, the prophetess, widow of Sir John, were of a most extraordinary kind. See a list of them in Watt's Bibliotheca Britannica. - J. B.]

Mr. Thomas Hobbes was born at Westport juxta Malmesbury, April the fifth, anno 1588, he told me, between four and six in the morning, in the house that faces or points to the horse-faire. He died at Hardwick in Darbyshire, Anno Domini 1679, ætatis 91. [See Aubrey's Life of Hobbes, appended to Letters from the Bodleian, vol. iii. p. 593. - J. B.]

Thomas Willis, M.D., was born at Great Bedwin in this county, anno [1621.] His father, he told me, was steward to my Lady Smyth there. He dyed in London, and lies interred with his wife in Westminster Abbey.

Thomas Piers, D.D., and Dean of Salisbury, formerly President of Magdalen College in Oxford, was born at the Devizes. His father was a woollen draper and an alderman there.

Sir Christopher Wren, Knt., Surveyor of his Majesties buildings, the eldest sonne of Dr. Christopher Wren, Deane of Windsor, was born at Knoyle, in this county, where his father was rector, in the parsonage-house, anno 1631; christened November the 10th; but he tells me that he was born October the 20th. His mother fell in labour with him when the bell rung eight.

[Richard] Blackmore, M.D., born in Cosham parish, the sonne of an attorney, went to schoole to Parson.... of Dracot. Scripsit an Epique poeme, called Prince Arthur, 1694.

Sir William Penn, Vice-Admirall, born at Minety, in the hundred of Malmesbury. His father was a keeper in Braden forest: the lodge is called Penn's lodge to this day. He was father to William Penn, Esq. Lord Proprietor of Pensylvania; it is a very ancient family in Buckinghamshire. This family in North Wilts had heretofore a dependence on the Abbey of Malmesbury as stewards or officers. [Sir William Penn was buried in Redcliffe Church, Bristol. See Britten's Account of Redcliffe Church. - J. B.]

T. Byfield, a physician, sonn of Adoniram Byfield, the Assembly man, born at Collingbourn Ducis, where his father was rector. He published a book of Waters about 1684.

Mr. Edward Whatman, of Mayden Bradley, practitioner in physick, and very successfull in his practise. By reason of the civill warrs he was of no university, but he was a young man of great parts and great hopes. He died shortly after his Majesties restauration, aged about 35. He onely printed "Funerall Obsequies on the Honourable the Ladie Elizabeth Hopton, wife to Sir Ralph Hopton," London, 1647.

Mr. William Gardiner, the eminent schoolemaster at Blandford, about twenty yeares; born in this county; died about 1636, aetatis 47. ——

MUSICIANS.-The quire of Salisbury Cathedral hath produced as many able musicians, if not more, than any quire in this nation.

Andrew Markes, of Salisbury, where his father was a fiddle maker, was the best lutinist in England in his time - sc. the latter end of Queen Elizabeth and King James, and the best composer of lute lessons; and as to his compositions, Mr. Sam. Cowper, the famous limner, who was an excellent lutinist, did affirme that they are of great value to this time.

Jo. Coperario, whose reall name I have been told was Cowper, and Alfonso Ferrabosco, lived most in Wiltshire, sc. at Amesbury, and Wulfall, with Edward Earle of Hertford, who was the great patrone of musicians.

Davys Mell, born at Wilton, was the best violinist of any Englishman in England: he also took a fancy to make clocks and watches, and had a great name for the goodness of his work. He was of the King's musick, and died in London about 1663.

.... Bell, of Wilton, was sagbuttere to King Charles the First, and was the most excellent artist in playing on that instrument, which is very difficult, of any one in England. He dyed about the restauration of the King.

Humphrey Madge, of Salisbury, was servant bound to Sir John Danvers, and afterwards one of the violinists to King Charles the Second.

Will. Yokeney, a lutinist and a composer of songs, e. g. of Colonel Lovelace's songs, &c. was born at Lacock, 1646. Among other fine compositions of songs by Will. Yokeney, this following ought to be remembred, made 1646 or 1647, viz.:-

"What if the King should come to the city,
Would he be then received I trow?
Would the Parliament treat him with rigor or pity?
Some doe think yea, but most doe think no, &c.'"

It is a lively, briske aire, and was playd by the lowd musick when King Charles the Second made his entry in London at his restauration.

Captain Thomas Stump, of Malmesbury. Tis pity the strange adventures of him should be forgotten. He was the eldest sonn of Mr. Will. Stump, rector of Yatton Keynell; was a boy of a most daring spirit; he would climbe towers and trees most dangerously; nay, he would walke on the battlements of the tower there. He had too much spirit to be a scholar, and about sixteen went in a voyage with his uncle, since Sir Thomas Ivy, to Guyana, in anno 1633, or 1632. When the ship put in some where there, four or five of them straggled into the countrey too far, and in the interim the wind served, and the sails were hoist, and the stragglers left behind. It was not long before the wild people seized on them and strip's them, and those that had beards they knocked their braines out, and (as I remember) did eat them; but the queen saved T. Stump, and the other boy. Stump threw himself into the river Pronoun to have drowned himself, but could not sinke; he is very full chested. The other youth shortly died. He lived with them till 1636 or 1637. His narrations are very strange and pleasant; but so many yeares since have made me almost forget all. He sayes there is incomparable fruite there, and that it may be termed the paradise of the world. He says that the spondyles of the backbones of the huge serpents there are used to sit on, as our women sitt upon butts. He taught them to build hovels, and to thatch and wattle. I wish I had a good account of his abode there; he is "fide dignus". I never heard of any man that lived so long among those salvages. A ship then sayling by, a Portughese, he swam to it; and they took him up and made use of him for a seaboy. As he was sayling near Cornwall he stole out of a port-hole and swam to shore; and so begged to his father's in Wiltshire. When he came home, nobody knew him, and they would not own him: only Jo. Harris the carpenter knew him. At last he recounted so many circumstances that he was owned, and in 1642 had a commission for a Captain of Foot in King Charles the First's army.

PART II. - CHAPTER II.

OF THE GRANDEUR OF THE HERBERTS, EARLES OF PEMBROKE.

WILTON HOUSE AND GARDENS.

[AUBREY'S account of the famous seat of the Pembroke family at Wilton, and of its choice and valuable contents, will be found exceedingly interesting. His statements are based upon his own knowledge of the mansion before the Civil Wars, and upon information derived from Thomas Earl of Pembroke, Dr. Caldicot, who had been chaplain to the Earl's family, and Mr. Unlades, who also held some appointment in the establishment.

As the ensuing narrative is occasionally somewhat obscure, owing to its want of method and arrangement, it may be useful to prefix a brief summary of the history of the mansion, with reference to dates, names, and other necessary particulars.

William Herbert, the founder of this branch of the family, married Anne, sister to Queen Katharine Parr, the last wife of Henry VIII. He was knighted by that monarch in 1544, and in the same year the buildings and lands of the dissolved Abbey of Wilton, with many other estates in different counties, were conferred upon him by the King. Being left executor, or "conservator" of Henry's will, he possessed considerable influence at the court of the young sovereign, Edward VI.; by whom he was created Earl of Pembroke (1551). He immediately began to alter and adapt the conventual's buildings at Wilton to a mansion suited to his rank and station. Amongst other new works of his time was the famous porch in the court-yard, generally ascribed to Hans Holborn (who died in 1554). To what extent this nobleman carried his building operations is not known. He was succeeded in 1570 by his son Henry, who probably made further additions to the house. This nobleman married Mary, the sister of Sir Philip Sidney, a lady whose name is illustrious in the annals of literature. He died in 1601.

William, his son (the second Earl of that name), who has been fully noticed in the last Chapter, succeeded him in the title, and was followed in 1630 by his brother Philip, who, in 1633, at the instigation of King Charles I., added a range of buildings at Wilton, forming the south front of the house, and facing an extensive garden which was laid out at the same time. In designing both the building and the gardens, he employed Solomon de Caus, a Gascon, on the recommendation of Inigo Jones. About fifteen years afterwards the south front so erected was destroyed by fire, and rebuilt by the same Earl in 1648, from the designs of John Webb, who had married the niece of Inigo Jones. This peer was a great lover of the fine arts, and a patron of Vandyck. He died in 1650.

Philip, his son (the second Earl of that name), experienced some pecuniary difficulties, and the valuable collection of pictures and books formed by his predecessor, was sold by auction, and dispersed for the benefit of his creditors. Aubrey's description, from his own familiar knowledge of them before the sale, is therefore the more curious and valuable.

In 1669 the second Earl Philip was succeeded by his son William (the third of that name), and on the death of the latter in 1674, the title and estates were inherited by his brother, a third Earl Philip. The two last-mentioned noblemen, according to Aubrey, "espoused not learning, but were addicted to field sports and hospitality". Their younger brother, Thomas, became Earl of Pembroke in 1683. He was a warm admirer and liberal patron of literature and the fine arts, and is famous as the founder of the magnificent collection of ancient marbles, coins, &c. which have given great celebrity to Wilton House. Aubrey dedicated the present work to that nobleman, soon after he succeeded to the title, and was honoured with his personal friendship. The Earl survived him many years, and was succeeded by Henry, the second of that name, in 1733. Of the latter nobleman and his works at Wilton, Horace Walpole wrote as follows:- "The towers, the chambers, the scenes which Holbein, Jones, and Vandyke had decorated, and which Earl Thomas had enriched with the spoils of the best ages, received the best touches of beauty from Earl Henry's hand. He removed all that obstructed the views to or from his palace, and threw Palladium's theatric bridge over his river. The present Earl has crowned the summit of the hill with the equestrian statue of Marcus Aurelius, and a handsome arch designed by Sir William Chambers.* No man had a purer taste in building than Earl Henry, of which he gave a few specimens besides his works at Wilton." (Anecdotes of Painting, &c.) The nobleman thus commended for his architectural taste, was succeeded as Earl of Pembroke, in 1751, by his son Henry, who employed Sir William Chambers as mentioned by Walpole; and George, who succeeded to the Earldom in 1794, caused other extensive additions and alterations to be made at Wilton, by the late James Wyatt. - J. B.]

*[I have in my possession a drawing of this arch by the architect. - J. B.]

THE old building of the Earl of Pembroke's house at WILTON was designed by an architect (Hans Holbein) in King Edward the Sixth's time.† The new building which faced the garden was designed by Monsieur Solomon de Caus, tempore Caroli {primi}, but this was burnt by accident and rebuilt 1648, Mr. Webb then being surveyor. [See next page.]

†[There is no authority for the assertion that Holbein designed more than the porch mentioned elsewhere.-J. B.]

The situation of Wilton House is incomparably noble. It hath not only the most pleasant prospect of the gardens and Rowlindon Parke, but from thence over a lovely flatt to the city of Salisbury, where that lofty steeple cuts the horizon, and so to Ivychurch; and to add further to the glory of this prospect the right honourable Thomas, Earle of Pembroke, did, anno 1686, make a stately canal from Quidhampton to the outer base-court of his illustrious palace.

The house is great and august, built all of freestone, lined with brick, which was erected by Henry Earle of Pembroke. [Holbein's porch, and probably other parts of the house, were anterior to the time of the first Earl Henry. See the introductory note to this chapter.- J. B.] Mr. Inigo Jones told Philip, first Earle of Pembroke, that the porch in the square court was as good architecture as any was in England. 'Tis true it does not stand exactly in the middle of the side, for which reason there were some would have perswaded his Lordship to take it down; but Mr. Jones disswaded him, for the reasons aforesayd, and that we had not workmen then to be found that could make the like work. - (From Dr. Caldicot.)

King Charles the first did love Wilton above all places, and came thither every summer. It was he that did put Philip first Earle of Pembroke upon making this magnificent garden and grotto, and to new build that side of the house that fronts the garden, with two stately pavilions at each end, all "al Italiano". His Majesty intended to have had it all designed by his own architect, Mr. Inigo Jones, who being at that time, about 1633, engaged in his Majesties buildings at Greenwich, could not attend to it; but he recommended it to an ingeniouse architect, Monsieur Solomon de Caus, a Gascoigne, who performed it very well; but not without the advice and approbation of Mr. Jones: for which his Lordship settled a pension on him of, I think, a hundred pounds per annum for his life, and lodgings in the house. He died about 1656; his picture is at Mr. Gauntlet's house at Netherhampton. I shall gladly surcease to make any further attempt of the description of the house, garden, stables, and approaches, as falling too short of the greatness and excellency of it. Mr. Loggan's graver will render it much more to the life, and leave a more fixt impression in the reader. [This refers to one of Aubrey's contemplated illustrations. See Chap. XX. (in a subsequent page), Draughts of the Seates and Prospects.-J. B.]

The south side of this stately house, that was built by Monsieur de Caus, was burnt ann. 1647 or 1648, by airing of the roomes. In anno 1648 Philip (the first) re-edifyed it, by the advice of Inigo Jones; but he, being then very old, could not be there in person, but left it to Mr. Webb, who married his niece.

THE PICTURES. In the hall (of old pieces) were the pictures of the Ministers of State in Queen Elizabeth's time, and some of King Henry the Eighth. There was Robert, Earle of Essex, that was beheaded, &c.

At the staircase, the picture of Sir Robert Naunton, author of "Fragmenta Regalia;" his name was writt on the frame. At the upper end was the picture of King Charles I. on horseback, with his French riding master by him on foot, under an arch; all as big as the life: which was a copie of Sir Anthony Vandyke, from that at Whitehall. By it was the picture of Peacock, a white race - horse, with the groom holding him, as big as the life: and to both which Sir Anthony gave many master touches. Over the skreen is a very long picture, by an Italian hand, of Aurora guiding her horses, neigheing, and above them the nymphes powring down out of phialls the morning showres. Here was the "Table" of Cebes, a very large picture, and done by a great master, which the genius describes to William, the first earl of this family, and lookes on him, pointing to Avarice, as to be avoyded by a noble person; and many other ancient pieces which I have now forgott.

The long gallery was furnished with the ministers of estate and heroes of Queen Elizabeth's time, and also some of the French. In one of the pictures of Sir Philip Sydney are these verses, viz.-

"Who gives himselfe may well his picture give, Els were it vain, since both short time doe live."

At the 'upper end is the picture of King James the First sitting in his throne, in his royall robes; a great piece, as big as the life; by him on the right hand wall is the picture of William Herbert, first earle, at length, as big as the life, and under it the picture of his little dog, of a kind of chesnut colour, that starved himselfe for his master's death. Here is the picture of Henry Earle of Pembroke and his Countesse; and of William Earle of Pembroke, Lord Chamberlain; severall Earles of Oxford; and also of Aubrey Earle of Oxford, now living; the pictures of Cardinal Wolsey; Archy (King James's jester);......, governour to Sir Philip Sydney; Mr. Secretary Walsingham, in his gown and wrought cap; Mary Countess of Pembrok, sister of Sir Philip Sydney; the last Lady Abbess of Wilton (Lady Anna Gawen), a pretty, beautiful, modest Penelope; with many others now forgotten by me and everybody else.

[The last mentioned name must be erroneous. The Abbess of Wilton at the time of the dissolution of monasteries was Cecily Bodenham, who had previously been Prioress of St. Mary's, Kington St. Michael. - J. B.]

I was heretofore a good nomenclator of these pictures, which was delivered to me from a child eight yeares old, by old persons relating to this noble family. It is a great and a generall fault that in all galleries of pictures the names are not writt underneath, or at least their coates of armes. Here was also the picture of Thomas Lyte, of Lytes Cary; and a stately picture of King Henry the eighth.

The genius of Philip (first) Earle of Pembroke lay much to painting and building, and he had the best collection of paintings of the best masters of any peer of his time in England; and, besides those pictures before mentioned, collected by his ancestors, he adorned the roomes above staires with a great many pieces of Georgeon [Giorgione], and some of Titian, his scholar. His lordship was the great patron of Sir Anthony Van Dyck, and had the most of his paintings of any one in the world; some whereof, of his family, are fixt now in the great pannells of the wainscot in the great dining roome, or roome of state; which is a magnificent, stately roome; and his Majesty King Charles the Second was wont to say, 'twas the best proportioned roome that ever he saw.* In the cieling piece of this great roome is a great peece, the Marriage of Perseus, drawn by the hand of Mr. Emanuel De Cretz; and all about this roome, the pannells below the windows, is painted by him, the whole story of Sir Philip Sydney's Arcadia,† Quaere, Dr. Caldicot and Mr. Uniades, what was the story or picture in the cieling when the house was burnt. At the upper end of this noble roome is a great piece of Philip (first) Earle of Pembroke and both his Countesses, and all his children, and the Earle of Carnarvon, as big as the life, with landskip beyond them; by the hand of that famous master in painting Sir Anthony Van Dyk, which is held one of his best pictures that ever he drew, and which was apprized at 1,000 li. by the creditors of Philip the third earle of Pembrok. Mr. Uniades told me that he heard Philip (first) Earle say, that he gave to Sir Anthony Van Dyk for it five hundred Jacobuses. 'Tis an heirloome, and the creditors had nothing to doe with it, but Mr. Davys the painter, that was brought from

London to apprize the goods, did apprize it at a thousand pounds. Captain Wind tells me that there is a tagliedome of this great picture: enquire for it. [A critical account of this picture, which is 17 feet in length by 11 feet in height, and contains ten full-length portraits, will be found in the Beauties of Wiltshire, vol. i. p. 180-187. It was engraved by Bernard Baron in 1740. - J. B.]

*[This refers to the "double-cube" room, as it is often called, from its proportions. The Great Hall at Kenilworth was also a double cube; and the same form was adopted in many other old buildings. - J. B.]

†[In "A Description of the Antiquities and Curiosities in Wilton House," 4to. these paintings are ascribed to Signer Tomaso and his brother.-J. B.]

The anti-roome to the great roome of state is the first roome as you come up staires from the garden, and the great pannells of wainscot are painted with the huntings of Tempesta, by that excellent master in landskip Mr. Edmund Piers.‡ He did also paint all the grotesco - painting about the new buildings.

‡[Ascribed to Tempesta junior in the "Description" already mentioned.-J. B.]

In the roome within this great roome is the picture of King Charles the First on his dun horse by Van Dyk; it hangs over the chimney. Also the Dutchess of Richmond by Van Dyk. Now this rare collection of pictures is sold and dispersed, and many of those eminent persons' pictures are but images without names; all sold by auction and disparkled by administratorship: they are, as the civilians term them, "bona caduca". But, as here were a number of pictures sold, with other goods, by the creditors of Philip (the second), so this earle [Thomas] hath supplied it with an admirable collection of paintings by great masters in Italy, when his lordship was there, and since; as he also did for prints, and bookes of fortification, &c.

THE LIBRARIE.- Here was a noble librarie of bookes, choicely collected in the time of Mary Countesse of Pembroke. I remember there were a great many Italian bookes; all their poets; and bookes of politic and historic. Here was Dame Julian Barnes of Hunting, Hawking, and Heraldry, in English verses, printed temp. Edward the Fourth. (Philip, third earle, gave Dame Julian Barnes to Capt. Edw. Saintlo of Dorsetshire.) A translation of the whole book of Psalmes, in English verse, by Sir Philip Sydney, writt curiously, and bound in crimson velvet and gilt; it is now lost. Here was a Latin poëme, a manuscript, writt in Julius Cæsar's time. [See ante, p. 60.] Henry Earle of Pembroke was a great lover of heraldrie, and collected curious manuscripts of it, that I have seen and perused; e. g. the coates of armes and short histories of the English nobility, and bookes of genealogies; all well painted and writt. 'Twas Henry that did sett up all the glasse scutchions about the house: quære if he did not build it? Now all these bookes are sold and dispersed as the pictures.

THE ARMORIE. The armory is a very long roome, which I guesse to have been a dorture heretofore. Before the civill warres, I remember, it was very full. The collection was not onely great, but the manner of obtaining it was much greater; which was by a victory at the battle of St. Quintin's, where William the first Earle of Pembroke was generall, Sir George Penruddock, of Compton Chamberlain, was Major Generall, and William Aubrey, LL.D. my great-grandfather, was Judge Advocat. There were armes, sc. the spoile, for sixteen thousand men, horse and foot. (From the Right Honourable Thomas Earle of Pembroke.)

Desire my brother William Aubrey to gett a copy of the inventory of it. Before the late civill warres here were musketts and pikes for .. . hundred men; lances for tilting; complete armour for horsemen; for pikemen, &c. The rich gilt and engraved armour of Henry VIII. The like rich armour of King Edward VI. In the late warres much of the armes was imbecill'd.

WILTON GARDEN: by Solomon de Caus. [See also in a subsequent page, Chap. IV. OF GARDENS.] "This garden, within the inclosure of the new wall, is a thousand foot long, and about four hundred in breadth; divided in its length into three long squares or parallellograms, the first of which divisions, next the building, hath four platts embroydered; in the midst of which are four fountaines, with statues of marble in their middle; and on the sides of those platts are the platts of flowers; and beyond them is a little terrass raised, for the more advantage of beholding those platts. In the second division are two groves or woods, cutt with divers walkes, and through those groves passeth the river Nader, having of breadth in this place 44 foote, upon which is built the bridge, of the breadth of the great walke: and in the middest of the aforesayd groves are two great statues of white marble of eight foot high, the one of Bacchus, and the other of Flora; and on the sides ranging with the platts of flowers are two covered arbours of three hundred foot long, and divers allies. At the beginning of the third and last division are, on either side of the great walke, two ponds with fountains, and two columnes in the middle, casting water all their height; which causeth the moving and turning of two crowns at the top of the same; and beyond is a compartment of green, with divers walkes planted with cherrie trees; and in the middle is the great ovall, with the Gladiator of brasse, the most famous statue of all that antiquity hath left. On the sides of this compartment, and answering the platts of flowers and long arbours, are three arbours of either side, with turning galleries, communicating themselves one into another. At the end of the great walke is a portico of stone, cutt and adorned with pyllasters and nyckes, within which are figures of white marble, of five foot high. On either side of the said portico is an ascent leading up to the terrasse, upon the steps whereof, instead of ballasters, are sea-monsters, casting water from one to the other, from the top to the bottome; and above the sayd portico is a great reserve of water for the grotto."

[The gardens of Wilton were illustrated by a series of twenty-six folio copper plates, with the following title; "Le Jardin De Wilton, construct par le trés noble et trés p. seigneur Philip Comte Pembroke et Montgomeri. Isaac de Caux invt." The above description is copied from one of these plates. Solomon de Caus was architect and engineer to the Elector Palatine, and constructed the gardens at Heidelberg in 1619. Walpole infers that Isaac and Solomon de Caus were brothers, and that they erected, in conjunction with each other, "the porticos and loggias of Gorhambury, and part of Campden house, near Kensington." (Anecdotes of Painting.) As the engravings of Wilton gardens bear the name of

Isaac, he had probably some share in the arrangement of the grounds, and perhaps also in building the house. In Campbell's Vitruvius Britannicus, vols. ii. and iii. are several views, plans, and sections of Wilton House and grounds. - J. B.]

The grotto is paved with black and white marble; the roofe is vaulted. The figures of the tritons, &c. are in bas-relieve, of white marble, excellently well wrought. Here is a fine jeddeau and nightingale pipes. Monsieur de Caus had here a contrivance, by the turning of a cock, to shew three rainbowes, the secret whereof he did keep to himself; he would not let the gardener, who shewes it to strangers, know how to doe it; and so, upon his death, it is lost. The grott and pipes did cost ten thousand pounds. The garden is twelve acres within the terrace of the grott.

The kitchin garden is a very good one, and here are good ponds and a decoy. By the kitchin garden is a streame which turnes a wheele that moves the engine to raise the water to the top of a cisterne at the corner of the great garden, to serve the water-workes of the grotto and fountaines in the garden.

Thomas, Earle of Pembroke, told me that his sister-in-law's priest, a Frenchman, made a pretty poem or poemation on Wilton House and Garden, in Latin verse, which Mr. Berford, his Lordship's Chaplain, can procure.

THE STABLES, of Roman architecture, built by Mons. de Caus, have a noble avenu to them, a square court in the middle; and on the four sides of this court were the pictures of the best horses as big as the life, painted in severall postures, by a Frenchman. Among others was the great black crop-eared stone horse on which Gustavus Adolphus, King of Sweden, was killed at the battle of Lutzen, two miles from Leipzig. Upon the comeing of the Scotts, in 1639, Sir. .. Fenwyck and. .. fearing their breeds of horses would be taken away by the Scotts, did sell their breeds of horses and mares to Philip (first) Earle of Pembroke. His Lordship had also Morocco horses, and for race horses, besides Peacock and Delavill, he had a great many more kept at the parke at Ramesbury and at Rowlinton. Then for his stagge-hunting, fox-hunting, brooke-hawking, and land-hawking, what number of horses were kept to bee fitt at all seasons for it, I leave the reader to guesse, besides his horses for at least halfe a dozen coaches. Mr. Chr. Wroughton guesses not lesse than an hundred horses. [In the notice of William, first Earl of Pembroke, in Aubrey's "Lives of Eminent Men," he says, "This present Earl (1680) has at Wilton 52 mastives and 30 greyhounds, some beares, and a lyon, and a matter of 60 fellowes more bestiall than they." - J. B.]

OF HIS LORDSHIP'S HOUNDS, GREYHOUNDS, AND HAWKES. His Lordship had all sorts of hounds, for severall disports: sc. harbourers (great hounds) to harbour the stagges, and also small bull-dogges to break the bayes of the stagge; fox-hounds, finders, harriers, and others. His Lordship had the choicest tumblers that were in England, and the same tumblers that rode behind him he made use of to retrieve the partridges. The setting-doggs for supper-flights for his hawkes. Grayhounds for his hare warren, as good as any were in England. When they returned from hawking the ladies would come out to see the hawkes at the highest flying, and then they made use of their setting dogges to be sure of a flight. His Lordship had two hawkes, one a falcon called Shrewsbury, which he had of the Earle of Shrewsbury, and another called the little tercel, which would fly quite out of sight, that they knew not how to shew the fowler till they found the head stood right. They had not little telescopes in those dayes; those would have been of great use for the discovery which way the hawke's head stood.

TILTING. Tilting was much used at Wilton in the times of Henry Earle of Pembroke and Sir Philip Sydney. At the solemnization of the great wedding of William, the second Earle of Pembroke, to one of the co-heires of the Earle of Shrewsbury, here was an extraordinary shew; at which time a great many of the nobility and gentry exercised, and they had shields of pastboard painted with their devices and emblemes, which were very pretty and ingenious. There are some of them hanging in some houses at Wilton to this day but I did remember many more. Most, or all of them, had relation to marriage. One, I remember, is a man standing by a river's side angling, and takes up a rammes-horne: the motto "Casus ubiq{ue} valet". - (Ovid de Arte Amandi.') Another hath the picture of a ship at sea sinking in a storm, and a house on fire; the motto "Tertia pestis abest"; meaning a wife. Another, a shield covered with black velvet; the motto "Par nulla figura dolori". This last is in the Arcadia, and I believe they were most of them contrived by Sir Philip Sydney. Another was a hawke lett off the hand, with her leashes hanging at her legges, which might hang her where'ere she pitcht, and is an embleme of youth that is apt to be ensnared by their own too plentifull estates. ——

'Tis certain that the Earles of Pembroke were the most popular peers in the West of England; but one might boldly say, in the whole kingdome. The revenue of his family was, till about 1652, 16,000li. per annum; but, with his offices and all, he had thirty thousand pounds per annum, and, as the revenue was great, so the greatnesse of his retinue and hospitality was answerable. One hundred and twenty family uprising and down lyeing, whereof you may take out six or seven, and all the rest servants and retayners. ——

FOR HIS LORDSHIP'S MUSICK. Alphonso Ferrabosco, the son, was Lord Philip (the first's) lutenist. He sang rarely well to the theorbo lute. He had a pension and lodgings in Baynard's Castle.

PART II. - CHAPTER III.

OF LEARNED MEN THAT HAD PENSIONS GRANTED TO THEM BY THE EARLES OF PEMBROKE.

IN the former Chapter I endeavoured to adumbrate Wilton House as to its architecture. We are now to consider it within, where it will appeare to have been an academie as well as palace; and was, as it were, the apiarie to which men that were excellent in armes and arts did resort and were caress't, and many of them received honourable pensions.

The hospitality here was very great. I shall wave the grandeur of William the first Earle, who married [Anne] sister to Queen Katharine Parre, and was the great favourite of King Henry 8th, and conservator of his will, and come to our grandfather's memorie, in the times of his sonne Henry Earle of Pembroke, and his Countess Mary, daughter of Sir Henry Sydney, and sister to that renowned knight Sir Philip Sydney, whose fame will never die whilest poetrie lives. His Lordship was the patron to the men of armes, and to the antiquaries and heralds; he took a great delight in the study of herauldry, as appeares by that curious collection of heraldique manuscripts in the library here. It was this earle that did set up all the painted glasse scutchions about the house. Many a brave souldier, no doubt, was here obliged by his Lordship; but time has obliterated their names.

Mr. Robert Barret dedicated the "Theorick and Practick of Moderne Warres", in folio, London, 1598, to this noble Earle, and William Lord Herbert of Cardiff, his son, then a youth. It seemes to have been a very good discourse as any writt in that time, wherein he shews much learning, besides experience. He had spent most of his time in foreigne warres, as the French, Dutch, Italian, and Spanish; and here delivers his military observations.

John Jones, an eminent physician in his tyme, wrote a treatise of the bathes at Bath, printed in a black letter, Anno Domini 1572, which he dedicated to Henry, Earle of Pembroke. [These dedications were doubtless acknowledged by pecuniary gifts from the patron to the authors. - J. B.] ——

I shall now passe to the illustrious Lady Mary, Countesse of Pembroke, whom her brother hath eternized by his Arcadia; but many or most of the verses in the Arcadia were made by her Honour, and they seem to have been writt by a woman. 'Twas a great pity that Sir Philip had not lived to have put his last hand to it. He spent much, if not most part of his time here, and at Ivychurch, near Salisbury, which did then belong to this family, when he was in England; and I cannot imagine that Mr. Edmund Spenser could be a stranger here. [See, in a subsequent page, Chap. VIII. "The Downes". - J. B.]

Her Honour's genius lay as much towards chymistrie as poetrie. The learned Dr. Mouffet, that wrote of Insects and of Meates, had a pension hence. In a catalogue of English playes set forth by Gerard Langbain, is thus, viz.: "Lady Pembrock, Antonius, 4to." [This was an English translation of "The Tragedie of Antonie. Doone into English by the Countesse of Pembroke. Imprinted at London, for William Ponsonby, 1595." 12mo. The Countess of Pembroke also translated "A Discourse of Life and Death, written in French, by Phil. Mornay", 1600, 12mo.- J. B.]

"Underneath this sable herse
Lies the subject of all verse,
Sydney's sister, Pembroke's mother,
Death! ere thou kill'st such another,
Fair, and wise, and learned as SHE,
Time will throw a dart at thee."

These verses were made by Mr. (William*) Browne, who wrote the "Pastoralls", and they are inserted there.

*(William, Governor afterwards to ye now E. of Oxford. - J. EVELYN.)

[In the Memoir of Aubrey, published by the Wiltshire Topographical Society in 1845, I drew attention to this passage, which shews that although the above famous epitaph on the Countess of Pembroke is almost always attributed to Ben Jonson, it was, in fact, written by William Browne. That such is really the case does not rest only on the authority of Aubrey and Evelyn; for we find this very epitaph in a volume of Poems written by Browne, and preserved amongst the Lansdowne MSS in the British Museum (No. 777), together with the following additional lines:

"Marble pyles let no man raise
To her name for after-dayes;
Some kind woman, borne as she,
Reading this, like Niobe,
Shall turne marble, and become
Both her mourner and her tombe."

To the epitaph is subjoined an "Elegie" on the Countess, of considerable length. When or by whom the epitaph was first ascribed to Jonson it is not easy to ascertain; but certainly no literary error has been more frequently repeated. Aubrey is wrong in stating that the lines were printed in Browne's Pastorals.- J. B.] ——

Mr. Adrian Gilbert, uterine brother to Sir Walter Raleigh, was a great chymist, and a man of excellent parts, but very sarcastick, and the greatest buffoon in the nation. He was housekeeper at Wilton, and made that delicate orchard where the stately garden now is. .... He had a pension, and died about the beginning of the reign of King Charles the First. Elias Ashmole, Esq. finds, by Dr. John Dee's papers, that there was a great friendship and correspondency between him and Adrian Gilbert, and he often mentions him in his manuscripts. Now there can be no doubt made but that his half-brother Sir Walter Raleigh, which was "tam Marti quam Mercurio", had a great acquaintance with the Earle Henry and his ingenious Countesse.

There lived in Wilton, in those dayes, one Mr. Boston, a Salisbury man (his father was a brewer there), who was a great chymist, and did great cures by his art. The Lady Mary, Countesse of Pembroke, did much esteeme him for his skill, and would have had him to have been her operator, and live with her, but he would not accept of her Ladyship's kind offer. But after long search after the philosopher's stone, he died at Wilton, having spent his estate. After his death they found in his laboratory two or three baskets of egge shelles, which I remember Geber saieth is a principall ingredient of that stone.

J. Donne, Deane of St. Paule's, was well known both to Sir Philip Sydney and his sister Mary, as appeares by those excellent verses in his poems, "Upon the Translation of the Psalmes by Sir Philip Sydney and the Countesse of Pembroke his sister." ——

Earl William [the second of that name] was a good scholar, and delighted in poetrie; and did sometimes, for his diversion, write some sonnets and epigrammes, which deserve commendation. Some of them are in print in a little book in 8vo. intituled "Poems writt by William Earle of Pembroke, and Sir Benjamin Ruddyer, Knight, 1660." [See ante, page 77. A new edition of these poems was published by Sir Egerton Brydges in 1817.] He was of an heroique and publick spirit, bountifull to his friends and servants, and a great encourager of learned men.

Philip Earle of Pembroke [the first of that name], his brother, did not delight in books or poetry; but exceedingly loved painting and building, in which he had singular judgment, and had the best collection of any peer in England. He had a wonderful sagacity in the understanding of men, and could discover whether an ambassadour's message was reall or feigned; and his Majesty King James made great use of this talent of his. Mr. Touars, an ingenious gentleman, who understood painting well, and did travell beyond sea to buy rare pieces for his lordship, had a pension of lOOli. per annum. Mr. Richard Gibson, the dwarfe, whose marriage Mr. Edm. Waller hath celebrated in his poëms, sc. the Marriage of the Dwarfs, a great master in miniture, hath a pension of an hundred pounds per annum. Mr. Philip Massinger, author of severall good playes, was a servant to his lordship, and had a pension of twenty or thirty pounds per annum, which was payed to his wife after his decease. She lived at Cardiffe, in Glamorganshire. There were others also had pensions, that I have forgot.

[Arthur Massinger, the father of the poet, was attached to the establishment of the Earl of Pembroke; and Gifford, in his Life of Massinger, seems inclined to think that Philip was born at Wilton. He was baptized in St. Thomas's Church, Salisbury, 24 Nov. 1583. His biographers have all been ignorant of the fact above recorded by Aubrey. A brief memoir of the life of Massinger will be found in Hatcher's History of Salisbury, p. 619.- J. B.]

William (third) and Philip (third) earles were gallant, noble persons, and handsome; they espoused not learning, but were addicted to field sports and hospitality. But Thomas Earle of Pembroke has the vertues and good parts of his ancestors concentred in him; which his lordship hath not been wanting to cultivate and improve by study and travell; which make his titles shine more bright. He is an honour to the peerage, and a glory and a blessing to his country: but his reall worth best speakes him, and it praises him in the gates.

PART II. - CHAPTER IV.

OF GARDENS: - LAVINGTON GARDEN, CHELSEY GARDEN.

[THE stately gardens of the seventeenth century were less remarkable for the cultivation of useful or ornamental plants than for the formal arrangement of their walks, arbours, parterres, and hedges. Amongst the various decorations introduced were jets d'eau, or fountains, artificial cascades, columns, statues, grottoes, rock-work, mazes or labyrinths, terraces communicating with each other by flights of steps, and similar puerilities. This style of gardening was introduced from France; where the celebrated Le Notre had displayed his skill in laying out the gardens of the palace of Versailles; the most important specimens of their class. The same person was afterwards employed by several of the English nobility.

The gardens at Wilton, described in the last chapter, were completely in the style referred to. Solomon de Caus, to whom they are attributed by Aubrey, is supposed by Mr. Loudon, in his valuable "Encyclopaedia of Gardening", to have been the inventor of greenhouses. The last mentioned work contains the best account yet published of the gardens of the olden time. Britton's "History of Cassiobury" (folio, 1837), p. 17, also contains some curious particulars of the original plantations and pleasure grounds of that interesting mansion.

The gardens at Lavington, which are described in the present chapter, were evidently of the same character with those of Wilton. Chelsey- garden is very minutely described by Aubrey, but our limits forbid its insertion, especially as it is irrelevant to a History of Wiltshire.- J. B.]

O janitores, villiciq{ue} felices:
Dominis parantur isti, serviunt vobis.
MARTIAL, Epigramm. 29, lib. x.

To write in the praise of gardens is besides my designe. The pleasure and use of them were unknown to our great-grandfathers. They were contented with pot-herbs, and did mind chiefly their stables. The chronicle tells us, that in the reign of King Henry the 8th pear- mains were so great a rarity that a baskett full of them was a present to the great Cardinall Wolsey.

Henry Lyte, of Lyte's Cary, in Somerset, Esq. translated Dodoens' Herball into English, which he dedicated to Q. Elizabeth, about the beginning of her reigne [1578]. He had a pretty good collection of plants for that age; some few whereof are yet alive, 1660: and no question but Dr. Gilbert, &c. did furnish their gardens as well as they could so long ago, which could be but meanly. But the first peer that stored his garden with exotick plants was William Earle of Salisbury, [1612-1668] at his garden at [Hatfield? - J. B.] a catalogue whereof, fairly writt in a skin of vellum, consisting of 830 plants, is in the hands of Elias Ashmole, Esq. at South Lambeth.

But 'twas Sir John Danvers, of Chelsey, who first taught us the way of Italian gardens. He had well travelled France and Italy, and made good observations.

He had in a fair body an harmonicall mind. In his youth his complexion was so exceeding beautiful and fine that Thomas Bond, Esq. of Ogbourne St. .... in Wiltshire, who was his companion in his travells, did say that the people would come after him in the street to admire him. He had a very fine fancy, which lay chiefly for gardens and architecture.

The garden at Lavington in this county, and that at Chelsey in Middlesex, as likewise the house there, doe remaine monuments of his ingenuity. The garden at Lavington is full of irregularities, both naturall and artificiall, sc. elevations and depressions. Through the length of it there runneth a fine cleare trowt stream; walled with brick on each side, to hinder the earth from mouldring down. In this stream are placed severall statues. At the west end is an admirable place for a grotto, where the great arch is, over which now is the market roade. Among severall others, there is a very pleasant elevation on the south side of the garden, which steales, arising almost insensibly, that is, before one is aware, and gives you a view over the spatious corn-fields there, and so to East Lavington: where, being landed on a fine levell, letteth you descend again with the like easinesse; each side is flanqued with laurells. It is almost impossible to describe this garden, it is so full of variety and unevenesse; nay, it would be a difficult matter for a good artist to make a draught of it. About An°. 1686, the right honourable James Earle of Abingdon [who had become possessed of the estate in right of his wife], built a noble portico, full of water workes, which is on the north side of the garden, and faceth the south. It is both portico and grott, and was designed by Mr. Rose, of ...... in Oxfordshire. ——

Wilton Garden was the third garden after these two of the Italian mode; but in the time of King Charles the Second gardening was much improved and became common. I doe believe I may modestly affirme that there is now, 1691, ten times as much gardening about London as there was Anno 1660 ; and wee have been, since that time, much improved in forreign plants, especially since about 1683, there have been exotick plants brought into England no lesse than seven thousand. (From Mr. Watts, gardener of the Apothecary's garden at Chelsey, and other botanists.)

As for Longleate Garden it was lately made. I have not seen it, but they say 'tis noble.

——

Till the breaking out of the civill warres, Tom ô Bedlam's did travell about the countrey. They had been poore distracted men that had been putt into Bedlam, where recovering to some sobernesse they were licentiated to goe a begging: e. g. they had on their left arm an armilla of tinn, printed in some workes, about four inches long; they could not gett it off. They wore about their necks a great horn of an oxe in a string or bawdrie, which, when they came to an house for almes, they did wind: and they did putt the drink given them into this horn, whereto they did putt a stopple. Since the warres I doe not remember to have seen any one of them. (I have seen them in Worcestershire within these thirty years, 1756. MS. NOTE, ANONYMOUS.)

[This account of the " bedlam beggars" so well known to our forefathers, is repeated by Aubrey in his "Remains of Gentilism," (Lansdowne MSS. No. 231,) portions of which have been printed in Mr. Thoms's Anecdotes and Traditions (1839). The passage corresponding with the above is quoted by Mr. Charles Knight from the manuscript referred to, in illustration of the character of "Mad Tom," assumed by Edgar, in Shakspere's play of King Lear.- J. B.]

PART II. - CHAPTER V.

ARTS: LIBERALL AND MECHANICK.

CRICKLAD, a market and borough town in this county, was an University before the Conquest, where were taught the liberall arts and sciences, as may appeare by the learned notes of Mr. Jo. Selden on Drayton's Poly-Olbion, and by a more convincing and undenyable argument out of Wheelock's translation of Bede's History.

This University was translated from hence to Oxford. But whereas writers swallow down the old storie that this place takes its name from certain Greek philosophers, who, they say, began here an university, it is a fond opinion.

[Aubrey here quotes Fuller as to the etymology of the names of Cricklade and Lechlade. That author, on the authority of Leland, had asserted in his Church History that the one was originally called Greek - lade, and the other Latin - lade, from "two schooles, famous both for eloquence and learning", which existed there anterior to the Conquest. But, on the report of his "worthy friend Dr. Peter Heylin," he afterwards stated in his Worthies that "Cricklade was the place for the professors of Greek; Lechlade for physick (Leech being an old English word for a physitian), and Latton, a small village hard by, the place where Latin was professed." It will be seen by the next sentence that Aubrey disputes even the amended theory of Fuller, and, with more probability, derives the names of the towns in question from words indicating the natural features of the localities.-J. B.]

But, as the saying is, "Bernardus non vidit omnia". Had the learned Dr. Heylin (that is Hoelin, little Howell) had a little knowledge of his ancestors' Welsh, he would not have made such a stumble, and so forced these etymologies; but would easily have found that Cricklad comes from kerig, stones; and glad, a country; which two words give a true description of the nature of the country on that side of Cricklad, which is, as wee term it, a stone-brash. Likewise Lechlade, from llech, plank-stones, or tile-stones. As for Latton, it may very well come from laith, which signifies a marsh, and is as much as to say Marshton, as there is a parish thereby called Marston. Hereabout are some few other places which retain their British names with a little disguise. ——

Without the close of Salisbury, as one comes to the town from Harnham-bridge, opposite to the hospitall, is a hop-yard, with a fair high stone wall about it, and the ruines of an old pidgeon house. I doe remember, 1642, and since, more ruines there. This was Collegium de Valle Scholarum (College de Vaux). It took its name from Vaux, a family. Here was likewise a magister scholarum, and it was in the nature of an university. It was never an endowed college. (From Seth Ward, Bishop of Sarum.)

[Some historical particulars connected with this scholastic establishment or college will be found in Hatcher's History of Salisbury, pp. 50, 92, 232, &c. The author gives a different etymology of its name to the above. Quoting Mosheim, cent. 13, p. ii. he states that the Professors of Divinity in the University of Paris, in the year 1234, assembled their pupils and fixed their residence in a valley of

Champagne, whence they acquired the name of Valli-scholares, or Scholars of the Valley. Mr. Hatcher adds, that the College at Salisbury, which was founded about 1260, derived its name, and probably its system of instruction, from this community in France. - J. B.] ——

The consistorie of this church (Salisbury) was as eminent for learning as any in England, and the choire had the best method; hence came the saying "secundum usum Sarum". Over every stall there was writt "hoc age". These old stalles were taken down about 1671, and now they sitt in the quire undistinguisht, without stalles.

But it was at the Abbey of Malmesbury where learning did most flourish in our parts, and where most writers were bred, as appeares by Pitseus, Baleus, &c.

——

MECHANICALL ARTS.- Cloathing. [See also subsequent chapters on this subject] At Salisbury the best whites of England are made. The city was ever also famous for the manufactures of parchment, razors, cizers, knives, and gloves. Salisbury mault is accounted the best mault, and they drive there a very considerable trade in maulting. Also it is not to be forgotten that the bottle ale of Salisbury (as likewise Wilton, upon the same reason, sc. the nitrous water) is the best bottle ale of this nation.

Malmesbury hath been an ancient cloathing town; where also is a considerable manufacture of gloves and strong waters. Also Troubridge, Calne, and Chippenham are great cloathing townes. ——

The Devises is famous for making excellent Metheglyn. Mr. Tho. Piers of the Swan did drive a great trade in it. [See ante, p. 68.]

Amesbury is famous for the best tobacco pipes in England; made by .... Gauntlet, who markes the heele of them with a gauntlet, whence they are called gauntlet pipes. The clay of which they are made is brought from Chiltern in this county. [See ante, p. 35.]

In King James the First's time coarse paper, commonly called whitebrowne paper, was first made in England, especially in Surrey and about Windsor.

At Bemarton near Salisbury is a paper mill, which is now, 1684, about 130 yeares standing, and the first that was erected in this county; and the workmen there told me, 1669, that it was the second paper mill in England. I remember the paper mill at Longdeane, in the parish of Yatton Keynell, was built by Mr. Wyld, a Bristow merchant, 1635. It serves Bristow with brown paper. There is no white paper made in Wiltshire.

At Crokerton, near Warminster, hath been since the restauration (about 1665) a manufacture of felt making, as good, I thinke, as those of Colbec in France. Crokerton hath its denomination from the crokery trade there; sc. making of earthen - ware, &c. Crock is the old English word for a pott. ——

It ought never to be forgott what our ingenious countreyman Sir Christopher Wren proposed to the silke stocking weavers of London, Anno Domini 16-, viz. a way to weave seven paire or nine paire of stockings at once (it must be an odd number). He demanded four hundred pounds for his invention; but the weavers refused it because they were poor; and besides, they sayd it would spoile their trade. Perhaps they did not consider the proverb, that "light gaines, with quick returnes, make heavy purses." Sir Christopher was so noble, seeing they would not adventure so much money, he breakes the modell of the engine all to pieces before their faces.

[This chapter contains many other remarks on trades, inventions, machinery, &c. similar in character to the above.- J. B.]

PART II - CHAPTER VI.

ARCHITECTURE.

[IN this chapter, the account of Aubrey's visit to Old Sarum, and the traditions connected with the erection of Salisbury Cathedral, although they furnish no new facts of importance, will be read with interest; especially on account of the reference they bear to the enlightened and munificent Bishop Ward. A memoir of that prelate was published by Dr. Walter Pope, in 1697 (8vo); and some further particulars of him, as connected with Salisbury, will be found in Hatcher's valuable History of that City. - J. B.]

THE celebrated antiquity of Stonehenge, as also that stupendious but unheeded antiquity at Aubury, &c. I affirme to have been temples, and built by the Britons. See my Templa Druidum. [The essay referred to was a part of Aubrey's Monumenta Britannica, the manuscript of which has strangely disappeared within the last twenty yeares. I have given an account of its contents in the Memoir of Aubrey, already frequently referred to,(page 87). Aubrey was the first who asserted that Avebury and Stonehenge were temples of the Britons. He was also the first person who wrote any thing about the forms, styles, and varieties of windows, arches, &c. in Church Architecture, and his remarks and opinions on both subjects were judicious, curious, and original. - J. B.] ——

Here being so much good stone in this countrey, no doubt but that the Romans had here, as well as in other parts, good buildings. But time hath left us no vestigia of their architecture unlesse that little that remains of the castle of Old Sarum, where the mortar is as hard as a stone. This must have been a most august structure, for it is situated upon a hill. When the high walles were standing, flanked at due distances with towers, about seven in all, and the vast keep (arx) in the middle crowned with another high fortification, it must needs afford a most noble view over the plaines.

(The following account I had from the right reverend, learned, and industrious Seth Ward, Lord Bishop of Sarum, who had taken the paines to peruse all the old records of the church, that had been clung together and untoucht for perhaps two hundred yeares.) Within this castle of Old Sarum, on the east side, stood the Cathedrall church; the tuft and scite is yet discernable: which being seated so high was so obnoxious to the weather, that when the wind did blow they could not heare the priest say masse. But this was not the only inconvenience. The soldiers of the castle and the priests could never agree; and one day, when they were gone without the castle in procession, the soldiers kept them out all night, or longer. Whereupon the Bishop, being much troubled, cheered them up as well as he could, and told them he would study to accommodate them better. In order thereunto he rode severall times to the Lady Abbesse at Wilton to have bought or exchanged a piece of ground of her ladyship to build a church and houses for the priests. A poor woman at Quidhampton, that was spinning in the street, sayd to one of her neighbours, "I marvell what the matter is that the bishop makes so many visits to my lady; I trow he intends to marry her." Well, the bishop and her ladyship did not conclude about the land, and the bishop dreamt that the Virgin Mary came to him, and brought him to or told him of Merrifield; she would have him build his church there and dedicate it to her. Merrifield was a great field or meadow where the city of New Sarum stands, and did belong to the Bishop, as now the whole city belongs to him.

This was about the latter end of King John's reigne, and the first grant or diploma that ever King Henry the Third signed was that for the building of our Ladies church at Salisbury. The Bishop sent for architects from Italy, and they did not onely build that famous structure, and the close, but layd out the streetes of the whole city: which run parallell one to another, and the market-place-square in the middle: whereas in other cities they were built by chance, and at severall times.

I know but one citie besides in England that was designed and layd out at once as this was; and that is Chichester: where, standing at the market-crosse, you may see the four gates of the city. They say there that it was built about the same time that New Salisbury was, and had some of those architects.* The town of Richelieu was built then by the great Cardinall, when he built his august chasteau there.

*[Salisbury has little parallelism to its neighbour Chichester, which is of Roman origin: the former being truly English, and perfectly unique in its history and arrangement. Aubrey has omitted to notice the rapid streams of water flowing through each of the principal streets, which form a remarkable feature of the city. - J. B.]

Upon the building of this cathedrall and close the castle of Old Sarum went to wrack, and one may see in the walles of the close abundance of stones, finely carved, that were perhaps part of the church there. After the church and close were built, the citizens had their freestone, &c. from thence. And in Edward the Sixth's time, the great house of the Earle of Pembroke, at Wilton, was built with the mines of it. About 1660 I was upon it. There was then remaining on the south side some of the walles of the great gate; and on the north side there was some remaines of a bottome of a tower; but the incrustation of freestone was almost all gone: a fellow was then picking at that little that was left. 'Tis like enough by this time they have digged all away.

Salisbury. - Edw. Leigh, Esq. "There is a stately and beautifull minster, with an exceeding high spered steeple, and double crosse aisle on both sides. The windowes of the church, as they reckon them, answer just in number to the dayes; the pillars, great and small, to the houres, of a full yeare; and the gates to the moneths." - ["England Described; or, Observations on the several Counties and Shires thereof, by Edw. Leigh." 1659. 8vo.]

"Mira canam, soles quot continet annus, in unâ
Tam numerosa ferunt sede fenestra micat.
Marmoreaq{ue} capit fusas tot ab arte columnas
Comprensus horas quot vagus annus habet.
Totq{ue}patent portæ, quot mensibus annus abundat,

Res mira, et vera, res celebrata fide." - DANIEL ROGERS.

'Tis strange to see how errour hath crept in upon the people, who believe that the pillars of this church were cast, forsooth, as chandlers make candles; and the like is reported of the pillars of the Temple Church, London, &c.: and not onely the vulgar swallow down the tradition gleb, but severall learned and otherwise understanding persons will not be perswaded to the contrary, and that the art is lost.[Among the rest Fuller, in his Worthies of England, gave currency to this absurd opinion.- J. B.] Nay, all the bishops and churchmen of that church in my remembrance did believe it, till Bishop Ward came, who would not be so imposed on; and the like errour runnes from generation to generation concerning Stoneheng, that the stones there are artificiall. But, to returne to the pillars of this church, they are all reall marble, and shew the graine of the Sussex marble (sc. the little cockles), from whence they were brought. [These pillars are not made of Sussex marble; but of that kind which is brought from a part of Dorsetshire called the Isle of Purbeck.- J. B.] At every nine foot they are jointed with an ornament or band of iron or copper. This quarrie hath been closed up and forgott time out of mind, and the last yeare, 1680, it was accidentally discovered by felling of an old oake; and it now serves London. (From Mr. Bushnell, the stone-cutter.)

The old tradition is, that this church was "built upon wooll-packs", and doubtlesse there is something in it which is now forgott. I shall endeavour to retrieve and unriddle it by comparison. There is a tower at Rouen in Normandie called the Butter Tower; for when it was built a toll was layd upon all the butter that was brought to Rouen, for and towards the building of this tower; as now there is a [duty] layd upon every chaldron of coales towards the building of St Paul's Church, London: so hereafter they may say that that church was built upon New- Castle coales. In like manner it might be that heretofore, when Salisbury Cathedral was building, which was long before wooll was manufactured in England (the merchants of the staple sent it then in woolpacks beyond sea, to Flanders, &c.), that an imposition might be putt on the Wiltshire wool-packs towards the carrying on of this magnificent structure. There is a saying also that London Bridge was built upon wooll-packs, upon the same account.

The height of Our Lady steeple at Salisbury was never found so little as 400 foot, and never more than 406 foot, by the observations of Thom. Nash, surveyor of the workes of this church: but Colonell John Wyndham did take the height more accurately, An° 1684, by a barometer: sc. the height of the weather-dore of Our Lady Church steeple at Salisbury from the ground is 4280 inches. The mercury subsided in that height 42/100 of an inch. He affirms that the height of the said steeple is 404 foot, which he hath tryed severall times; and by the help of his barometer, which is accurately made according to his direction, he will with great facility take the height of any mountain: quod N.B. [Col. Wyndham's measurement has been adopted as correct by most authors who have written on the subject since.- J. B.]

Memorandum. About 1669 or 1670 Bishop Ward invited Sir Christopher Wren to Salisbury, out of curiosity, to survey the church there, as to the steeple, architecture, &c. He was above a weeke about it, and writt a sheet or a sheet and a halfe, an account of it, which he presented to the bishop. I asked the bishop since for it, and he told me he had lent it, to whom he could not tell, and had no copy of it. 'Tis great pity the paines of so great an artist should be lost. Sir Christopher tells me he hath no copie of it neither.

This year, 1691, Mr. Anth. Wood tells me, he hath gott a transcript of Sir Chr. Wren's paper; which obtain, and insert here. I much doubted I should never have heard of it again.

[Soon after writing this passage Aubrey probably obtained a copy of Sir Christopher Wren's report, which he has inserted in his original manuscript. It is dated in 1669, and occupies eleven folio pages. In The History and Antiquities of the Cathedral of Salisbury, &c. (1723, 8vo.), it is printed, and described as "An Architectonical Account of this Cathedral", by "an eminent gentleman". Part of the same report was printed in Wren's Parentalia (1750); and a short abstract of it will also be found in Dodsworth's Salisbury Cathedral (written by the late Mr. Hatcher), p. 172. In a communication from the last named gentleman in 1841, when he was engaged upon his History of Salisbury, he wrote to me as follows: "I have lately fallen upon what appears to have been Sir C. Wren's original report relative to the cathedral; a very elaborate report on the state of the building in 1691, by a person named Naish; some good observations on the bending of the piers (anonymous); and several estimates and observations made by Price. What I shall do with them I have not yet determined." - J. B.] — —

Wardour Castle was very strongly built of freestone. I never saw it but when I was a youth; the day after part of it was blown up: and the mortar was so good that one of the little towers reclining on one side did hang together and not fall in peeces. It was called Warder Castle from the conserving there the ammunition of the West. ——

Sir William Dugdale told me, many years since, that about Henry the Third's time the Pope gave a bull or patents to a company of Italian Freemasons to travell up and down over all Europe to build churches. From those are derived the fraternity of adopted Masons. They are known to one another by certain signes and watch-words: it continues to this day. They have severall lodges in severall counties for their reception, and when any of them fall into decay the brotherhood is to relieve him, &c. The manner of their adoption is very formall, and with an oath of secresy.

Memorandum. This day, May the 18th, being Munday, 1691, after Rogation Sunday, is a great convention at St. Paul's Church of the fraternity of the adopted Masons, where Sir Christopher Wren is to be adopted a brother, and Sir Henry Goodric, of the Tower, and divers others. There have been kings of this sodality. ——

At Pottern, a great mannour belonging to the Bishop of Sarum, is a very faire strong built church, with a great tower in the middest of the crosse aisle. It is exactly of the same architecture of the cathedrall church at Sarum, and the windowes are painted by the same hand, in that kind of Gothick grotesco. Likewise the church at Kington St. Michael's, and that at Sopworth, are of the same fashion, and built about the same time, sc. with slender marble pillars to the windowes; and just so the church of Glastonbury Abbey, and Westminster Abbey. Likewise the architecture of the church at Bishop's Cannings is the same, and such pillars to the windowes. ——

At Calne was a fine high steeple which stood upon four pillars in the middle of the church. One of the pillars was faulty, and the churchwardens were dilatory, as is usual in such cases. - Chivers, Esq. of that parish, foreseeing the fall of it, if not prevented, and the great charge they must be at by it, brought down Mr. Inigo Jones to survey it. This was about 1639 or 1640: he gave him 30 li. out of his own purse for his paines. Mr. Jones would have underbuilt it for an hundred pounds. About 1645 it fell down, on a Saturday, and also broke down the chancell; the parish have since been at 1,000 li. Charge to make a new heavy tower. Such will be the fate of our steeple at Kington St. Michael; one cannot perswade the parishioners to goe out of their own way. [In another of Aubrey's MSS. (his "Description of North Wiltshire"), is a sketch of the tower and spire of the church of Kington St. Michael, shewing several large and serious cracks in the walls. The spire was blown down in 1703, its neglected state no doubt contributing to its fall. The following manuscript note by James Gilpin, Esq. Recorder of Oxford (who was born at Kington in 1709), may be added, from my own collections for the history of this, my native parish. "In ye great storm in ye year 1703, ye spire of this church was blown down, and two of ye old bells I remember standing in ye belfry till ye tower was pulled down in 1724, in order to be rebuilt It was rebuilt accordingly, and the bells were then new cast, with ye assistance of Mr. Harington ye Vicar, who gave a new bell, on which his name is inscribed, so as to make a peal of six bells. On these bells are the following inscriptions:- 1. Prosperity to this parish, 1726. 2. Peace and good neighbourhood, 1726. 3. Prosperity to ye Church of England, 1726. 4. William Harington, Vicar. A. R. 1726 (A. R. means Abraham Rudhall, ye bell founder). 5. Has no inscription, but 1726 in gilt figures. 6. Jonathan Power and Robert Hewett, Churchwardens, 1726." - J. B.] ——

Sir William Dugdale told me he finds that painting in glasse came first into England in King John's time. Before the Reformation I believe there was no county or great town in England but had glasse painters. Old ...... Harding, of Blandford in Dorsetshire, where I went to schoole, was the only countrey glasse-painter that ever I knew. Upon play dayes I was wont to visit his shop and furnaces. He dyed about 1643, aged about 83, or more.

In St. Edmund's church at Salisbury were curious painted glasse windowes, especially in the chancell, where there was one window, I think the east window, of such exquisite worke that Gundamour, the Spanish Ambassadour, did offer some hundreds of pounds for it, if it might have been bought. In one of the windowes was the picture of God the Father, like an old man, which gave offence to H. Shervill, Esq. then Recorder of this city (this was about 1631), who, out of zeale, came and brake some of these windowes, and clambering upon one of the pews to be able to reach high enough, fell down and brake his leg. For this action he was brought into the Starr-Chamber, and had a great fine layd upon him [£500. J. B.] which, I think, did undoe him. [See a minute and interesting account of Sherfield's offence, and the proceedings at the trial, in Hatcher's History of Salisbury, p. 371-374. - J. B.] ——

There was, at the Abbey of Malmesbury, a very high spire-steeple, as high almost, they at Malmesbury say, as that of St. Paul's, London; and they further report, that when the steeple fell down the ball of it fell as far as the Griffin Inne. ——

The top of the tower of Sutton Benger is very elegant, there is not such another in the county. It much resembles St Walborough's [St. Werburg's] at Bristoll. [The tower of Sutton Benger church, here alluded to, has a large open-work'd pinnacle, rising from the centre of the roof; a beautiful and very singular ornament. See the wood-cut in the title-page of the present volume.- J. B.]

The priory of Broadstock was very well built, and with good strong ribbs, as one may conclude by the remaines that are left of it yet standing, which are the cellar, which is strongly vaulted with freestone, and the hall above it. It is the stateliest cellar in Wiltshire. The Hall is spatious, and within that the priour's parlour, wherein is good carving. In the middle of the south side of the hall is a large chimney, over which is a great window, so that the draught of the smoake runnes on each side of the chimney. Above the cellars the hall and parlours are one moietie; the church or, chapell stood on the south side of the hall, under which was a vault, as at St. Faithes under Paules. The very fundations of this fair church are now, 1666, digged up, where I saw severall freestone coffins, having two holes bored in the bottome, and severall capitalls and bases of handsome Gothique pillars. On the west end of the hall was the King's lodgeings, which they say were very noble, and standing about 1588. [Aubrey records some further particulars of Bradenstoke Priory; a short account of which edifice will be found in the third volume of the Beauties of Wiltshire. The Gentleman's Magazine, Nov. 1833, contains a wood-cut and account of this old religious house. See also Bowles's History of Lacock Abbey.-J. B.]

The church of Broad Chalke was dedicated to All-Hallowes, as appeares by the ancient parish booke. The tradition is that it was built by a lawyer, whose picture is in severall of the glasse-windowes yet remaining, kneeling, in a purple gowne or robe, and at the bottome of the windowes this subscription: "Orate pro felici statu Magistri Sieardi Lenot". This church hath no pillar, and the breadth is thirty and two feete and two inches. Hereabout are no trees now growing that would be long enough to make the crosse beames that doe reach from side to side. By the fashion of the windowes I doe guesse that it was built in the reigne of King Henry the Sixth. [The church of Broad Chalk is described in Hoare's Modern Wiltshire, Hundred of Chalk, p. 148.] ——

The market-crosses of Salisbury, Malmesbury, and Trowbridge, are very noble: standing on six pillars, and well vaulted over with freestone well carved. On every one of these crosses above sayd the crest of Hungerford, the sickles, doth flourish like parietaria or wall-flower, as likewise on most publique buildings in these parts, which witnesse not onely their opulency but munificency. I doe think there is such another crosse at Cricklade, with the coate and crests of Hungerford. Quaere de hoc. [There is not any cross remaining in Trowbridge; and that at Cricklade, in the high street, is merely a single shaft, placed on a base of steps. The one at Salisbury is a plain unadorned building; but that of Malmesbury is a fine ornamented edifice. It is described and illustrated in my "Dictionary of the Architecture and Archaeology of the Middle Ages". - J. B.] ——

The Lord Stourton's house at Stourton is very large and very old, but is little considerable as to the architecture. The pavement of the chapell there is of bricks, annealed or painted yellow, with their coat and rebus; sc. a tower and a tunne. These enamelled bricks have not been in use these last hundred yeares. The old paving of Our Lady Church at Salisbury was of such; and the choire of Gloucester church is paved with admirable bricks of this fashion. A little chapell at Merton, in the Earle of Shaftesbury's house, is paved with such tiles, whereon are annealed or enamelled the coate and quarterings of Horsey. It is pity that this fashion is not revived; they are handsome and far more wholesome than marble paving in our could climate, and much cheaper. They have been disused ever since King Edward the Sixth's time. [Aubrey would have rejoiced to witness the success which has attended the revived use of ornamental paving tiles within the last few years. Messrs. Copeland and Garrett, and Mr. Minton, of Stoke- upon-Trent, as well as the Messrs. Chamberlain of Worcester, are engaged in making large numbers of these tiles, which are now extensively employed by church architects. Those individuals have produced tiles equal in excellence and beauty to the ancient specimens.-J. B.] ——

Heretofore all gentlemen's houses had fish ponds, and their houses had motes drawn about them, both for strength and for convenience of fish on fasting days.

The architecture of an old English gentleman's house, especially in Wiltshire and thereabout, was a good high strong wall, a gate house, a great hall and parlour, and within the little green court where you come in, stood on one side the barne: they then thought not the noise of the threshold ill musique. This is yet to be seen at severall old houses and seates, e. g. Bradfield, Alderton, Stanton St. Quintin, Yatton-Keynell, &c.

Fallersdowne, vulgo Falston, was built by a Baynton, about perhaps Henry the Fifth. Here was a noble old-fashioned house, with a mote about it and drawbridge, and strong high walles embatteled. They did consist of a layer of freestone and a layer of flints, squared or headed; two towers faced the south, one the east, the other the west end. After the garrison was gonn the mote was filled up, about 1650, and the high wall pulled down and one of the towers. Baynton was attainted about Henry the Sixth. Afterwards the Lord Chief Justice Cheyney had it About the beginning of Queen Elizabeth, ... Vaughan of Glamorganshire bought it; and about 1649, Sir George Vaughan sold it to Philip Earle of Pembroke.

Longleate House is the most august building in the kingdome. It was built by [Edward] Seymor, Duke of Somerset, Lord Protector,* tempore Edward VI., who sent for the architects out of Italy. The length is 272 foot, the breadth 172 foot; measured by Mr. Moore, Clericus. It is as high as the Banqueting house at Whitehall, outwardly adorned with Dorick, lonick, and Corinthian pillars. Mr. Dankertz drew a landskip of it, which was engraved. Desire Mr. Rose to gett me a print of it.

*[This statement is erroneous. Maiden Bradley, which is not far from Longleat, has been a seat of the noble family of Seymour for many centuries, and they have an old mansion there; but the family never possessed Longleat. The latter estate, on the contrary, was granted by King Henry VIII. to Sir John Horsey, and Edward Earl of Hertford, from whom it was purchased by Sir John Thynne, ancestor of its present proprietor, the Marquess of Bath. In 1576, Sir John commenced the splendid mansion at Longleat, which some writers assert was designed by John of Padua. The works were regularly prosecuted during the next twelve years, and completed by the two succeeding owners of the property. See Architectural Antiquities of Great Britain, vol. ii. - J. B.]

Longford House was built by the Lord Georges, after the fashion of one of the King of Swedland's palaces. The figure of it is triangular, and the roomes of state are in the round towers in the angles. These round roomes are adorned with black marble Corinthian pillars, with gilded capitalls and bases. 'Twas sold to the Lord Colraine about 1646. [It now belongs to the Earl of Radnor. Plans, views, and accounts of this mansion, as well as of Longleat and Charlton Houses, are published in the "Architectural Antiquities", vol. ii.-J. B.]

Charlton House was built by the Earl of Suffolk, Lord High Treasurer, about the beginning of King James the First, when architecture was at a low ebbe. ——

At Broad Chalke is one of the tunablest ring of bells in Wiltshire, which hang advantageously; the river running near the churchyard, which meliorates the sound. Here were but four bells till anno 1616 was added a fifth; and in anno 1659 Sir George Penruddock and I made ourselves church-wardens, or else the fair church had fallen, from the niggardlinesse of the churchwardens of mean condition, and then we added the sixth bell.

The great bell at Westminster, in the Clockiar at the New Palace Yard, 36,OOOlib. weight. See Stow's Survey of London, de hoc. It was given by Jo. Montacute, Earle of (Salisbury, I think). Part of the inscription is thus, sc. "...... annis ab acuto monte Johannis."

PART II.-CHAPTER VII.

AGRICULTURE.

[THE late Mr. Thos. Davis, of Longleat, Steward to the Marquess of Bath, drew up an admirable "View of the Agriculture of the County of Wilts", which was printed by the Board of Agriculture in 1794. 8vo. -J. B.]

CONSIDERING the distance of place where I now write, London, and the distance of time that I lived in this county, I am not able to give a satisfactorie account of the husbandry thereof. I will only say of our husbandmen, as Sir Thom. Overbury does of the Oxford scholars, that they goe after the fashion; that is, when the fashion is almost out they take it up: so our countrey-men are very late and very unwilling to learne or be brought to new improvements.

[It was scarcely a reproach to the Wiltshire husbandmen to be far behind those of more enlightened counties, when, in the seat of learning, where the mental faculties of the students ought to have been continually exercised and cultivated, and not merely occupied in learning useless Greek and Latin, the "Oxford scholars" followed, rather than led, the fashion. Agricultural societies were then unknown, farmers had little communication with distant districts, and consequently knew nothing of the practice of other places; rents were low, and the same families continued in the farms from generation to generation, pursuing the same routine of Agriculture which their fathers and grandfathers had pursued "time out of mind". In the days of my own boyhood, nearly seventy years ago, I spent some time at a solitary farmhouse in North Wiltshire, with a grandfather and his family, and can remember the various occupations and practices of the persons employed in the dairy, and on the grazing and corn lands. I never saw either a book or newspaper in the house; nor were any accounts of the farming kept. - J. B.]

The Devonshire men were the earliest improvers. I heard Oliver Cromwell, Protector, at dinner at Hampton Court, 1657 or 8, tell the Lord Arundell of Wardour and the Lord Fitzwilliams that he had been in all the counties of England, and that the Devonshire husbandry was the best: and at length we have obtained a good deal of it, which is now well known and need not to be rehearsed. But William Scott, of Hedington, a very understanding man in these things, told me that since 1630 the fashion of husbandry in this country had been altered three times over, still refining.

Mr. Bishop, of Merton, first brought into the south of Wiltshire the improvement by burn-beking or Denshiring, about 1639. He learnt it in Flanders; it is very much used in this parish, and their neighbours doe imitate them: they say 'tis good for the father, but naught for the son, by reason it does so weare out the heart of the land.

[The reader will find many observations of this nature, and on analogous subjects, in the manuscript, which it has not been thought desirable to print. Among the rest are several pages from John Norden's "Surveyor's Dialogue", containing advice and directions respecting agriculture, of which Aubrey says, "though they are not of Wiltshire, they will do no hurt here; and, if my countrymen know it not, I wish they might learn". - J. B.] ——

The wheate and bread of this county, especially South Wilts, is but indifferent; that of the Vale of White Horse is excellent. King Charles II. when he lay at Salisbury, in his progresse, complained that he found there neither good bread nor good beer. But for the latter, 'twas the fault of the brewer not to boil it well; for the water and the mault there are as good as any in England. ——

The improvement by cinque-foile, which now spreads much in the stone-brash lands, was first used at North Wraxhall by Nicholas Hall, who came from Dundery in Somersetshire, about the yeare 1650.

George Johnson, Esq. counsellour-at-law, did improve some of his estate at Bowdon-parke, by marling, from 6d. an acre to 25sh. He did lay three hundred loades of blew marle upon an acre. ——

Sir William Basset, of Claverdoun, hath made the best vinyard that I have heard of in England. He sayes that the Navarre grape is the best for our climate, and that the eastern sunn does most comfort the vine, by putting off the cold. Mr. Jo. Ash, of Teffont Ewyas, has a pretty vineyard of about six acres, made anno 1665. Sir Walter Erneley, Baronet, told me, a little before he died, that he was making one at Stert, I thinke, neer the Devizes. ——

The improvement of watering meadows began at Wyley, about 1635, about which time, I remember, we began to use them at Chalke. Watering of meadows about Marleburgh and so to Hungerford was, I remember, about 1646, and Mr. John Bayly, of Bishop's Down, near Salisbury, about the same time made his great improvements by watering there by St. Thomas's Bridge. This is as old as the Romans; e.g. Virgil, "Claudite jam rivos, pueri, sat prata biberunt". Mr. Jo. Evelyn told me that out of Varro, Cato, and Columella are to be extracted all good rules of husbandry; and he wishes that a good collection or extraction were made out of them. ——

INCLOSING.- Anciently, in the hundreds of Malmesbury and Chippenham were but few enclosures, and that near houses. The north part of Wiltshire was in those dayes admirable for field-sports. All vast champian fields, as now about Sherston and Marsfield. King Henry the 7 brought in depopulations, and that inclosures; and after the dissolution of the abbeys in Hen. 8 time more inclosing. About 1695 all between Easton Piers and Castle Comb was a campania, like Coteswold, upon which it borders; and then Yatton and Castle Combe did intercommon together. Between these two parishes much hath been enclosed in my remembrance, and every day more and more. I doe remember about 1633 but one enclosure to Chipnam-field, which was at the north end, and by this time I thinke it is all inclosed. So all between Kington St. Michael and Dracot Cerne was common field, and the west field of Kington St. Michael between Easton Piers and Haywood was inclosed in 1664. Then were a world of labouring people maintained by the plough, as they were likewise in Northamptonshire. 'Tis observed that the inclosures of Northamptonshire have been unfortunate since, and not one of them have prospered. ——

Mr. Toogood, of Harcot, has fenced his grounds with crab-tree hedges, which are so thick that no boare can gett through them. Captain Jones, of Newton Tony, did the like on his downes. Their method is thus: they first runne a furrow with the plough, and then they sow the cakes of the crabbes, which they gett at the verjuice mill. It growes very well, and on many of them they doe graffe. ——

Limeing of ground was not used but about 1595, some time after the comeing in of tobacco. (From Sir Edw. Ford of Devon.) ——

Old Mr. Broughton, of Herefordshire, was the man that brought in the husbandry of soap ashes. He living at Bristoll, where much soap is made, and the haven there was like to have been choak't up with it, considering that ground was much meliorated by compost, &c. did undertake this experiment, and having land near the city, did accordingly improve it with soap ashes. I remember the gentleman very well. He dyed about 1650, I believe near 90 yeares old, and was the handsomest, well limbed, strait old man that ever I saw, had a good witt and a graceful elocution. He was the father of Bess Broughton, one of the greatest beauties of her age. ——

Proverb for apples, peares, hawthorns, quicksetts, oakes:

"Sett them at All-hallow-tyde, and command them to grow;
Sett them at Candlemass, and entreat them to grow."

——

Butter and Cheese. At Pertwood and about Lidyard as good butter is made as any in England, but the cheese is not so good. About Lidyard, in those fatt grounds, in hott weather, the best huswives cannot keep their cheese from heaving. The art to keep it from heaving is to putt in cold water. Sowre woodsere grounds doe yield the best cheese, and such are Cheshire. Bromefield, in the parish of Yatton, is so - sower and wett - and where I had better cheese made than anywhere in all the neighbourhood.

Somerset proverb:

"If you will have a good cheese, and hav'n old, You must turn'n seven times before he is cold."

Jo. Shakespeare's wife, of Worplesdowne in Surrey, a North Wiltshire woman, and an excellent huswife, does assure me that she makes as good cheese there as ever she did at Wraxhall or Bitteston, and that it is meerly for want of art that her neighbours doe not make as good; they send their butter to London. So it appeares that, some time or other, when there in the vale of Sussex and Surrey they have the North Wiltshire skill, that halfe the cheese trade of the markets of Tedbury and Marleborough will be spoiled.

Now of late, sc. about 1680, in North Wiltshire, they have altered their fashion from thinne cheeses about an inch thick, made so for the sake of drying and quick sale, called at London Marleborough cheese, to thick ones, as the Cheshire cheese. At Marleborough and Tedbury the London cheese-mongers doe keep their factors for their trade. [At the close of the last century Reading was the principal seat of the London cheese factors, who visited the different farms in Wiltshire once in each year to purchase the cheese, which was sent in waggons to Reading: often by circuitous routes in order to save the tolls payable on turnpike roads. - J. B.] ——

Maulting and Brewing. It is certain that Salisbury mault is better than any other in the West; but they have no more skill there than elsewhere. It is the water there is the chiefest cause of its goodnesse: perhaps the nitrousnesse of the maulting floores may something help.

[Aubrey devotes several pages to these subjects. He particularly commends "The History of Malting, or the method of making Malt, practised at Derby, described for R. T. Esq. by J. F. (John Flamsteed), January 1682-3", which was printed in "A Collection of Letters for ye Improvement of Husbandry and Trade", No. 7, Thursday, June 15, 1682. This paper by Flamsteed, which is of considerable length, is inserted by Aubrey in both his manuscripts: a printed copy in the original at Oxford, and a transcript in the Royal Society's fair copy. - J. B.]

It may be objected how came that great astronomer, Mr. John Flamsteed, to know so much the mystery of malsters. Why, his father is a maulster at Derby; and he himself was a maulster, and did drive a trade in it till he was about twenty yeares of age, at what time Sir Jonas Moore invited him to London. [The best memoir of Flamsteed will be found in "An Account of the Rev. John Flamsteed, the first Astronomer Royal, compiled from his own manuscripts and other authentic documents never before published. To which is added his British Catalogue of Stars, corrected and enlarged. By Francis Baily, Esq. &c. &c. Printed by order of the Lords Commissioners of the Admiralty. London, 1835". Such is the title of a large quarto volume which my late esteemed friend and neighbour Mr. Baily edited and wrote, con amore; and which contains not only a curious autobiography of the first Astronomer Royal of Great Britain, but numerous letters, documents, and miscellaneous information on the science of astronomy as it was known in Flamsteed's time, and up to the time of the publication of the volume. This work was printed at the expense of the government, and presented to public colleges and societies, to royal and public libraries, and to many persons distinguished in science and literature. Hence it may be regarded as a choice and remarkable literary production. Some curious particulars of Flamsteed's quarrel with Sir Isaac Newton, respecting the printing of his "Historia Coelestis", are given in Mr. Baily's volume, which tend to shew that the latter, in conjunction with Halley and other persons, perseveringly annoyed and injured Flamsteed in various ways, and for a considerable time. Some of the admirers of Newton's moral character having attempted to extenuate his conduct, Mr. Baily published a Supplement to his work, in which he shews that such attempts had completely failed. - J. B.]

PART II. - CHAPTER VIII.

THE DOWNES.

WE now make our ascent to the second elevation or the hill countrey, known by the name of the Downes, or Salisbury Plaines; and they are the most spacious plaines in Europe, and the greatest remaines that I can heare of of the smooth primitive world when it lay all under water.

These downes runne into Hampshire, Berkshire, and Dorsetshire; but as to its extent in this county, it is from Red-hone, the hill above Urshfont, to Salisbury, north and south, and from Mere to Lurgershall, east and west. The turfe is of a short sweet grasse, good for the sheep, and delightfull to the eye, for its smoothnesse like a bowling green, and pleasant to the traveller; who wants here only variety of objects to make his journey lesse tedious: for here is "nil nisi campus et aer", not a tree, or rarely a bush to shelter one from a shower.

The soile of the downes I take generally to be a white earth or mawme. More south, sc. about Wilton and Chalke, the downes are intermixt with boscages that nothing can be more pleasant, and in the summer time doe excell Arcadia in verdant and rich turfe and moderate aire, but in winter indeed our air is cold and rawe. The innocent lives here of the shepherds doe give us a resemblance of the golden age. Jacob and Esau were shepherds; and Amos, one of the royall family, asserts the same of himself, for he was among the shepherds of Tecua [Tekoa] following that employment. The like, by God's own appointment, prepared Moses for a scepter, as Philo intimates in his life, when he tells us that a shepherd's art is a suitable preparation to a kingdome. The same he mentions in his Life of Joseph, affirming that the care a shepherd has over his cattle very much resembles that which a King hath over his subjects. The same St. Basil, in his Homily de St. Mamme Martyre has, concerning David, who was taken from following the ewes great with young ones to feed Israel. The Romans, the worthiest and greatest nation in the world, sprang from shepherds. The augury of the twelve vultures plac't a scepter in Romulus's hand, which held a crook before; and as Ovid sayes:-

"His own small flock each senator did keep."

Lucretius mentions an extraordinary happinesse, and as it were divinity in a shepherd's life: -

"Thro' shepherds' care, and their divine retreats."

And, to speake from the very bottome of my heart, not to mention the integrity and innocence of shepherds, upon which so many have insisted and copiously declaimed, methinkes he is much more happy in a wood that at ease contemplates the universe as his own, and in it the sunn and starrs, the pleasing meadows, shades, groves, green banks, stately trees, flowing springs, and the wanton windings of a river, fit objects for quiet innocence, than he that with fire and sword disturbs the world, and measures his possessions by the wast that lies about him.

These plaines doe abound with hares, fallow deer, partridges, and bustards. [The fallow deer and bustards have long since disappeared from these plains; but hares and partridges abound in the vicinity of gentlemen's seats, particularly around Everleigh, Tidworth, Amesbury, Wilbury, Wilton, Earl-Stoke, Clarendon, &c. - Vide ante, p.64. - J. B.] In this tract is ye Earle of Pembroke's noble seat at Wilton; but the Arcadia and the Daphne is about Vernditch and Wilton; and these romancy plaines and boscages did no doubt conduce to the hightening of Sir Philip Sydney's phansie. He lived much in these parts, and his most masterly touches of his pastoralls he wrote here upon the spott, where they were conceived. 'Twas about these purlieus that the muses were wont to appeare to Sir Philip Sydney, and where he wrote down their dictates in his table book, though on horseback.* For those nimble fugitives, except they be presently registred, fly away, and perhaps can never be caught again. But they were never so kind to appeare to me, though I am the usufructuary:† it seemes they reserve that grace only for the proprietors, to whom they have continued a constant kindnesse for a succession of generations of the no lesse ingenious than honorable family of the Herberts. These were the places where our Kings and Queens used to divert themselves in the hunting season. Cranbourn Chase, which reaches from Harnham Bridge, at Salisbury, near to Blandford, was belonging to Roger Mortimer, Earle of March: his seate was at his castle at Cranbourne. If these oakes here were vocall as Dodona's, some of the old dotards (old stagge- headed oakes, so called) could give us an account of the amours and secret whispers between this great Earle and the faire Queen Isabell.

*I remember some old relations of mine and [other] old men hereabout that have seen Sir Philip doe thus.

†[Aubrey held the manor farm of Broad Chalk under a lease from the Earl of Pembroke. - J. B.]

To find the proportion of the downes of this countrey to the vales, I did divide Speed's Mappe of Wiltshire with a paire of cizars, according to the respective hundreds of downes and vale, and I weighed them in a curious ballance of a goldsmith, and the proportion of the hill countrey to the vale is as .... to .... sc. about 3/4 fere. ——

SHEEP. As to the nature of our Wiltshire sheep, negatively, they are not subject to the shaking; which the Dorsetshire sheep are. Our sheep about Chalke doe never die of the rott. My Cos. Scott does assure me that I may modestly allow a thousand sheep to a tything, one with another. Mr. Rogers was for allowing of two thousand sheep, one with another, to a tything, but my Cosin Scott saies that is too high. ——

SHEPHERDS. The Britons received their knowledge of agriculture from the Romans, and they retain yet many of their customes. The festivalls at sheep-shearing seeme to bee derived from the Parilia. In our western parts, I know not what is done in the north, the sheep-masters give no wages to their shepherds, but they have the keeping of so many sheep, pro rata; soe that the shepherds' lambs doe never miscarry. I find that Plautus gives us a hint of this custome amongst the Romans in his time; Asinaria, Act III. scene i. Philenian (Meretrix):

" Etiam opilio, qui pascit (mater) alienas ovis, Aliquani habet peculiarem qua spem soletur suam."

Their habit, I believe, (let there be a draught of their habit) is that of the Roman or Arcadian shepherds; as they are delineated in Mr. Mich. Drayton's Poly-olbion; sc. a long white cloake with a very deep cape, which comes halfway down their backs, made of the locks of the sheep. There was a sheep-crooke (vide Virgil's Eclogues, and Theocritus,) a sling, a scrip, their tar-box, a pipe or flute, and their dog. But since 1671, they are grown so luxurious as to neglect their ancient warme and useful fashion, and goe a la mode. T. Randolph in a Pastoral sayes;-

" What clod-pates, Thenot, are our British swaines, How lubber-like they loll upon the plaines." *

* [See "Plays and Poems, by Thomas Randolph, M.A." 12mo. 1664, p. 90. The lines quoted are at the commencement of a dialogue between Collen and Thenot; which is described as "an Eglogue on the noble assemblies revived on Cotswold Hills by Mr. Robert Dover". An able criticism of Randolph's works, with extracts, will be found in the sixth volume of the "Retrospective Review". - J. B.]

Before the civill warres I remember many of them made straw hatts, which I thinke is now left off, and our shepherdesses of late yeares (1680) doe begin to worke point, whereas before they did only knitt coarse stockings. (Instead of the sling they have now a hollow iron or piece of horne, not unlike a shoeing horne, fastened to the other end of the crosier, by wch they take up stones and sling, and keep their flocks in order. The French sheperdesses spin with a rocque. - J. EVELYN.) ——

Mr. Ferraby, the minister of Bishop's Cannings, was an ingenious man, and an excellent musician, and made severall of his parishioners good musicians, both for vocall and instrumentall musick; they sung the Psalmes in consort to the organ, which Mr. Ferraby procured to be erected.

When King James the First was in these parts he lay at Sir Edw. Baynton's at Bromham. Mr. Ferraby then entertained his Majesty at the Bush, in Cotefield, with bucoliques of his own making and composing, of four parts; which were sung by his parishioners, who wore frocks and whippes like carters. Whilst his majesty was thus diverted, the eight bells (of which he was the cause) did ring, and the organ was played on for state; and after this musicall entertainment he entertained his Majesty with a foot-ball match of his own parishioners. This parish in those dayes would have challenged all England for musique, foot-ball, and ringing. For this entertainment his Majesty made him one of his chaplains in ordinary.

When Queen Anne† returned from Bathe, he made an entertainment for her Majesty on Canning's-down, sc. at Shepherds-shard,‡ at Wensditch, with a pastorall performed by himself and his parishioners in shepherds' weeds. A copie of his song was printed within a compartment excellently well engraved and designed, with goates, pipes, sheep hooks, cornucopias, &c. [Aubrey has transcribed it into his manuscript. It appears that it was sung as above mentioned on the llth of June 1613; being "voyc't in four parts compleatly musicall"; and we are told that "it was by her Highnesse not only most gratiously accepted and approved, but also bounteously rewarded; and by the right honourable, worshipfull, and the rest of the generall hearers and beholders, worthily applauded". See this also noticed in Wood's "Fasti Oxonienses", under "Ferebe", and in Nichols's Progresses, &c. of King James the First, ii. 668. In this curious chapter, Aubrey has further transcribed "A Dialogue between two Shepherds uttered in a Pastorall shew at Wilton", and written by Sir Philip Sidney. See the Life of Sidney, prefixed to an edition of his Works in three volumes, 8vo, 1725.-J. B.]

†[Anne of Denmark, Queen of James I. was married to that monarch in 1589, and died in 1619.-J. B.]

‡[Shard is a word used in Wiltshire to indicate a gap in a hedge. Ponshard signifies a broken piece of earthenware.-J. B.]

PART II-CHAPTER IX.

WOOLL.

[THE author appears to have merely commenced this chapter; which, as it now stands in the manuscript, contains little more than is here printed. The three succeeding chapters are connected in their subjects with the present. - J. B.]

THIS nation is the most famous for the great quantity of wooll of any in the world; and this county hath the most sheep and wooll of any other. The down-wooll is not of the finest of England, but of about the second rate. That of the common-field is the finest.

Quaere, if Castle Comb was not a staple for wooll, or else a very
great wooll-market?

——

Mr. Ludlowe, of the Devises, and his predecessours have been wooll-breakers [brokers] 80 or 90 yeares, and hath promised to assist me. ——

Quaere, if it would not bee the better way to send our wooll beyond the sea again, as in the time of the staple? For the Dutch and French doe spinn finer, work cheaper, and die better. Our cloathiers combine against the wooll-masters, and keep their spinners but just alive: they steale hedges, spoile coppices, and are trained up as nurseries of sedition and rebellion.

[For a long series of years the clothiers, or manufacturers, and the wool-growers, or landowners, entertained opposite opinions respecting the propriety of exporting wool; and numerous acts of parliament were passed at different times encouraging or restricting its exportation, as either of these conflicting interests happened to prevail for the time with the legislature. The landowners were generally desirous to export their produce, without restriction, to foreign markets, and to limit the importation of competing wool from abroad. The manufacturers, on the contrary, wished for the free importation of those foreign wools, without an admixture of which the native produce cannot be successfully manufactured; whilst they were anxious to restrain the exportation of British wool, from an absurd fear of injury to their own trade. Some curious particulars of the contest between these parties, and of the history of legislation on the subject, will be found in Porter's Progress of the Nation and McCulloch's Commercial Dictionary and Statistical Account of the British Empire; and more particularly in Bischoff's History of Wool (1842). The wool trade is now free from either import or export duties. - J. B.]

PART II. - CHAPTER X.

FALLING OF RENTS.

[AUBREY addressed to his friend Mr. Francis Lodwyck, merchant of London, a project on the wool trade; proposing, amongst other things, a duty on the importation of Spanish wool, with a view to raise the price of English wool, and consequently the rent of land. (See the Note on this subject in the preceding page.) Mr. Lodwyck's letter in reply, fully discussing the question, may be consulted in Aubrey's manuscript by any one interested in the subject It is inserted in the chapter now under consideration; which contains also a printed pamphlet with the following title:- "A Treatise on Wool, and the Manufacture of it; in a letter to a friend: occasioned upon a discourse concerning the great abatements and low value of lands. Wherein it is shewed how their worth and value may be advanced by the improvement of the manufacture and price of our English wooll. Together with the Presentment of the Grand Jury of the County of Somerset at the General Quarter Sessions begun at Brewton the 13th day of January 1684. London. Printed for William Crooke, at the Green Dragon without Temple Bar. 1685." (Sm. 4to. pp. 32.) - J. B.]

THE falling of rents is a consequence of the decay of the Turky-trade; which is the principall cause of the falling of the price of wooll. Another reason that conduces to the falling of the prices of wooll is our women's wearing so much silk and Indian ware as they doe. By these meanes my farme at Chalke is worse by sixty pounds per annum than it was before the civill warres.

The gentry living in London, and the dayly concourse of servants out of the country to London, makes servants' wages deare in the countrey, and makes scarcity of labourers.

Sir William Petty told me, that when he was a boy a seeds-man had five pounds per annum wages, and a countrey servant-maid between 30 and 40s. wages. [40s. per ann. to a servant-maid is now, 1743, good wages in Worcestershire.- MS. NOTE, ANONYMOUS.] ——

Memorandum. Great increase of sanfoine now, in most places fitt for itt; improvements of meadowes by watering; ploughing up of the King's forrests and parkes, &c. But as to all these, as ten thousand pounds is gained in the hill barren countrey, so the vale does lose as much, which brings it to an equation.

——

The Indians doe worke for a penny a day; so their silkes are exceeding cheap; and rice is sold in India for four pence per bushell.

PART II - CHAPTER XI

HISTORIE OF CLOATHING.

[THE following are the only essential parts of this chapter, which is very short.-J. B.]

KING Edward the Third first settled the staples of wooll in Flanders. See Hollinshead, Stowe, Speed, and the Statute Book, de hoc.

Staple, "estape", i e. a market place; so the wooll staple at Westminster, which is now a great market for flesh and fish. ——

When King Henry the Seventh lived in Flanders with his aunt the Dutchess of Burgundie, he considered that all or most of the wooll that was manufactured there into cloath was brought out of England; and observing what great profit did arise by it, when he came to the crown he sent into Flanders for cloathing manufacturers, whom he placed in the west, and particularly at Send in Wiltshire, where they built severall good houses yet remaining: I know not any village so remote from London that can shew the like. The cloathing trade did flourish here till about 1580, when they removed to Troubridge, by reason of (I thinke) a plague; but I conjecture the main reason was that the water here was not proper for the fulling and washing of their cloath; for this water, being impregnated with iron, did give the white cloath a yellowish tincture. Mem. In the country hereabout are severall families that still retaine Walloun names, as Goupy, &c. ——

The best white cloaths in England are made at Salisbury, where the water, running through chalke, becomes very nitrous, and therefore abstersive. These fine cloathes are died black or scarlet, at London or in Holland.

Malmesbury, a very neat town, hath a great name for cloathing.

The Art of Cloathing and Dyeing is already donn by Sir William Petty, and is printed in the History of the Royall Society, writt by Dr. Spratt, since Bishop of Rochester.

PART II.-CHAPTER XII.

EMINENT CLOATHIERS OF THIS COUNTY.

[IN this chapter there is a long "Digression of Cloathiers of other Counties," full of curious matter, which is here necessarily omitted. - J. B.]

.. . SUTTON of Salisbury, was an eminent cloathier: what is become of his family I know not.

[John] Hall, I doe believe, was a merchant of the staple, at Salisbury, where he had many houses. His dwelling house, now a taverne (1669), was on the Ditch, where in the glasse windowes are many scutchions of his armes yet remaining, and severall merchant markes. Quaere, if there are not also wooll-sacks in the pannells of glass? [Of this house and family the reader will find many interesting particulars in a volume by my friend the Rev. Edward Duke, of Lake House, near Amesbury. Its title will explain the work, viz. "Prolusiones Historicæ; or, Essays Illustrative of the Halle of John Halle, citizen and merchant of Salisbury in the reigns of Henry VI. and Edward IV.; with Notes illustrative and explanatory. By the Rev. Edward Duke, M.A., F.S.A., and L.S. in two vols. 8vo. 1837." (Only one volume has been published.) - J. B.] ——

The ancestor of Sir William Webb of Odstock, near Salisbury, was a merchant of the staple in Salisbury. As Grevill and Wenman bought all the Coteswold wooll, so did Hall and Webb the wooll of Salisbury plaines; but these families are Roman Catholiques.

The ancestor of Mr. Long, of Rood Ashton, was a very great cloathier. He built great part of that handsome church, as appeares by the inscription there, between 1480 and 1500.

[William] Stump was a wealthy cloathier at Malmesbury, tempore Henrici VIII. His father was the parish clarke of North Nibley, in Gloucestershire, and was a weaver, and at last grew up to be a cloathier. This cloathier at Malmesbury, at the dissolution of the abbeys, bought a great deale of the abbey lands thereabout. When King Henry 8th hunted in Bradon Forest, he gave his majesty and the court a great entertainment at his house (the abbey). The King told him he was afraid he had undone himself; he replied that his own servants should only want their supper for it. [See this anecdote also in Fuller's Worthies, Wiltshire. - J. B.] Leland sayes that when he was there the dortures and other great roomes were filled with weavers' loomes. [The following is the passage referred to (Leland's Itincrary, vol. ii. p. 27.) "The hole logginges of th' abbay be now longging to one Stumpe, an exceeding rich clothiar, that boute them of the king. This Stumpe was the chef causer and contributor to have th' abbay chirch made a paroch chirch. At this present tyme every corner of the vaste houses of office that belongid to th' abbay be full of lumbes to weeve cloth yn, and this Stumpe entendith to make a strete or 2 for cloathiers in the back vacant ground of the abbay that is withyn the town waulles. There be made now every yere in the town a 3,000 clothes." See "Memorials of the Family of Stumpe", by Mr. J. G. Nichols, in "Collectanea Topographica et Genealogica", vol. vii. - J. B.] ——

Mr. Paul Methwin of Bradford succeeded his father-in-law in the trade, and was the greatest cloathier of his time (tempore Caroli 2nd). He was a worthy gentleman, and died about 1667. Now (temp. Jacobi II.) Mr. Brewer of Troubridge driveth the greatest trade for medleys of any cloathier in England.

PART II.-CHAPTER XIII.

FAIRES AND MARKETTS.

FAIRES. The most celebrated faire in North Wiltshire for sheep is at Castle Combe, on St. George's Day (23 April), whither sheep-masters doe come as far as from Northamptonshire. Here is a good crosse and market-house; and heretofore was a staple of wooll, as John Scrope, Esq. Lord of this mannour, affirmes to me. The market here now is very inconsiderable. [Part of the cross and market-house remain, but there is not any wool fair, market, or trade at Castle Combe, which is a retired, secluded village, of a romantic character, seated in a narrow valley, with steep acclivities, covered with woods. The house, gardens, &c. of George Poulett Scrope, Esq. M.P., the Lord of the Manor, are peculiar features in this scene. - J. B.]

At Wilton is a very noted faire for sheepe, on St. George's Day also; and another on St. Giles's Day, September the first. Graziers, &c. from Buckinghamshire come hither to buy sheep.

Wilton was the head town of the county till Bishop Bingham built the Bridge at Harnham which turned away the old Roman way (in the Legier- booke of Wilton called the heþepath, i. e. the army path), and brought the trade to New Sarum, where it hath ever since continued.

At Chilmarke is a good faire for sheep on St. Margaret's day, 20th July.

Burford, near Salisbury, a faire on Lammas day; 'tis an eminent faire for wooll and sheep, the eve is for wooll and cheese.

At the city of New Sarum is a very great faire for cloath at Twelf- tyde, called Twelfe Market. In the parish of All-Cannings is St Anne's Hill, vulgarly called Tann Hill, where every yeare on St. Anne's Day (26th July), is kept a great fair within an old camp, called Oldbury.* The chiefe commodities are sheep, oxen, and fineries. This faire would bee more considerable, but that Bristow Faire happens at the same time.

* [Aubrey errs in stating "Oldbury Camp" to be on St. Anne's Hill; those places being nearly two miles apart. - J. B.]

At the Devises severall faires; but the greatest is at the Green there, at Michaelmas: it continues about a week. ——

MARKETTS. - Warminster is exceeding much frequented for a round corn-market on Saturday. Hither come the best teemes of horses, and it is much resorted to by buyers. Good horses for the coach: some of 20li. + It is held to be the greatest corn-market by much in the West of England. My bayliif has assured me that twelve or fourteen score loades of corne on market-dayes are brought thither: the glovers that work in their shops at the towne's end doe tell the carts as they come in; but this market of late yeares has decayed; the reason whereof I had from my honored friend Henry Millburne, Esq. Recorder of Monmouth. [The reason assigned is, that Mr. Millburne "encouraged badgars" to take corn from Monmouthshire to Bristol; whereupon the bakers there, finding the Welsh corn was better, and could be more cheaply conveyed to them than that grown in Wiltshire, forsook Warminster Market. - J. B.] ——

My bayliff, an ancient servant to our family, assures me that, about 1644, six quarters of wheat would stand, as they terme it, Hindon Market, which is now perhaps the second best market after Warminster in this county. ——

I have heard old men say long since that the market at Castle Combe was considerable in the time of the staple: the market day is Munday. Now only some eggs and butter, &c. ——

Marleborough Market is Saturday: one of the greatest markets for cheese in the west of England. Here doe reside factors for the cheesemongers of London. ——

King Edgar granted a charter to Steeple Ashton. [Aubrey has transcribed the charter at length, from the original Latin. - J. B.] The towne was burnt about the yeare .... before which time it was a market-town; but out of the ashes of this sprang up the market at Lavington, which flourisheth still. [Lavington market has long been discontinued in consequence of its vicinity to the Devizes, which has superior business attractions.-J. B.] ——

At Highworth was the greatest market, on Wednesday, for fatt cattle in our county, which was furnished by the rich vale; and the Oxford butchers furnished themselves here. In the late civill warres it being made a garrison for the King, the graziers, to avoid the rudeness of the souldiers, quitted that market, and went to Swindon, four miles distant, where the market on Munday continues still, which before was a petty, inconsiderable one. Also, the plague was at Highworth before the late warres, which was very prejudiciall to the market there; by reason whereof all the countrey sent their cattle to Swindown market, as they did before to Highworth. ——

Devises. - On Thursday a very plentifull market of every thing: but the best for fish in the county. They bring fish from Poole hither, which is sent from hence to Oxford. ——

[At this place in Aubrey's manuscript is another "digression"; being "Remarks taken from Henry Milburne, Esq. concerning Husbandry, Trade, &c. in Herefordshire". - J. B.]

PART 1I.-CHAPTER XIV.

OF HAWKS AND HAWKING.

[A PAPER "Of Hawkes and Falconry, ancient and modern", is here transcribed from Sir Thomas Browne's Miscellanies, (8vo. 1684.) It describes at considerable length (from the works of Symmachus, Albertus Magnus, Demetrius Constantinopolitanus, and others), the various rules which were acted upon in their times, with regard to the food and medicine of hawks; and it also narrates some historical particulars of the once popular sport of hawking.-J. B.] QUÆRE, Sir James Long of this subject, for he understands it as well as any gentleman in this nation, and desire him to write his marginall notes.

——

[From Sir James Long, Dracot.] Memorandum. Between the years 1630 and 1634 Henry Poole, of Cyrencester, Esquire (since Sir Henry Poole, Baronet), lost a falcon flying at Brook, in the spring of the year, about three a'clock in the afternoon; and he had a falconer in Norway at that time to take hawks for him, who discovered this falcon, upon the stand from whence he was took at first, the next day in the evening. This flight must be 600 miles at least.

Dame Julian Barnes, in her book of Hunting and Hawking, says that the hawk's bells must be in proportion to the hawk, and they are to be equiponderant, otherwise they will give the hawk an unequall ballast: and as to their sound they are to differ by a semitone, which will make them heard better than if they were unisons. ——

William of Malmesbury sayes that, anno Domini 900, tempore Regis Alfredi, hawking was first used. Coteswold is a very fine countrey for this sport, especially before they began to enclose about Malmesbury, Newton, &c. It is a princely sport, and no doubt the novelty, together with the delight, and the conveniency of this countrey, did make King Athelstan much use it. I was wont to admire to behold King Athelstan's figure in his monument at Malmesbury Abbey Church, with a falconer's glove on his right hand, with a knobbe or tassel to put under his girdle, as the falconers use still; but this chronologicall advertisement cleares it. [The effigy on the monument here referred to, as well as the monument itself, have no reference to Athelstan, as they are of a style and character some hundreds of years subsequent to that monarch's decease. If there were any tomb to Athelstan it would have been placed near the high altar in the Presbytery, and very different in form and decoration to the altar tomb and statue here mentioned, which are at the east end of the south aisle of the nave.-J. B.] Sir George Marshal of Cole Park, a-quarry to King James First, had no more manners or humanity than to have his body buried under this tombe. The Welsh did King Athelstan homage at the city of Hereford, and covenanted yearly payment of 20li. gold, of silver 300, oxen 2,500, besides hunting dogges and hawkes. He dyed anno Domini 941, and was buried with many trophies at Malmesbury. His lawes are extant to this day among the lawes of other Saxon kings.

PART II.-CHAPTER XV.

THE RACE.

HENRY Earle of Pembroke [1570-1601] instituted Salisbury Race;* which hath since continued very famous, and beneficiall to the city. He gave ..... pounds to the corporation of Sarum to provide every yeare, in the first Thursday after Mid-Lent Sunday, a silver bell [see note below], of ...... value; which, about 1630, was turned into a silver cup of the same value. This race is of two sorts: the greater, fourteen miles, beginnes at Whitesheet and ends on Harnham-hill, which is very seldom runn, not once perhaps in twenty yeares. The shorter begins at a place called the Start, at the end of the edge of the north downe of the farme of Broad Chalke, and ends at the standing at the hare-warren, built by William Earle of Pembroke, and is four miles from the Start. ——

*[In the civic archives of Salisbury, under the date of 1585, is the following memorandum:- "These two years, in March, there was a race run with horses at the farthest three miles from Sarum, at the which were divers noble personages, and the Earl of Cumberland won the golden bell, which was valued at 501. and better, the which earl is to bring the same again next year, which he promised to do, upon his honour, to the mayor of this city". See Hatcher's History of Salisbury, p. 294. In the Appendix to that volume is a copy of an Indenture, made in 1654, between the Mayor and Commonalty of the city and Sir Edward Baynton of Bromham, relative to the race-cup. It recites that Henry Earl of Pembroke in his lifetime gave a golden bell, to be run for yearly, "at the place then used and accustomed for horse races, upon the downe or plaine leading from New Sarum towards the towne of Shaston [Shaftesbury], in the county of Dorset". This would imply that the nobleman referred to was not the founder of Salisbury Races. - J. B.]

It is certain that Peacock used to runn the four-miles course in five minutes and a little more; and Dalavill since came but little short of him. Peacock was first Sir Thomas Thynne's of Long-leate; who valued him at 1,000 pounds. Philip Earle of Pembrock gave 51i. but to have a sight of him: at last his lordship had him; I thinke by gift. Peacock was a bastard barb. He was the most beautifull horse ever seen in this last age, and was as fleet as handsome. He dyed about 1650.

"Here lies the man whose horse did gaine
The bell in race on Salisbury plaine;
Reader, I know not whether needs it,
You or your horse rather to reade it."

At Everly is another race. Quære, if the Earle of Abington hath not set up another?

——

Stobball-play is peculiar to North Wilts, North Gloucestershire, and a little part of Somerset near Bath. They smite a ball, stuffed very hard with quills and covered with soale leather, with a staffe, commonly made of withy, about 3 [feet] and a halfe long. Colerne-downe is the place so famous and so frequented for stobball-playing. The turfe is very fine, and the rock (freestone) is within an inch and a halfe of the surface, which gives the ball so quick a rebound. A stobball-ball is of about four inches diameter, and as hard as a stone. I doe not heare that this game is used anywhere in England but in this part of Wiltshire and Gloucestershire adjoining.

PART II.-CHAPTER XVI.

OF THE NUMBER OF ATTORNIES IN THIS COUNTIE NOW AND HERETOFORE.

[A STATUTE was passed in the reign of Edward I. which gave the first authority to suitors in the courts of law to prosecute or defend by attorney; and the number of attorneys afterwards increased so rapidly that several statutes were passed in the reigns of Henry IV. Henry VI. and Elizabeth, for limiting their number. One of these (33 Hen. VI. c. 7) states that not long before there were only six or eight attorneys in Norfolk and Suffolk, and that their increase to twenty-four was to the vexation and prejudice of those counties; and it therefore enacts that for the future there shall be only six in Norfolk, six in Suffolk, and two in Norwich. (Penny Cycle, art. Attorney.) Aubrey adopts the inference that strife and dissension were promoted by the increase of attorneys; which he accordingly laments as a serious evil. He quotes at some length from a treatise "About Actions for Slander and Arbitrements, what words are actionable in the law, and what not", &c. by John March, of Gray's Inn, Barrister (London, 1674, 8vo.); wherein the great increase of actions for slander is shewn, by reference to old law books. The author urges the propriety of checking such actions as much as possible, and quaintly observes, "as I cannot balk that observation of that learned Chief Justice (Wray), who sayes that in our old bookes actions for scandal are very rare; so I will here close with this one word: though the tongues of men be set on fire, I know no reason wherefore the law should be used as bellows". Aubrey remarks upon this:- "The true and intrinsic reason why actions of the case were so rare in those times above mentioned, was by reason that men's consciences were kept cleane and in awe by confession"; and he concludes the chapter with an extract from "Europæ Speculum", by Sir Edwin Sandys, Knight, (1637,) in which the advantages and disadvantages of auricular confession are discussed. - J. B.]

ME. BAYNHAM, of Cold Ashton, in Gloucestershire, bred an attorney, sayes, that an hundred yeares since there were in the county of Gloucester but four attorneys, and now (1689) no fewer than three hundred attorneys and sollicitors; and Dr. Guydot, Physician, of Bath, sayes that they report that anciently there was but one attorney in Somerset, and he was so poor that he went a'foot to London; and now they swarme there like locusts.

Fabian Philips tells me (1683) that about sixty-nine yeares since there were but two attorneys in Worcestershire, sc. Langston and Dowdeswell; and they be now in every market towne, and goe to marketts; and he believes there are a hundred.

In Henry 6th time (q. if not in Hen. 7?) there was a complaint to the Parliament by the Norfolk people that whereas formerly there were in that county but five or six attorneys, that now they are exceedingly encreased, and that they went to markets and bred contention. The judges were ordered to rectify this grievance, but they fell asleep and never awak't since. - Vide the Parliament Roll. [See the above note. In page 12 (ante) Aubrey states that the Norfolk people are the "most litigious" of any in England. - J. B.] 'Tis thought that in England there are at this time near three thousand;* but there is a rule in hawking, the more spaniells the more game. They doe now rule and governe the lawyers [barristers] and judges. They will take a hundred pounds with a clarke.

*[There are now upwards of three thousand attorneys in practice in the metropolis alone, to whom the celebrated remark of Alderman Beckford to King George the Third may be justly applied, with the substitution of another word for "the Crown", - "the influence of lawyers has increased, is increasing, and ought to be diminished." - J. B.]

PART II.-CHAPTER XVII.

OF FATALITIES OF FAMILIES AND PLACES.

[NEARLY the whole of this chapter, with some additions, is included under the head of "Local Fatality" in Aubrey's Miscellanies. 12mo. 1696.-J. B.]

"Omnium rerum est vicissitudo". Families, and also places, have their fatalities,

"Fors sua cuiq' loco est." OVID, PAST. lib. iv.

This verse putts me in mind of severall places in this countie that are or have been fortunate to their owners, or e contra.

The Gawens of Norrington, in the parish of Alvideston, continued in this place four hundred fifty and odd yeares. They had also an estate in Broad Chalke, which was, perhaps, of as great antiquity. On the south downe of the farme of Broad Chalke is a little barrow called Gawen's-barrow, which must bee before ecclesiastical lawes were established. [Aubrey quotes a few lines from the "Squire's Tale" in Chaucer, where Gawain, nephew to King Arthur, is alluded to.-J. B.] ——

The Scropes of Castle-Comb have been there ever since the time of King Richard the Second. The Lord Chancellor Scrope gave this mannour to his third son; they have continued there ever since, and enjoy the old land (about 800li per annum), and the estate is neither augmented nor diminished all this time, neither doth the family spred.

The Powers of Stanton St. Quintin had that farme in lease about three hundred yeares. It did belong to the abbey of Cyrencester. ——

The Lytes had Easton Piers in lease and in inheritance 249 yeares; sc. from Henry 6th. About 1572 Mr. Th. Lyte, my mother's grandfather, purchased the inheritance of the greatest part of this place, a part whereof descended to me by my mother Debora, the daughter and heire of Mr. Isaac Lyte. I sold it in 1669 to Francis Hill, who sold it to Mr. Sherwin, who hath left it to a daughter and heir. Thos. Lyte's father had 800li. per annum in leases: viz. all Easton, except Cromwell's farm (20li), and the farmes of Dedmerton and Sopworth. ——

The Longs are now the most flourishing and numerous family in this county, and next to them the Ashes; but the latter are strangers, and came in but about 1642, or since. ——

Contrarywise there are severall places unlucky to the possessors. Easton Piers hath had six owners since the reigne of Henry 7th, where I myself had a share to act my part; and one part of it called Lyte's Kitchin hath been sold four times over since 1630.

'Tis certain that there are some houses lucky and some that are unlucky; e.g. a handsome brick house on the south side of Clarkenwell churchyard hath been so unlucky for at least these forty yeares that it is seldom tenanted; nobody at last would adventure to take it. Also a handsome house in Holbourne that looked into the fields, the tenants of it did not prosper; about six, one after another.

PART II.-CHAPTER XVIII.

ACCIDENTS.

["ACCIDENTS" was a term used in astrology, in the general sense of remarkable events or occurrences. From a curious collection of Aubrey's memoranda I have selected a few of the most interesting and most apposite to Wiltshire. Several of the anecdotes in this chapter will be found in Aubrey's Miscellanies, 12mo. 1696. J. B.]

IN the reigne of King James 1st, as boyes were at play in Amesbury- street, it thundred and lightened. One of the boyes wore a little dagger by his side, which was melted in the scabbard, and the scabbard not hurt. This dagger Edward Earle of Hertford kept amongst his rarities. I have forgott if the boy was killed. (From old Mr. Bowman and Mr. Gauntlett) ——

The long street, Marleborough, was burned down to the ground in five houres, and the greatnesse of the fire encreased the wind. This was in 165-. This account I had from Thomas Henshaw, Esq. who was an eye- witness as he was on his journey to London.

["Marlborough has often suffered by fire; particularly in the year 1690. Soon afterwards the town obtained an act of Parliament to prohibit the covering of houses with thatch." Beauties of Wiltshire, vol. ii. p. 177. A pamphlet was published in 1653 (12mo.) with the following title:- "Take heed in time; or, a briefe relation of many harmes that have of late been done by fire in Marlborough and other places. Written by L. P." - J. B.]

In the gallery at Wilton hangs, under the picture of the first William Earl of Pembroke, the picture of a little reddish picked-nose dog (none of the prettiest) that his lordship loved. The dog starved himself after his master's death. ——

Dr. Ralph Bathurst, Dean of Wells, and one of the chaplains to King Charles 1st, who is no superstitious man, protested to me that the curing of the King's evill by the touch of the King doth puzzle his philosophie: for whether they were of the house of Yorke or Lancaster it did. 'Tis true indeed there are prayers read at the touching, but neither the King minds them nor the chaplains. Some confidently report that James Duke of Monmouth did it. ——

Imposture. - Richard Heydock, M.D., quondam fellow of New College in Oxford, was an ingenious and a learned person, but much against the hierarchie of the Church of England. He had a device to gaine proselytes, by preaching in his dreame; which was much noised abroad, and talked of as a miracle. But King James 1st being at Salisbury went to heare him. He observed that his harrangue was very methodicall, and that he did but counterfeit a sleep. He surprised the doctor by drawing his sword, and swearing, "God's waunes, I will cut off his head"; at which the doctor startled and pretended to awake; and so the cheat was detected. ——

One M{istress} Katharine Waldron, a gentlewoman of good family, waited on Sir Francis Seymor's lady, of Marleborough. Shee pretended to be bewitched by a certain woman, and had acquired such a strange habit that she would endure exquisite torments, as to have pinnes thrust into her flesh, nay under her nailes. These tricks of hers were about the time when King James wrote his Demonologie. His Majesty being in these parts, went to see her in one of her fitts. Shee lay on a bed, and the King saw her endure the torments aforesayd. The room, as it is easily to be believed, was full of company. His Majesty gave a sodain pluck to her coates, and tos't them over her head; which surprise made her immediately start, and detected the cheate. ——

[Speaking of the trial of Aim Bodenham, who was executed at Salisbury as a witch in 1653, Aubrey says:-] Mr. Anthony Ettrick, of the Middle Temple, a very judicious gentleman, was a curious observer of the whole triall, and was not satisfied. The crowd of spectators made such a noise that the judge [Chief Baron Wild] could not heare the prisoner, nor the prisoner the judge; but the words were handed from one to the other by Mr. R. Chandler, and sometimes not truly reported. This memorable triall was printed about 165-. 4to. [See full particulars in Hatcher's History of Salisbury, p. 418. - J. B.] ——

In the time of King Charles II. the drumming at the house of Mr. Monpesson, of Tydworth, made a great talke over England, of which Mr. Joseph Glanvill, Rector of Bath, hath largely writt; to which I refer the reader. But as he was an ingenious person, so I suspect he was a little too credulous; for Sir Ralph Bankes and Mr. Anthony Ettrick lay there together one night out of curiosity, to be satisfied. They did heare sometimes knockings; and if they said "Devill, knock so many knocks"; so many knocks would be answered. But Mr. Ettrick sometimes whispered the words, and there was then no returne: but he should have spoke in Latin or French for the detection of this.

Another time Sir Christopher Wren lay there. He could see no strange things, but sometimes he should heare a drumming, as one may drum with one's hand upon wainscot; but he observed that this drumming was only when a certain maid-servant was in the next room: the partitions of the rooms are by borden-brasse, as wee call it. But all these remarked that the Devill kept no very unseasonable houres: it seldome knock't after 12 at night, or before 6 in the morning.

[In Hoare's Modern Wiltshire, (Hundred of Amesbury,) p. 92, is a narrative, quoted from Glanvil, of the nocturnal disturbances in the house of Mr. Mompesson at North Tidworth, Wilts, in the year 1661, which excited considerable interest at the time, and led to the publication of several pamphlets on the subject. The book by Mr. Glanvil, referred to by Aubrey, is called "A blow at modern Sadducism; or Philosophical considerations touching the being of Witches and Witchcraft; with an account of the Demon of Tedworth." Lond. 1666, 4to. There are other editions in folio and 8vo. in 1667 and 1668. Addison founded his comedy of "The Drummer, or the Haunted House," on this occurrence. - J. B.] ——

About 167- there was a cabal of witches detected at Malmsbury. They ere examined by Sir James Long of Draycot-Cerne, and by him committed to Salisbury Gaol. I think there were seven or eight old women hanged. There were odd things sworne against them, as the strange manner of the dyeing of H. Denny's horse, and of flying in the aire on a staffe. These examinations Sir James hath fairly written in a book which he promised to give to the Royall Societie. ——

At Salisbury a phantome appeared to Dr. Turbervill's sister severall times, and it discovered to her a writing or deed of settlement that was hid behind the wainscot ——

Phantomes. - Though I myselfe never saw any such things, yet I will not conclude that there is no truth at all in these reports. I believe that extraordinarily there have been such apparitions; but where one is true a hundred are figments. There is a lecherie in lyeing and imposeing on the credulous; and the imagination of fearfull people is to admiration: e.g. Not long after the cave at Bathford was discovered (where the opus tessellatum was found), one of Mr. Skreen's ploughboyes lyeing asleep near to the mouth of the cave, a gentleman in a boate on the river Avon, which runnes hard by, played on his flajolet. The boy apprehended the musique to be in the cave, and ran away in a lamentable fright, and his fearfull phancy made him believe he saw spirits in the cave. This Mr. Skreen told me, and that the neighbourhood are so confident of the truth of this, that there is no undeceiving of them.

PART II.-CHAPTER XIX.

SEATES.

[This chapter comprises only a few scattered notes; of which the following are specimens. -J. B.]

I TAKE Merton to be the best seated for healthy aire, &c., and sports, of any place in this county. The soile is gravelly and pebbly.

Ivy Church, adjoining to Clarendon Parke, a grove of elms, and prospect over the city of Salisbury and the adjacent parts. The right honorable Mary, Countess of Pembroke, much delighted in this place.

At Longford is a noble house that was built by Lord Georges, who married a Swedish lady. [See before, p. 102. Sir Thomas Gorges was the second husband of Helena dowager Marchioness of Northampton, daughter of Wolfgang Snachenburg, of Sweden: see Hoare's Modern Wiltshire, Hundred of Cawden, p. 31.-J. B.]

Little-coat, in the parish of Rammysbury, is a very great house. It was Sir Thomas Dayrell's, who was tryed for his life for burning a child, being accessory. It is now Sir Jo. Popham's, Lord Chief Justice. [The murder here alluded to is said to have been committed in Littlecot-house. The strange and mysterious story connected with it is recorded in a note to Scott's poem of "Rokeby," and also in the account of Wiltshire, in the Beauties of England. - J. B.]

Longleat, the dwelling place of the Thynnes, a very fair, neat, elegant house, in a foul soile. It is true Roman architecture, adorned on the outside with three orders of pillars, Dorique, Ionique, and Corinthian.

Tocknam [Tottenham] Parke, a seate of the Duke of Somerset, is a most parkely ground, and a romancey place. Severall walkes of trees planted of great length. Here is a new complete pile of good architecture. It is in the parish of Great Bedwin. [The domain comprises the whole extent of Savernake Forest. - J. B.]

Wardour Castle, the seate of the Lord Arundell, was kept by Col. Ludlow: a part of it was blown up by Sir F. Dodington in 1644 or 1645. Here was a red-deer parke and a fallow-deer parke. [Some of the ruins of the old castle still remain. The present mansion, belonging to the Arundell family of Wardour, was erected about seventy years ago. - J. B.]

Knighton Wood, the Earle of Pembroke's, is an exceeding pleasant place, both for the variety of high wood and lawnes, as well as deer, as also the prospect over the New Forest to the sea, and the whole length of the Isle of Wight It is a desk-like elevation, and faces the south, and in my conceit it would be the noblest situation for a grand building that this countrey doth afford.

PART II.-CHAPTER XX.

DRAUGHTS OF THE SEATES AND PROSPECTS.

[I HAVE thought it desirable to print the concluding Chapter of Aubrey's work verbatim. It is merely a list of remarkable buildings and views, which he wished to be drawn and engraved, for the illustration of his work. The names attached to each subject are those of persons whom he thought likely to incur the expence of the plates, for publication; and his own name being affixed to two of them shews that he was willing to contribute. It is impossible not to concur in his closing observations on this subject, or to avoid an expression of regret that he was not enabled to publish such a "glorious volume" of engravings as would have been formed by those here enumerated. - J. B.]

MY WISH. - AN APPENDIX.

"Multorum manibus grande levatur onus."-Ovid.

ADVICE TO THE PAINTER OR GRAVER.

1. Our Ladies Church at Salisbury; the view without, and in perspective within: and a mappe of the city. - Bishop Ward. And of Old Sarum from Harnham hill. - (Sir Hugh Speke gave to the Monasticon Angliæ the prospect of Salisbury Church, excellently well done by Mr. Hollar. Quaere, who hath the plate? I doe believe, my Lady Speke.)

2. Prospect of Malmesbury Abbey; and also (3) of the Town, and (4) a Mappe of the Town. - Mr. Wharton, &c.- Sir James Long. (Take the true latitude and longitude of Malmesbury.)

5. And also King Athelston's tombe. [See ante, p. 116.]

6. Prospect of the borough of Chippenham. - Duke of Somerset.

7. The Castle at Marleborough, and the prospect of the

8. Town. - D. of Somerset.

9. The Ruines of Lurgershall Castle. - Sir George Brown.

10. Bradstock Priorie. - James, Earle of Abingdon.

11. Wardour Castle. - The Lord Arundel of Wardour.

12. Lacock Abbey. - Sir Jo. Talbot.

13. Priory St. Maries, juxta Kington St. Michael.

14. Ivy Church.

15. Sturton House. - The Lord Sturton.

16. Wilton House, and (17) Garden: sc. from the House and from Rowlingdon Parke. The garden was heretofore drawn by Mr. Solomon de Caus, the architect, that was the surveyor of it, and engraved [ante, p. 86]; but the plates were burnt in the Fire of London. - E. of Pembrok

18. Longleate House and Garden. - I have seen a print of the house: it was engraved after Mr. Dankertz' painting. Quære, Mr. Thompson, the printseller, for it? Perhaps he hath the plates. - Lord Weymouth. (Desire Mr. Beech, the

Lord Weymouth's steward, to enquire what is become of the copper plate that was engraved after Mr. Dankertz' painting of this house; also enquire of Mr. Rose, my Lord's surveyor, for it).

19. Longford House. - Lord Colraine. (Engraved by Thacker. Quære, my Lord Colraine, if he hath the plate or a copie.)

20. The Duke of Beauford's house at Amesbury. - His Grace.

21. Tocknam Parke House. - E. of Alesbury.

22. Funthill House. - Mr. Cottington.

23. Charlton House. - Earle of Barkshire.

24. Lavington House and Garden. - Earle of Abingdon.

25. Mr. Hall's house at Bradford. - J. Hall, Esq.

26. Lidyard-Tregoze House and Scite. - Sir Walter St. John.

27. Sir John Wyld's House at Compton Basset. - Sir Jo. Wyld.

28. Ramesbury House. - Sir Wm. Jones, Attorney-General.

HOUSES OF LESSER NOTE.

29. Edington House. - .... Lewis, Esq.

30. Sir Jo. Evelyn's House at Deane. - Earle of Kingston.

31. Dracot-Cerne House. - Sir James Long, Baronet.

32. Cosham House. - .... Kent, Esq.

33. Lakham House. - .... Montague, Esq.

34. Cadnam House. - Sir George Hungerford.

The Mannour House of Kington St. Michael. - .... Laford.

The Mannour House at .....- Sir Henry Coker.

Gretenham House. - George Ayliff, Esq.

PROSPECTS.

1. From Newnton (Mr. Poole's garden-house) is an admirable prospect. It takes in Malmesbury, &c. and terminates with the blew hills of Salisbury plaines. 'Tis the best in Wiltshire.- Madam Estcourt, or Earle of Kent.

2. From Colern Tower, or Marsfield downe, eastwards; which takes in Bradstock Priory, several steeples and parkes, and extends to Salisbury plaine. - D. of Beauford, or Marq. of Worcester.

3. From the garret at Easton Piers, a delicate prospect. - J. Aubrey.

4. From Bradstock Priory, over the rich green tuff-taffety vale to Cyrencester, Malmesbury, Marsfield, Colern, Mendip-hills; and Coteswold bounds the north horizon. - Earle of Abingdon.

5. From Bowdon Lodge, a noble prospect of the north part of Wilts. - Hen. Baynton, Esq.

6. From Spy Park, westward. - Hen. Baynton, Esq.

7. From Westbury Hill to the vale below, northward. - Lord Norris.

8. From the south downe of the farme of Broad Chalke one sees over Vernditch, Merton, and the New Forest, to the sea; and all the Isle of Wight, and to Portland. - J. Aubrey. (Memorandum. A quarter of a mile or lesse from hence is Knighton Ashes, which is a sea marke, which came into this prospect. The Needles, at the west end of the Isle of Wight, beare from it south and by east; but try its bearings exactly.)

9. From Knoll Hill, a vast prospect every way. - The Lord Weymouth.

10. From Cricklade Tower, a lovely vernall prospect. - Sir George Hungerford, or Sir Stephen Fox. (This prospect is over the rich green country to Marston-Mazy, Down-Ampney, Cyrencester, Minchinghampton, and Coteswold.)

11. From the leads of Wilton House to Salisbury, Ivy-church, &c. - Sir R. Sawyer, Attorney-Genl.

12. The prospect that I drew from Warren, above Farleigh-castle Parke; and take another view in the parke. - Sir Edward Hungerford. (This prospect of Farleigh is in my book A, at the end; with Mr. Anthony Wood.)

13. The prospect of Malmesbury from the hill above Cowbridge. This I have drawn.

14. I have drawn the prospect of Salisbury, and so beyond to Old Sarum, from the lime-kills at Harnham. (Memorandum. Mr. Dankertz did make a very fine draught of Salisbury. Enquire of Mr. Thompson, the printseller, who bought his draughts, if he hath it) - Seth Ward, Bishop of Sarum. (Set down the latitude and longitude of Salisbury.)

15. A draft of the toft of the castle and keep of Castle Comb. - Jo. Scroop, Esq.

16. A Mappe of Wiltshire, to be donne by Mr. [Brown?] that did Staffordshire. (Advertisement to the surveyor of Wiltshire, as to the mappe. - Let him make his two first stations at the south downe at Broad Chalke, which he may enlarge two miles or more; from whence he may ken with his bare eye to Portsmouth, all the Isle of Wight, to Portland, to the towers and chimny's of Shaftesbury, to Knoll-hill, to the promontory of Roundway-down above the Devises: to St. Anne's hill, vulgo Tanne hill, to Martinsoll hill, to Amesbury becon-hill, to Salisbury steeple, &c. When he comes into North Wiltshire his prospect will not be much shorter. There he will take in Glastenbury-torre and Gloucestershire, and Cumnor Lodge in Barkshire).

IF these views were well donn, they would make a glorious volume by itselfe, and like enough it might take well in the world. It were an inconsiderable expence (charge) to these persons of qualitie, and it would remaine to posterity, when their families are gonn and their buildings ruin'd by time or fire, as we have seen that stupendous fabrick of Paul's Church, not a stone left on a stone, and lives now onely in Mr. Hollar's Etchings in Sir William Dugdale's History of Paul's. I am not displeased with this thought as a desideratum, but I doe never expect to see it donn; so few men have the hearts to doe publique good, to give 3, 4, or 5li. for a copper plate.

" Thus Poets like to Kings (by trust deceiv'd) Give oftner what is heard of than receiv'd."

SIR WILLIAM DAVENANT to the Lady Olivia Porter;
"A New Yeares Gift."

——

(There are noble prospects in Gloucestershire, but that concernes not me. The city of Gloucester is one of the best views of any city in England; so many stately towers and steeples cutting the horizon. From Broadway-downe one beholds the vale of Evesham, and so to Malvern hills, to Staffordshire, Monmouthshire, Warwickshire, the cities of Gloucester and Worcester, and also Tukesbury, the city of Coventry, and, I thinke, of Lichfield. From Kimsbury, a camp, is a very pleasant prospect to Gloucester over the vale. From Dundery is a noble prospect of the city of Bristow and St. Vincent's Rocks, &c., quod NB.)

FINIS.

Printed in the United States
134525LV00002B/59/A

9 781406 807165